Judi Loren has woven a mother's story about life and death and the everlasting repercussions of a child's death on the rest of the family. This well-written book can help parents, especially those with a particularly challenging child, become aware of how daily life imprints on the mental health and development of a child growing up in a complex world. Hug your kids and tell them how much you love them.

    James B. Wood, M.D.

    Pediatrician

    Chico, CA

Judi Loren Grace has the ability to grab you by the stacking swivels as she shares her most deep and personal reflections of the pain she bore in losing her son to suicide. Such loss comes so close to the heart, forcing survivors to second-guess what could have been done to prevent such a tragedy. Judi tackled this challenge by recalling important events in her life with her son, covering each topic with candor that just may give all of us notice to reach out to those we love. Thanks, Judi, for sharing with us.

    Captain Jack Long

    Irish Eyes, Pearl Harbor, Hawaii

The suicide of a child is one of the most traumatic events that could ever occur in a parent's life. The author of *Dreamscape in A minor* takes the reader through a courageous journey whereby she and her family grieve yet ultimately grow from the suicide of a son and brother. This is a MUST READ for anyone who has suffered through this kind of loss.

> Roger B. Graves PhD
> Licensed Psychologist
> Anchorage, Alaska

In her book *The Third Floor*, author Judi Loren Grace introduced her readers to the strongest passion and feeling known to humankind: a mothers' love. This passion fueled a desire to seek answers and write a second book about her son Jeffrey, a free-spirited and talented youth whose life ended too soon. Judi's latest book, *Dreamscape in A minor*, will tug at your heart strings!

> Alvin Bonds
> Industrial Relations Specialist
> Winchester, Kentucky

I understand the issues in this book as darkness and light. Darkness closes in on a single person of immense talent and potential, and the light is the struggle of those who loved him to understand their loss. Thank you, my friend Judi, for having the courage to bring your emotions to life, and for turning on the light so others may see.

> Stockton Kelly, USAF Veteran and Patriot,
> Porterville, California

In her book *Dreamscape in A minor*, Judi Loren Grace rises beyond her profound grief to bring her son's life to us, and her captivating story will leave an everlasting impression. Judi writes with humor, but you will also feel her passion like no other.

Shawn Stinson
Attorney at Law/Mediator

This is the story of a disaster created by politicians, perpetuated by budget-focused administrators, and witnessed by powerless agency therapists, all of whom ignored the one person who knew the victim's needs best: his mother!

Jerry D. Bakus, PsyD. MFT, Bay City, Michigan.

Ms. Loren writes with purposeful clarity, drawing the reader into her memories and enabling us to see events through her eyes. With humor, parental love, sadness, and complete honesty, she provides insight for others, addressing issues many parents and loved ones face. With her style of writing, one can relate perfectly, and hopefully her message will save another life. Bravo!

Helen Baker, Honolulu, Hawaii

Everyone knows someone who is involved with depression which could lead to suicide. *Dreamscape in A minor* will be a guide to professionals, parents, and clergy based on a mother's firsthand experience with her own son's suicide. Judi Loren Grace takes us to the innermost thoughts and insights of her journey as she recalls their mother-son relationship and strives to heal from his loss. Please read so you can be a part of the solution to this growing problem.

Duke, Prison Chaplain, New Jersey

Dreamscape in Aminor
JUDI LOREN GRACE

Published by **Jetstream Publishing** in association with Memoir Books
Chico, California

Publications by Jetstream Publishing:
The Third Floor, Judi Loren Grace
Dreamscape in A minor, Judi Loren Grace

Contact Judi Loren Grace: kepi@sunset.net

Follow Judi Loren Grace on Facebook

www.jetstreampublishing.com

ISBN: 978-1-937748-04-3
Library of Congress Control Number: 2013951584
Printed in the United States of America

Cover and Interior Design and Layout: Connie Ballou, Back Alley Graphics
Copy Editor: Ruth Younger
Front Cover Photo: Judi, Spencer, Dana, and Jeff looking at Half Dome,
Yosemite 1978. Photo by Don Adkisson.

Contents

DEDICATION AND ACKNOWLEDGEMENTS

This book is dedicated to the nieces and nephews of Uncle Jeff.

Audrey, Gemma, Anders, Josiah

Ask your parents to tell you an Uncle Jeff bedtime story.

A life to be lived has ended, with many different endings.

In Remembrance

Courtney Cathleen and Whitney Ann-Marie—*twin infant daughters of my friends Marlys and Allen*

Billy and Marilyn—*adult son and adult daughter of Uncle Anslie and Aunt Verna*

Michelle Leanne—*teen daughter of classmate Mardell and Richard*

Diane Alzora—*baby daughter of my pal Shirley and her former husband Duke*

Beau—*young adult son of close friend's daughter Kristi*

Dodd—*young son of high school friends Susan and Maurice*

Sharon Elaine—*young adult daughter of Aunt Lydia and Uncle Elbert*
Michael—*adult son of dear friends Sharon and Ed*
Marguerite—*infant daughter of grandparents Lena and Roey*
Gia—*teen daughter of family friends Linda and Ken*
Jason—*adult son of our neighbors Debbie and Steve*

Acknowledgements

Connie Ballou, Back Alley Graphics—*The front cover is stunning, as is the inside art. Thank you, Connie.*

Ruth Younger, Editor—*You are amazing. Thank you for understanding and working with me so carefully.*

Shannon Iris Photography—*Shannon, you captured the mood with your author photo for the back cover, and I thank you.*

Pete Grace—*Thank you for giving me the space I needed to retreat and relive this part of my life, and for allowing me private time to brood and sort papers.*

Dana and Spencer—*I so appreciate your understanding of my ongoing need to keep your brother's memory alive. Each of you said little, but both gave a nod to write about Jeff. In doing so, we brought him back to life for the rest of the world to know.*

Kari and Alex—*Being step-children of a mother who was grieving must have been a difficult path for you to walk. Thank you for your patience and love during our family's long-term grief.*

George Kilker—*I'm so grateful to you for patiently sharing your understanding of what happened that fateful day, despite your claim of "memory loss." I also appreciate your opening up about our blended family, especially your mother Marion and my father from your next-door vantage point. You are continually supportive and helpful, dear brother. Love and kisses.*

Tammy Taylor—*Thank you for driving all the way to the North State to help me cope in my early stages of grief.*

Lisa Boettger—*Girl, you have brought so much peace to our family with your gift of an open heart and mind! I value your amazing friendship and ongoing correspondence more than I can say.*

Susan Allwardt—*Thank you, dear friend, for returning Jeff's long-lost baseball bat that you discovered in your garage. You have no idea how much it meant to me to see his youthful signature on the handle after so many years. I look forward to passing it on to Spencer and Cassie's son Anders when he gets big enough to play ball.*

Stockton Kelly—*Thank you for being the confidant I needed to get this book started. Your suggestion that I pretend we are simply visiting and to "just talk" enabled me to finally let the story about my son flow.*

Keith Guernsey—*Thank you for always being Jeff's friend and for sharing your musical talents with him. Whether you simply let him watch your fingers move effortlessly and quickly across the keys as you played classical piano pieces, or showed him finger placement and technique, your generosity enabled Jeff to discover his talent and love for music. You are the coolest guy I know.*

*Death makes us angels, all of us and gives us wings
where we had shoulders smooth as a raven claws.
Jim Morrison of the Doors*

MY LIFE AS A YOUNG WOMAN began with baggage and a dark secret. I had been forced to relinquish an infant as a teen mom. We unwed mothers happily glided along and pretended to be well-equipped young ladies, ready to marry and become *legal mothers*. Nothing could be further from the truth. The chain had been broken. The life line from Grandmother to Mother to Daughter had been stretched to the point of shreds. Everything I learned about mothering was a blur. *Dreamscape in A minor* is about my second son, the oldest of the three children whom I had the privilege to raise. This is about a lost life, one that fell through the cracks.

His name is Jeff. We called him Jet, or Jeffrey, or Jeffrey Paul when he was in trouble. I'm bringing my son back to life for you to get to know and love as we, his family, did. Jeff died too soon, far too young, leaving an unfinished life. He left no note, but as I look back I realize that in his own way, he did say a proper goodbye. Here is the story of our family—the joy and grief, the anger and love, the frustration and pride, the comedy and tragedy, the laughs and tears, and the coincidences and the memories that follow. The conflicting emotions and apparent inconsistencies in this story are the twenty-four year aftermath of living with Jeff's suicide and my father's connected death. You're invited for the ride as I explore many avenues of healing in my lengthy search for peace.

Imagine first a strong-willed boy with golden blond hair and green eyes. Meet my son, Jeffrey. Picture Jeff at age eight, as he sits at the piano and begins to play classical music simply by watching and listening to his friend play. Jeff was blessed with an amazing musical talent. Whether it was piano, guitar, trumpet, or percussion, he seemed able to make music with whatever he picked up.

Yet in school, Jeff struggled with his lessons and got in trouble for silly antics. He thought he was invincible, and the super hero cape I sewed for him when he was seven didn't help. In those days, before the common labels of today, adults surmised Jeff must be a dreamer, or craved attention, or liked to get into trouble. He was one of the misunderstood generation. Jeff was either silly, quiet, or doing something—constructive or destructive. He was born with no boundaries, and he was fearless. I visualize Jeff, continually stating his claims and facts, and always questioning. *Why does thunder follow lightning? Where does Darth Vader live? Why does your hair* look like a Trojan helmet? Why are some clouds fluffy and some long and flat? Why is there a big moon and sometimes a broken moon? When will I grow man hairs? He was fascinated by nature and science, and he worried about many things in life.

Jeff and I created a special bond as he was the only child from my fairy tale marriage to Gene, a marriage that was not destined to make me happy ever after. He was the oldest child I raised, and he witnessed my life unfolding as I matured and expanded our family with two more babies. He also served as a witness to the eventual decline of my second marriage to Don, and then I became both mom and dad. Jeff gave off the aura of being strong and independent. Granted, he was a quick thinker, and he was born to argue, but he was sensitive and longed for a dad to nurture him.

Jeff's life was far from perfect. Still, for his first nineteen years and into his twenties, I could see the makings of a great husband, an attentive father, and a son who always came back home. He would have been an amazing uncle, had he chosen to live his life.

Who can say what leads someone to commit suicide? I have blamed Jeff's taking drugs as a teen, and I have blamed myself. Sometimes I feel certain that it was his fantasy of death that sprouted somewhere along the way and ultimately ended his life. To this day I have moments when his reasons seem crystal clear, then times when I find myself questioning his decision over and over.

Towards the end of his life, Jeff was showing signs of mental illness, and this was extremely difficult for me to acknowledge. The phrase *mental illness* put a very dark picture in my mind, one that had nothing to do with the bright, funny, sweet boy I raised. Yet I do know this: Jeff's life went into a dark place the year before he turned twenty-one. Today I am ready to stand tall, tell the painful truth, and let Jeff's story fly with wings.

This one's for you, Jet.

Your pain is the breaking of the shell that
encloses your understanding.
Khalil Gibran

SEPTEMBER NIGHT

ON A BEAUTIFUL SATURDAY IN SEPTEMBER OF 1990, my boyfriend John and I took my daughter Dana, son Spencer, and Dana's friend Meilani to Oakland for a New Kids on the Block concert. As John and I enjoyed an elegant fish dinner while the kids attended the concert and bought tapes and t-shirts, I wished Jeff had wanted to join us. He of all people in the family would have loved the chance to hear the popular band live, even though he claimed they weren't cool. The next day, we slowly packed our things and said goodbye to the Bay Area after a morning at Pier 39 in San Francisco, shopping and eating and enjoying the view. Before we left, John and I walked to the end of the pier for one last look at the Bay. When we rounded the corner, the wind was sharp and cold. I flipped up my collar and mumbled to John that I hoped Jeff is warm, wherever he is.

Halfway home we decided to stop at the Vacaville outlets since we were in no hurry to get home. We climbed out of John's large truck and headed in separate directions—John and I towards a clothing store; Dana, Meilani, and Spencer to look at shoes. Out of character, John said he needed some better dress clothes, like a new suit he could wear to a wedding or a funeral. He tried on a couple and bought a dark charcoal suit, a pin-striped shirt, tie, black shoes and socks. We put these in the back of his truck, along with what we had purchased at Pier 39, which for me was a new angel for the top of a Christmas tree and a sunglass holder that looked like cowhide. Then we spotted the kids just finishing ice cream, so the five of us piled back into the truck and headed home.

Sunday evening at dusk, we turned down the long gravel road to the home John had built for us a few years before. We'd only been gone since the morning before, but it seemed much longer. As we drove along, with gravel crunching under the tires, I was telling John that my worst nightmare is that I'll live to be an old lady and Jeff would be the one who will be my care giver. We laughed a little because everyone knew that Jeff and I have this ongoing relationship of laughter and arguments.

King cab doors opened, and we jumped out of John's diesel truck, gathered our packages and gifts, except John who said to leave his bags in the truck, and went into the house. We happily walked down the short hallway and everyone dispersed to their rooms. The answering machine next to my bed was blinking faster than I had ever seen. Instantly, I knew it was trouble. Dana and her friend Meilani came in and lay across my pillows on the bed to listen to the messages that continued to roll in. I turned towards the bathroom, went in and thought about this for a moment, splashed cold water on my face, patted it dry, and came out.

I told the girls and John that I felt it would be bad news—perhaps a death in the family, and I think it might be Aunt Harriett. I clicked on the message machine and we listened. Lucinda, a hairdresser from my salon, kept leaving messages over and over that said nothing in particular, only that she needs to find me, she loves me, and to please call back. This was interspersed with messages from my sister, who sounded stern and said to call her immediately at Dad's house; it is an emergency. Over and over the same messages rolled in with pleas to return the calls. George, my step-brother, also left a message to please call my dad's house, his voice calm but desperate. Everyone was looking for me and begging me to call Dad's house. Even Tammy, my niece, left a message saying she was in Lakeport (she lived a five-hour drive south) and that I should call there as soon as possible. I thought to myself, yep, it's Aunt Harriett. I just knew it.

I told the girls to brace themselves. When the phone rang again, John answered and listened. I quickly went back into the bathroom to catch my breath and prepare for bad news. When I walked out, I searched for answers in John's face, which had grown red and tense. He kept his head down, not making eye contact with me, but I could see the veins throbbing in his neck. It's bad news for sure. He turned to me, held out the phone, and said, "It's your sister." As I walked towards him, he physically sat me down on the edge of the bed, handed me the phone, and tightly gripped each of my shoulders to hold me down. Then I listened as my sister blurted out the horrible news: "Jeff shot Dad; he's in the hospital. And Jeff shot himself; he's dead."

My arms flew up with such force that I knocked John's strong arms up and away. Blinded by these horrific blunt words, my hands were on the walls, rubbing through a dark maze as though searching for a way out, and I screamed a blood-curdling animal cry. Dana later described it as a deep primal animal cry for help, and told me it was a sound she had never heard before, and a sound she never wants to hear again. The girls were terrified, crying and hugging each other, still not knowing what the news was. Spencer ran in, saw the chaos, and asked John what happened. John gently told this sweet fourteen-year-old that his brother had killed himself. Dana and Meilani overheard this and ran into Dana's bedroom crying.

I was soon to hear more mind-numbing detail. Before I was told the news, my sister had told John that the transplant hospital wanted to harvest Jeff's organs at midnight and they would be phoning any minute to get permission. He was to prepare me for the call.

Within two minutes the phone rang again. It was indeed the transplant hospital in San Francisco. I had to choke my sobs and somehow say Jeff's full name, his date of birth, and my full name, and give them permission to harvest my son's soft tissue and organs.

The once-happy, now traumatized travelers somehow gathered back together. John was instrumental in helping us all pack suitable clothes for a funeral, so we could climb back into the truck and head to Lakeport where my family waited. The scene was already in place. John, of course, remembered that he had a full set of new dress clothes in his truck. Before we'd left for Oakland, I had laid a nice blue linen dress out on the bed and said to him, "I'll never wear this dress. I think I'll give it to someone." John grabbed that dress and Dana grabbed dress shoes for me. Then John helped Spencer gather nice clothes and told Dana to get a dress and shoes. John got on the phone and gave instructions to a secretary friend who began to take shorthand as he gave orders: Do this, call this person, cancel Judi's week at the salon, take my dogs to a neighbor, water plants, and keep an eye on the house.

Soon we were back in the truck, headed for Lakeport. Spencer sat in the front seat with John. Dana and I lay on a mattress in the camper, holding each other tight and sobbing. The ride seemed to be in slow motion, our sobbing endless. I have no idea how Meilani got home. John turned off Highway 5 onto Highway 20 and headed west through the mountain range, and eventually to Lakeport, a drive I had taken a thousand times. A full moon came up and seemed to follow us. I stared out the back camper window and noticed a translucent face forming in the back window from the condensation. My body moved forward and I rearranged the pillow to prop my head up so I could study the vision while the face stared back. I dared not mention what I saw to my daughter—a man with shoulder-length curly hair and what seemed to be a beard, or perhaps it was clouds just under his chin. I could see his eyes, high cheekbones, and a longer-shaped face. I continued to stare. Dana put her long thin arms around me, gently laid her head on my chest, and in her very soft voice asked, "Mommy, do you see the man's face in the window?" I calmly whispered back, "Yes, Dana, I do see him." At first we didn't talk about what we saw as we lay arm in arm but simply watched the face that was watching us. Finally Dana began to describe what she saw, and I realized she was seeing the same exact face.

Halfway to Lakeport, John pulled over to let Spencer stretch and join me, while Dana moved to the front seat with him. As Spencer curled up next to me, I thought it best not to mention what Dana and I had witnessed in the window, so I said nothing. My youngest son lay next to me and I comforted him, rubbed his hair, and tried to soothe him by patting his back and holding him tight. He then asked if I had noticed the image in the window. "It's the image of a man's face," he said. "Yes, I see him, honey, and Dana did too." My son and I watched the man in the window in silence as John drove us closer to a living nightmare.

When we arrived at my dad's house at 9:30 P.M., we entered using the back door that led into the kitchen. When I saw my family, I burst into tears and buckled, along with my kids and family. Finally we calmed down and walked next door, where George had arranged for us to sleep at his place. He had laid out two sleeping bags in his living room for John and me, and two in the front bedroom for the kids. He'd notified his wife Shari, who was traveling in London, about the news. He said she felt alone and isolated being so far away. Shari was also the person who cooked most of the meals so we were on our own. My sister had told me on the phone that the team of doctors would be harvesting my son's organs at precisely midnight. I wish I had been spared that brutal and painful information. John and I crawled into sleeping bags with comfortable pads underneath, but I couldn't sleep. I kept watching the clock numbers glowing in the dark. As the time drew nearer, I became more restless. Then at 11: 50 P.M., John could not keep me in the sleeping bag. I fought him away as I tried frantically to get outside. Finally he let me go, following as I ran through the house and out the sliding doors, jumped off the deck, went through the gate that led to my dad's side yard, then kept running until I was out from under the roof and the shadow of trees, branches, and leaves. I looked up at the stars and knew that at any moment the doctors would make their first cut. I screamed with all I had. John tried to calm me but I was inconsolable; he put his arms around me and held me tight, saying he loved me as I screamed a muffled tortured howl into his shoulder.

The next day we planned Jeff's funeral as I walked around in a daze. My father lay in ICU from the effects of a bullet through his lung. I didn't know which way to turn. I needed to console my children, visit my father, tend to business at the funeral home, and somehow deal with a house full of relatives in an atmosphere that had gone from chaos to silence.

John, not as emotionally crippled as I was, came to the rescue. He took Dana and Spencer under his wing. Gene and Patty, Jeff's father and step-mother, came over, and Gene and I cried as we planned our son's funeral and discussed picking up his ashes at the funeral home. I can't remember how long I was numb; I still am in some ways. I had lost a son to adoption as a teen, but losing a son to death was life-crippling. I couldn't get my mind wrapped around the reality of Jeff's death. It would take years of questioning everyone in a 1,000-mile radius to begin to decipher what happened and why. I would become a detective, searching for clues as I recalled every single day of my son's life.

Our trip to the Bay Area now seems like a dream, and the reality of what actually happened while we were enjoying a great weekend still makes my heart pound. My kids never listened to the tapes of the *New Kids on the Block* they bought at the concert and never wore their new t-shirts. We never mentioned our trip. I never thanked my friends, hairdressers, or neighbors for taking care of my business, house, land, and dogs. And Meilani never came over to stay with Dana again. Time stood still through that weekend, as though it had never happened.

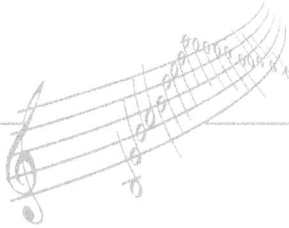

Never ask why, spread your winds and fly.
Jeff Harris, 1987

FÜR JEFF

YOUR FUNERAL WAS LOVELY. One would think we had prepared for weeks instead of just three days. It was held at the Episcopal Church across the street from Grandpa's house in Lakeport, the church with red brick, stained glass windows, and a high-pitched roof. Since you had been an acolyte in our church in Chico, it seemed best for us to say goodbye to you in Lakeport. Later I was sorry I didn't have a service for you in Chico, too, but I hope you understand that Lakeport felt like our best choice at the time.

The day before your service I sat with the priest on Grandpa's patio for a private moment and told him to please not go into a sermon about heaven and golden streets, wings of angels, and the love and warmth you now feel while resting in the loving arms of God. I said, please be respectful but, Jeff would prefer your eulogy to be truthful and straightforward, so please don't color-coat it. Jeff, you carried a heavy burden and made some poor choices, your sendoff needed to fit your lifestyle, your talent, and your tragic end.

The minister spoke with a keen sense of respect and insight. He described life as a tapestry that each of us weaves, then when we turn our art work over, we see all the knots and mistakes and re-dos that happened along the way. "This was the life pattern for Jeffrey's tapestry," he said.

Music began to fill the church and magnified the loss and suffering we felt, especially for our family who knew so well your musical talents. Many of us had experienced the pleasure of hearing you play Ludwig van Beethoven's *Für Elise in A minor*, a tune you played so beautifully in our family room on our antique upright piano. Grandma Marion had loaned me a tape of *Für Elise* as she knew the significance of this piece Keith had taught you so long ago, when you two were young kids. At your funeral, this music filled the chapel and our eyes brimmed with tears. John sat next to me, closest to the aisle. Dana was on my other side and Spencer next to her, all of us crying as the music played.

The rest of your funeral was a blur. I have only snippets of memories and conversations of that day. The church, I recall, was filled to capacity. A few friends I'd graduated with from Lakeport were there, which was a nice surprise. The reception followed and was held across the street in

Dad and Marion's back yard, though your grandfather lay in ICU recovering from being shot. He had no idea what had transpired as we filed out of the church.

The day before your funeral John took Dana for a ride around the lake and stopped for ice cream, the exact diversion she needed, an exit from the drama and sadness. Next he took Spencer to a soccer game where his childhood friend Mike was playing. Mike had moved across the street from our house in Chico to Lakeport, and now he lived one block down the street from my dad's house. John paid for the funeral and I paid him back when I was able. I don't recall for sure, but I think your dad sent half the cost.

I remember, too, that your Uncle George placed a pill in the palm of my hand, handed me a glass of water and waited until I swallowed. Then later, in the afternoon he handed me a second pill along with another glass of water. In the evening he handed me the small amber plastic bottle of pills and reminded me to be careful and read the directions. I have no idea what the doctor had given him, but the pain in my heart diminished and my tears were on hold. This was a wonderful insightful gift for a very dark day.

Your step-dad Don walked into the garage where you had shot yourself and said his goodbyes. He related this to me at the reception, but I was somewhat numb from the medication and looked at him as he described his moment of clarity and closure. Carolyn, Don's wife, told me she was very sorry and together we began to cry.

The food was laid out on one of Marion's vintage lace tablecloths. Many people must have sent meals and helped with the reception, as I don't recall any cooking at Dad's. I don't remember if the kids ate. Another small table was set up with a nice tablecloth and an 8 x 10 photo of you in a dark striped long-sleeved shirt with a library of books behind you as a backdrop, another photo of you with your little league baseball team, along with a bouquet of flowers. Your grandparents were here from Corning and your dad's family, your aunt, uncles, and cousins from Vacaville, but I have no recall of conversations—only red eyes and sad faces and hugs, maybe words of wisdom that I no longer remember. Your step-dad Don's sister and her husband drove over from Durham. Maybe your cousins came too. Patty's parents were there. Sarah was too young and must have been with a sitter. I hope I'm not missing anyone else who came over as I relive this day.

Grandma Harris was there—so tiny, stout, and as sweet as pie. I'm sure your death was the most horrible nightmare she had ever encountered. I can't forget that she stepped up to me and asked, "What happened?" I could hardly look her in the eye.

Do you remember, the week before when we went on a road trip to Grandma and Grandpa Harris' house, just thirty minutes away? We sat at their tiny kitchen table, while your grandpa lay on the couch because he wasn't feeling well. Grandma asked if we wanted a little something to eat and she put a tiny blob of tuna onto the corner of a tiny baguette, then placed the two bite-sized snacks on a teacup-sized plate. Then she asked if we wanted a little tea and we nodded yes, so she filled a tiny porcelain tea cup for each of us. You sipped the tea and put your little finger out. We tried not to chuckle because this was so silly. On her kitchen counter was the tiniest fire extinguisher I'd ever seen. Then she called in her dog, whose name was Tiny. You looked at me and we giggled as we sipped our tiny spot of tea.

This was on a Monday, September 3, just five days before you died. Did you suggest we go there to say goodbye to your grandparents? Did you know then that you were going to end your life? How were you able to sit there and smile and enjoy this day, knowing your end was so near?

The morning of your funeral, your dad and I had to make the terrible trip to the funeral home to retrieve your ashes. I remember leaving the funeral home, your dad carrying your ashes as we walked out the wide front doors, down the steps to the car. Gene opened the car door and I slipped into the front seat, then he placed the square cardboard box on my lap. It struck me as déjà vu; this was almost exactly the same scenario as twenty-one years and five weeks prior—the day you were born in Bakersfield. One difference was that it had been 113° when we stepped out of the hospital's double doors twenty-one years ago, the heat had been stifling. I'd carried you in my arms while Gene walked next to me, then I handed you back to your dad while I sat down in the passenger seat before he placed you in my arms for the ride home. When he handed me your ashes, the weather was perfect, a beautiful day.

The box that held what remained of you was heavier than one would imagine. Here we were, driving along the narrow shady streets lining old Victorian and bungalow houses; you, me, and your father. We said nothing, both looking straight ahead as we rounded the corner and pulled into my dad's wide driveway.

Years later, I would experience another weird coincidence that occurred after your departure from earth. When I was carrying you in 1969, my gynecologist in Bakersfield was Dr. Mundy. After your death in 1990, I was on a quest to find out what happened to your donor parts and was finally routed to the phone number for the Transplant Center located in San Francisco.

My phone call was forwarded to the doctor who harvested your donor parts and found recipients patiently waiting to receive them. He had your file and he told me that your eyes were in Northern California, your skin and femur bones were also in California, and cartilage from your ribs in Northern California. In those days it was not possible to give out names or numbers, but his little bit of information gave me a smidge of compassion to whomever received your donated parts, and I was pleased that parts of you helped people who needed them and were kept in Northern California. The doctor then introduced himself as Dr. Mundy. Startled, I sat back as my face went cold and I swallowed hard, then I asked him if he was from the Bakersfield area. He hesitated before turning the question around and asking me why I wanted to know. I told him about my doctor with the same last name who had delivered you twenty-one years ago and his startled reply was, "He's my father." So the father delivered you and the son accepted your donor gifts. The younger Dr. Mundy was as stunned to learn this as I was.

Für Jeff

The day after your funeral, John drove us home. Dana and Spencer had left directly after the funeral reception with their dad and Carolyn. It seemed too soon for your grieving brother and sister to return to school, but they thought it was best to keep busy and be with their friends. I was not in a position to argue, and perhaps they were right. Jeffrey, your family, aye, we are weak lot .... The length of time eludes me, but sometime fairly soon after we returned to our home, the kids settled back into school, and I went back to work, we became increasingly curious about your ashes. The box was heavy and it seemed an oddity that this was what remained of you. One late Saturday morning in early winter, your sister, brother, and I opened the lid of the nondescript sealed cardboard box and disturbed your ashes. Sorry. We undid the twisty and opened the thick plastic bag inside. Dana put in her hand and let the soft ash fall through her fingers, then she spotted a small bone fragment and kept it. I touched your ashes, ran my hands deep to the bottom and back up again, and then I sat back and melted into a clump. Your little brother, only fourteen years old, gently reached in and touched you; he looked closely at the wonder of a human body transformed into ashes. We folded up the bag, re-secured it, placed it back into the box, closed the lid, and put you back into my bedroom.

The kids and I kept to our routines, and tried to heal. Looking back, I knew I had to stay busy to keep my sanity. I still couldn't imagine how we would ever come out of this and be a normal family without you. Our life in a new home on an acre was splintered and nothing much seemed funny anymore. Not until four months after the funeral, when your cousin Tammy called to say she wanted to spend the weekend with me. She requested I cook a stew, and then we'd enjoy having time to curl up under a blanket and talk.

Tammy came into town to help and be my companion. She is the best wingman because she is organized, quiet, and helpful. So while the kids were in school, she and I went to a funeral home to buy an urn for your ashes. We waited, sitting in matching maroon velvet French provincial chairs while our eyes took in the design of the Victorian wallpaper and we breathed the scent of flowers that filled the room. The funeral director, dressed in a somber black suit and tie, entered through gathered curtains on French doors. He introduced himself, shook our hands, then sat down behind his large mahogany desk. The entire scene was a bit over the top and pretentious; we were intimated and nervous.

I collected myself, put on my business face, then cleared my throat and told him that my son had recently passed away and had been cremated in another town, Lakeport. I told him I would like to look at his selection and purchase a urinal. Tammy quickly leaned forward and corrected me, but I was confused and didn't know what she was doing, so I repeated myself, a bit louder this time. Tammy again leaned towards me, even closer this time, and ever so softly said, "It's called an urn." I sat stone-faced and confused, being in the zone and all, so she had to shake me back to my senses by repeating my faux pas, making me aware that I had referred to an urn as a urinal. I put my hand over my mouth, and we both tried to stifle ourselves. We were both red in the face, trying hard to regain our composure, and simply couldn't look at each other. The director smiled and said, "You'd be surprised how many people say that."

Oh Jeff, you'd have loved that moment, a moment of stupidity and embarrassment.

Eventually, we picked out a tall urn made of oak with rounded edges. On each side of the front were carvings of tall redwoods with an eagle flying above. The brass plaque to be placed on the lower part of the trees would be inscribed with your name, date of birth, date of death, and your own creative words, which we found in your binder of music lyrics. This was a huge task for me, but was only the first; I had a second decision to make.

Tammy and I prepared for the next phase: purchasing a casket for my mother who was gravely ill. I cleared my throat, took a deep breath, and told the staunch director that I was the conservator for my mother and needed to purchase a coffin in advance to disperse the money she'd received from my father's military pension after his recent death. Although my dad had been married to Marion for twenty-five years or more, his pension money went directly into my mom's checking account because she had been his spouse at the time he was in the service. This lump sum of money blew Mother out of her medicare supplement. Tammy leaned over to me once again, and began to whisper in her soft and matter-of-fact way, "Aunt Judi, it's called a casket; vampires sleep in coffins." Here we go again: *Ethel and Lucy* at a funeral home.

I'm sure the director heard what Tammy said, but being the pro he was, simply told me I could pay for the casket, plot, and a headstone in advance, and hold the paperwork until the time of her death. As he took us to the back room to choose mother's casket, Tammy poked me in the ribs, but I shook my head no, not daring to look her way. We kept our faces as straight as we could while we chose a sturdy casket of dark wood with blue silk inside.

Our business concluded, we were emotionally drained so headed to Big Al's and ordered a well-deserved treat: two double frosties dipped in chocolate. Then we drove back to my house in Durham, and as the stew continued to simmer, we took a nap.

Note: Your grandmother recovered and has already lived twenty-four more years since we purchased her casket. She is now ninety-four years old.

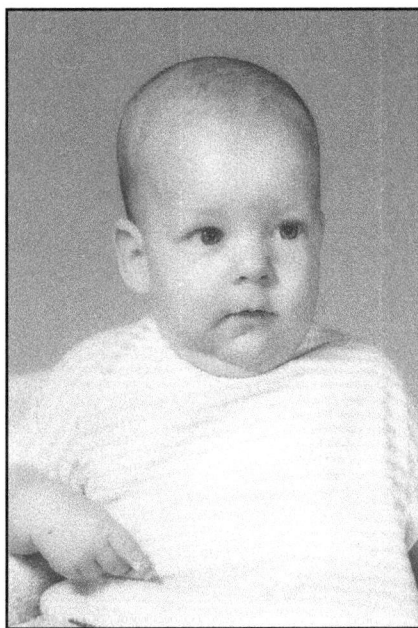

Twenty-some years earlier.

Music is the mediator between spiritual and the sensual life.
Ludwig van Beethoven

THE SUMMER OF '69

I'D MET A GREAT GUY WHEN I MOVED NORTH TO CHICO. His name was Gene, and he had a degree in civil engineering, drove an MGB, and had a sailboat. This was my dream come true.

Gene and I met at a party. He and another guy were measuring all the girls that came in. I was an inch taller than Gene, and when he measured me he stood on a box and said "Wow!" I melted as I looked at his big green eyes and the dimple in his chin, and then I smiled. He said he lived in an upstairs apartment and outside his window was a schoolyard and baseball field. I told him I lived in a basement apartment and outside my front window was a baseball field, then both of us said at the same time: "Citrus School!" Yes. We joked about meeting on third base. Jeff, this is the story of how I met your dad, fell in love, and married. You were to join us about two years later.

Forward two years

The following year we attended a picnic for Department of Water Resources on an extra warm day for May. I loved being pregnant and able to show my swollen stomach with pride. Of course, back then I wore smocks, but I was as skinny as a stick except for you growing inside of me.

Your dad was one of the concrete inspectors, and others were design and construction supervisors working in all aspects of this water resources project. Most of us attending the picnic were re-plants from Chico and Oroville in Northern California. After the Oroville Dam was complete, we had only a few months' notice to transfer to Southern California, specifically the desert. I'd told Gene at the beginning of our relationship that I couldn't move with him if we were not married. So we had a beautiful wedding in October followed by a reception in my dad and Marion's backyard, then a honeymoon in Mexico City and Acapulco. I was so proud to have Gene as my husband and to show my dad I could make something of myself by picking a good guy and becoming a respectable daughter. We moved to Bakersfield in January of 1968.

The new project in Bakersfield was to build an aqueduct that would bring water up and over the mountain range and into the Los Angeles basin from Northern California. There was much controversy in the news about Southern California taking Northern California water, then filling up their swimming pools and leaving their sprinklers on overnight so water overflowed onto their yards and filled the gutters. I remember watching Walter Cronkite on television as he showed photos of gutters filled with water and people swimming in lavish pools, evidence of how wasteful Southern California was. This was a time in history when many things began to change, everyone wanted peace. The Viet Nam War was a hot a topic. There were protests led by conscientious objectors who didn't want us in the war, or who were afraid to fight; and there were veterans who hated the ones who fled to Canada rather than enlist. The shootings at Kent State University were only a few years away, the hippy revolution had already arrived, and so had the Beatles and other British groups. Music was in full swing in the summer you were to be born. Artists who performed on the stage of the outrageous rock concert in Woodstock, New York, are icons today.

I was just twenty-two years old and had been married eighteen months when you came into our lives. It was a dry heat in Bakersfield, I felt at home in this area, but out of place as one of the youngest people at the picnic. I felt naïve and shy. In a crowd of hometown friends, I could laugh and talk all day; but in a crowd of new fresh friends, most with college degrees, I withdrew so as not to say something telling about my education, or lack of education, so I kept to myself. I sat and watched the women gossip, play with their kids, and eat hot dogs while the men talked and cooled off with a beer or two. Meanwhile the afternoon sun beat down on us, and I felt sick to my stomach. I could feel you kicking and rolling inside of me and sometimes watched my pale yellow smock move with you.

Your dad and I decided to leave early, and I was very happy to do so. The desert heat was starting to wear me down as the shade moved away. Your dad hadn't had a beer, but we were both new to this area, and this accounts for what happened to us next.

We left the park and headed back into town, winding up towards the freeway in our new forest green Pontiac Lemans. There were two streets that crossed the freeway; one had a four-way stop, the other a two-way stop. Gene thought we were farther down the road and that this was the one with the four stop signs. He pulled up, stopped, and looked both ways. I could see a car racing towards us from the right, but he assumed it would stop so he put his foot on the gas and drove into the intersection. The oncoming car was moving quickly towards us, and I watched in horror as it smashed into the side of our car, my side. I put my arms out to protect you as the car spun around in circles and came to rest on someone's yard on the corner lot. My head hit the passenger window and my stomach was jolted back and forth because of the seatbelt that went across my lap. Thank God we weren't in my Volkswagen, which didn't even have seatbelts. Gene was in a daze when we heard sirens in the distance. The date was May 31, 1969. You weren't due until late July and no one examined me. Gene talked to the police and honestly, I have no idea who brought us home or what happened to our car. I suppose it was towed away and repaired. I just wanted to rest and calm my baby.

You began to kick and move around violently. This kicking and rolling lasted for twenty-four hours non-stop. The next morning I went to my doctor. He listened to your heart, he checked my blood pressure, and as I look back on this, I realize he did nothing more. He told me to go home and lie flat and rest and said that my unborn child would soon settle down. I returned home, relieved that I wasn't going to miscarry, but uneasy with the doctor's lack of interest. The next two months I continued to worry about my pregnancy, that something might go wrong.

We drove to the hospital on July 31 at 6:00 A.M. The grid and location of our home meant there was only one way to the hospital, no shortcuts or alternate routes. All roads led back to this single throughway. Your dad put my little pre-packed overnight bag into the car and off we drove, excited that the day had arrived. We were naturally pensive, and drove with caution. We went just a few short blocks, and as the sun began to rise, we turned the corner towards the main road and were startled to see a house right in the middle of the street. I thought, who moves a house? We followed along at a snail's pace in disbelief. Gene had driven this route to the hospital with a timer so our grand finale to the hospital would be with impeccable timing, down to the minute. As we crept along, Gene was getting really impatient. Finally we reached the intersection that led to more streets that were part of the maze to nowhere. Your dad slowly drove around the side of the moving house, up and over the curb onto someone's lawn, and off we went.

I had a ten-hour labor, and then the doctor had to go up inside and cut the cord as it was wrapped around your neck several times. Every time I had a contraction and you moved farther down the birth canal, you were choking yourself. He was a wonderful doctor; he felt his way to your neck and cut the cord sight unseen and essentially saved your life. When you finally emerged, the doctor smiled and said, "It's a strong baby boy!" I named you Jeffrey Paul.

I stayed in the hospital for four days and tried to nurse you, but it was a nightmare for me. I looked at your beautiful face and wondered what kind of baby would suck so hard. The nurses said they could hear us all the way down the hall at the nurses' station—you sucking and me crying for help. I felt so much pain that I checked inside my nursing bra for blood, but there was no sign of red. I guess I was just too young and had no information to guide me. But you were starving, so they put you on a bottle and you gulped it all down.

While I struggled to adjust to motherhood, Gene was out celebrating at a Basque café, telling his friends and everyone else that he was a dad. In his inebriated enthusiasm, he spilled his bowl of soup onto his lap. My friends who witnessed this said Gene laughed at himself, and the proprietor gave him another bowl of soup.

Gene came to the hospital to take us home, back through the maze of streets, then on to the north and up the only hill for miles. My mother was waiting on the porch when we pulled into the driveway. You were born into this world on her fiftieth birthday. She always lied about her age, saying every year that she was twenty-nine, so now I could keep track by adding your age plus fifty years. Your grandmother had suffered a stroke when I was three and another, a massive stroke, when I was fifteen. As a result, she had been steadily going downhill in her strength and ability to function and be of any help. Although she tried and loved us so much, I was not sure if her being with me at this time was a good idea. For example, the day after I brought you home, she did a load of laundry while I lay down to catch some sleep. She had also been soaking some baby clothes, which plugged up the drain when the water went into the basin from the washing machine. Eventually the sink overflowed onto a fifty-pound bag of dry dog food. I left this soggy mess for Gene to clean up and continued to function with little sleep, afraid of what Mother might do while I slept.

My mother also kept picking you up after I asked her not to, and she almost fell down more than once; but slowly she would make it to the rocker, which was very old. I would be resting, almost asleep, when I would hear the creak of the rocker, and my eyelids would flip open. Fortunately, your grandmother's friend came into town two days later and took her back home. It was sweet for your grandmother to try to help, but it was a very stressful few days for me.

I should have felt happier than I did, but I was too scared to enjoy the first few weeks of your life. Most young mothers have their own capable mothers or someone else with experience to guide them. I had no one to offer an opinion or to prepare a meal, or to knock at the door with groceries. I delivered you, and after a few days, we were on our own. Gene worked all week and my only support was my girlfriend, Sharon, who was a new mother three months ahead of me.

The night after your grandmother left, I had to phone the doctor because you had developed a high fever. The answering service found him at a pool party. I could tell he was very irritated by the way he asked certain questions point blank. I told him you were listless and very hot. When he asked me if I had given you any water, I said no I had not. He snapped, yelling, "Then give your baby a bottle of water!" Then he asked what you were wearing. I told him a cotton long-sleeved gown with a tie at the bottom and socks, and that you were wrapped in a blanket. He yelled, "Get those clothes off your baby; he's dehydrated! It is 110° outside!" I felt sure he wanted to jump through the phone and slap me. He repeated for me to immediately remove all your clothes, give you a nice lukewarm bath, and let you sleep in a diaper only. I quickly did all this, and once you'd emptied the water bottle and were placed back into your crib, you slept for four hours. I had no idea that babies could just wear a diaper. Sorry.

The hospital had given me a free 5 x 7 professional photo to be taken when you turned three months. The end of October, off we went— you in your cutest jumper. The photographer sat you on a blanket and began to do silly antics to make you smile, but you just stared back. He dropped a green stuffed squeaky frog on top of his head and yelled,

"Ah boo!" He squeaked more toys; he jumped forward and back again and again. You stared. He finally turned to me, and with a serious face told me he had been photographing babies for twenty years and he had never seen a baby give him such a deadpan stare. He asked me if you ever smiled or giggled. I said, "Not too much, but he does smile and laugh with me and his dad." He then turned back towards you and snapped a photo, and to this day when I look at this one photo, I see you, Mr. Deadpan, and it makes me smile. I have very few pictures of you smiling; you preferred to stare into the lens.

You were a strong and bright boy; you began to pull yourself up and side-step around the coffee table at five months. When you were seven months old, we left you with my sister and went snow skiing for the weekend. It was a much-needed break, and Bobbie was happy to have a baby in the house. When we came back to pick you up, she told me to sit down on the floor and said, "Look at this!" She stood you up and you walked over to me. What should have been a joyous moment was not so much. Your dad and I wanted to teach you to walk, which we knew would happen early, but not this early. Plus, now I had a seven-month-old baby who was walking around with no idea what the words *no* or *stop* or *hot* meant, nor any concept of danger. I would have prolonged your crawling and kept you side-stepping around the coffee table for much longer, as you were happy to side-step and reach for toys. Naturally we bought a playpen with toys and *babyfied* the entire house.

Sharon, my best girlfriend, had a baby girl named Holli. We took you babies everywhere, and we walked through the mall most days then back to my house or to hers. I had a black buggy like the ones in the movie *Mary Poppins,* I stacked two buggy mattresses so you could see out and off we went. We were young girls with babies, and it was a fun time. Also, because I learned from Sharon and her mother's instructions, I began to slide into confident mother mode. I can say that you and I were growing up together. I have a vivid memory of Sharon and me sitting on her couch, holding our babies and watching this new singer on television, Janis Joplin. Then Tom Jones did a duet with her. It was a blessing for each of us to have a very silly and funny friend sharing our journey.

As you know, you weren't my first baby. When I was just fifteen, I discovered I was pregnant and was sent to a home for unwed mothers where your half-brother was born. I was forced to relinquish that baby when he was nine weeks old after your grandmother suffered her second stroke and I became ill with the Asian flu. What I have since learned is that in most cases, the young mother who suffered separation and forced relinquishment tends to marry young and become pregnant soon after to replace the baby that was taken from her. I fit this observation perfectly, but didn't recognize my motives for wanting a child so early in my marriage to Gene. I loved Gene; he was a wonderful husband and we had a good life. But when you were born, Jeff, I was a mother with scar tissue and baggage. You were sweet and precious, but you were not the baby boy I had lost those years ago. I not only went into post-partum depression that's caused by a hormone drop after birthing a child, but I was once again reliving and grieving for the son I'd birthed seven years prior. I know now that's why I suffered a breakdown when you were fifteen months old.

Jeff, although you didn't like to be cuddled or sit on laps, you and I developed a close bond because we were alone so much of the time, but we also butted heads early on. You were very sweet, but you were also strong-willed. When you were about seventeen months old, I put you in your crib for a nap. You cried and struggled with me and refused to lie down. You'd pop right back up like a Jack-in-the-Box. I'd put you down again, and the power struggle went on and on. Finally I put you in the crib one last time and closed the door. You jumped up and down, turning your crib mattress into a trampoline, and vaulted over the edge, opened the door, and ran down the hall. Wow, impressive! I gave up.

Then there was the time I decided to potty train you when you were twenty-four months old. I put you on the wooden potty chair, secured a little strap across your lap, turned on Captain Kangaroo, and began to wash dishes. Then I heard a squeak and knew it was the front door opening. I looked out the door to see you running down the sidewalk with a potty chair strapped to your back. This scene of you leaving me standing with a surprised look on my face was to be repeated many times.

I bought you a nice large picture book that you loved. I ran bath water and told you to hop in. When I went into check on you, I discovered that you had put your book under water to show me how the pictures magnified. This remained your favorite book, even though the pages were wavy and crinkled, and you continued to look at this ruined book for a long time.

Jeff, we soon left Bakersfield, where our shared journey had begun. The project your dad was working on ended, so we moved to Windsor, a small town ten miles north of Santa Rosa, where Gene had found a job. We lived on an acre on a country road, and I felt isolated and suffered terribly. I missed my friendship with Sharon, I missed my retired neighbors who were my security for raising a baby, and I hated being in a town so far from my hometown and childhood friends. I stayed in bed most of the day; you stayed close to me and became used to me lying in bed with no energy. I'd give you a handful of Cheerios and you would eat them one by one, then snuggle up next to me and sleep. Finally I began to recover somewhat. My relationship with Gene was not as wonderful as I had hoped; he didn't spend much time with us. He came home from work, put his lunch box on the counter, then would head for the garage to work on his projects. I cooked and napped, did the laundry and napped, bathed you and napped. I was a mess, and lonely. I totally blame our divorce on me. I was too young to be married. I'd married for the wrong reasons, and I was ill-equipped to be a mother. I had no one to help me and show me what comes natural to so many mothers. I lost my confidence, my pride, and my passion for life. I had a beautiful baby boy but I was too emotionally crippled to cope.

I left this marriage when you were only three; you and I moved back to Chico to begin a new life. Gene soon met a young woman who was his perfect mate, married her, and gave you your wonderful step-mom Patty. Life moves on. You continued to be a very sweet boy, but I could see you were different when you were with other little children, especially when I went to work and enrolled you in the Kings Christian Nursery School. They told me that you played alone, but next to kids. The teachers found you a handful, and I had many talks with them about your not napping during *nap time*, and you trying to climb the cyclone fence to escape. E-gad!

The following year I met Don on a blind date. I worked with his sister and she set us up. Soon we were dating and serious. I told him he looked like *Adam Cartwright* on *Bonanza*, and he loved that. Don was tall and large-framed, had black wavy hair that was thinning on top, and had a wide smile. The winning kicker was this: he knew how to dance. He grew up in a family of twelve children—second to the last and the last boy. I thought I was marrying into the *Walton's*, like the TV series. Life was good and Don agreed to be a good stepfather to you. Because this was my second marriage, we had a chocolate wedding cake. Jeff, you were just four when I married Don and now had many cousins, aunts, and uncles.

Don and I bought a small house and got you a dog named *Maggie Mae*. We had been married just seven months when Don's mother passed away. Don grieved terribly over his loss and longed for change. We began searching for a new town.

One day, in early spring, I asked Don to bring home a coconut. He laughed and said okay. I told him, "I don't care where you have to go, but please find one." He came home for lunch and put a coconut on the kitchen counter. I ran outside with the coconut and a hammer, sat down in the middle of our driveway and smashed it open. Jeff, you sat next to me, and together we ate the fresh coconut meat and drank the juice ... ahhhhhh, perfect. This was what I needed, and it was sooooooo refreshing. I never tasted another coconut with such intensity. Three weeks later we packed up and moved south, to Rancho Mirage, a small desert town just three miles north of Palm Springs.

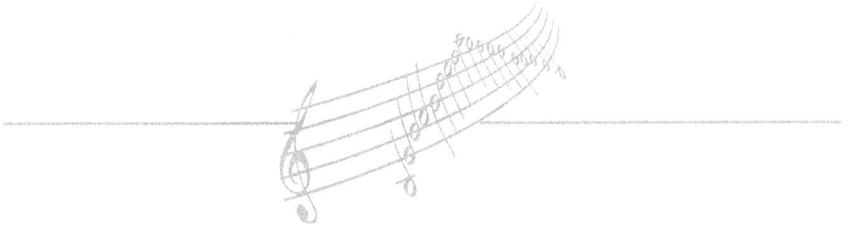

If there must be trouble, let it be in my day,
that my child may have peace.
Thomas Paine

GOOD TICKETS

OUR MOVE TO RANCHO MIRAGE proved to be a test of wills. The day Don and I lined up to caravan to the desert, he drove the moving truck. You wanted to ride in the truck with your daddy so I followed behind in my Datsun 510. On the news that day, the President had ordered gasoline rationing. One could get in line for gasoline depending on whether your car license plate ended in an odd or even number. I vaguely remember driving, sitting in the shade to eat and rest, and putting you into my car as we continued south. The first day only even-numbered plates could get gas. Luckily, both our license plates had an even number so we drove as far as we dared before filling up our tanks, then we refueled before midnight to take advantage of the even number rationing day to get us to our destination.

Very late that night, we pulled into our new home. Don flipped on the lights, and I went into the kitchen to check out storage and put away what food we had packed. I opened the cabinet doors to wipe everything down with a damp cloth and the smell of *new* made me sick. I had to run outside for a gulp of fresh air. Two weeks later, you and Don took me to the doctor. As we left our appointment, you held my hand and Don held the pink and blue vitamins the doctor had put inside the baby bottle, and down we went on the elevator in shock. I was due in November.

We settled into our new home, and began to adapt to the never-ending 70° daily weather. Every day your dad woke up, smiled, and said the same thing: "Well, it's another balmy 72° today." Then the summer desert heat began to close in, followed by beautiful evenings. At night the skies were filled with the sounds of coyote howls. The moon was always bright and the breeze kept the temperature at ... a balmy 72°.

I was into the third month of my pregnancy when Don asked me to help him lift our TV over the threshold so he could take it in to a repair shop. We argued a bit about me lifting but finally I gave in and lifted one end of the large console. We managed to get it into his El Camino using a makeshift ramp. On our way back home, he drove us around to look at unfinished homes. We stepped out of the car to look at the construction when the world around me began to swirl, and down I went. Your dad carried me back to the car, and you, Jeff, crawled in and sat between us as he sped toward the emergency room.

There was a large amount of blood at the scene, which I tried to conceal from you. I was sure I had begun to dilate and was about to miscarry.

In the emergency room, the doctor checked me. I had indeed begun to dilate slightly, and he suggested I let him remove the fetus. I balked at this idea, opting to be sent home and take my chances. His advice was to stay flat, do no activity whatsoever, except to walk slowly to use the bathroom, and to contact my own doctor immediately. I did as told for two months while you, my active son, terrorized the neighborhood. My neighbor Sherry was an angel. She watched over you, as did some other mothers who also had young children. Some days a watchful mother would bring you home and you'd watch cartoons, or play with building blocks, or snuggle up next to me and nap. Yes, you actually napped sometimes. But just as often you would go outside and get into mischief.

Summertime on the desert was not an easy time to stay indoors in the mornings and late afternoons. There was a pool just down the path, but you couldn't go there without an adult. Kindergarten was still three months away. Meanwhile, I received a shot in my hip every day and then once every other day, then once a week, and finally just once a month to keep my baby from aborting. It was a very long recovery for me, and I'm sure a hard time for you too.

But Jeff, you were so sweet, helping care for me. I thank you for the water you'd bring to me in your red plastic cowboy boot cup. Sometimes you brought me crackers and once an apple; but the one cracker with peanut butter really hit the spot. One day you noticed the Japanese fan on my dresser and you fanned my face, which was at first very annoying as I waited for you to hit my nose, but you never did. Then you fanned my belly and my feet; you gave me a full body fanning. When I'd get a call from another mother offering to help, I knew I could trust you not to stray but walk straight down the short path to her home, where she would be waiting for you. You sensed this was not a game and understood your mom had to lie still. Later when I was able to sit up, I'd go into the living room and you'd sit right next to me and watch my hands work the needle as I did stitchery and produced a colorful picture out of threads. You were mesmerized by this, and liked to watch for long periods of time. Later, as I grew in size, you liked to put your little hand on my smock and feel the movement underneath. You told me many times that you wanted a brother.

Eventually I was able to walk down the path to the swimming pool with you. You loved to swim and were as fast as a little fish. I'd slip down into the refreshing water to relieve my backaches and to cool down. You and I were as brown as berries that summer. And, dear one, your antics continued. You had good days mixed with crazy days, but never a really bad day. I never knew what to expect. There were times, not just once but twice, when you ran out in front of cars as we waited on a busy intersection for the bus to take you to kindergarten. I think you did his for attention and to shock the other kids waiting patiently for the school bus. I had prepared you for this day, we had visited your school and you met your teacher, who was young and pretty. But you continued on with your comic show with the traffic. I had to hold your hand, and then watch you step onto the bus, and then hope you would be stepping off at noon where I waited.

Jeffrey, you caused such a stir, and I didn't understand why you were drawn to death-defying stunts. For example, there was a tall hill in front of our house that I told you to never climb because of the unsteady terrain of dirt and small to medium rocks straight up to a sharp peak. I was doing dishes directly across the street and had just told you to watch out for sidewinders. You'd yelled back, "I will" as you rode your bicycle with training wheels back and forth. Then I heard a "Hi Mom!" I looked out the window but didn't see you. But when I walked out the front door and looked up, there you are, sitting at the top of the hill, smiling and waving. I rubbed my swollen belly and softly said, "Please come down!" When you'd scrambled down, you got another lecture about rolling rocks and injuries.

Once you were chased down the path by a gang of little boys. When I heard the commotion, I stepped out onto the porch and ushered you into our house. The boys backed away. What had you done? I've always wondered.

I recall a letter sent to everyone in our complex saying that someone had removed ten sprinkler heads and that such vandalism would not be tolerated. I looked at your step-dad and we said in unison, "No way." We walked into your bedroom, looked in the closet, lifted the lid to the toy box, then finally lifted your *Mickey Mouse* bedspread and looked under your bed. There they were. You got another lecture, this time about replacement and thievery. Don took you to the office and you apologized and returned the sprinkler heads. After many such incidents, we decided to take you to a pediatrician at the Eisenhower Medical Center for evaluation.

Shoo fly

I took you in to see our pediatrician in late spring and mentioned the difficulties we were experiencing. The doctor suggested an EEG. In two weeks you and I, along with your new baby sister, Dana, went to your appointment for testing. The receptionist told me to walk down the path to the testing area. "You'll see the sign," she said. It happened to be a single-wide trailer behind the looming Prestigious Medical Center. A nurse showed us the way to the testing area, and once inside the technician told you to lie still on a examining table as she placed electrodes all over your head. "This won't hurt, but don't move." Jeff, you looked over towards me and remained still. Your eyes looked big and green, but you weren't scared. For some reason, it felt like a scam to me. I wondered why we weren't in a private room with an air conditioner.

I spotted a fly in the room. The nurse had left the door open as it was a warm winter day on the desert and airflow, even hot air, was needed. I watched the readout of your brain function on the machine, and I also watched the fly. It landed on your forehead, but you rolled your eyes upwards toward the fly and never moved a muscle. It buzzed my head, landed on my knee, then returned and landed on your nose. You twitched as it walked down your cheek. I couldn't stand this another second so I told the technician about the fly. She told me not to talk or disrupt the patient because he might move. I repeated, "But the fly ...." She shushed me so I waved my hand across your face; you looked at me and smiled. Too bad I didn't bring the Japanese fan along with me, I thought. Finally your test was complete. The technician told us the doctor would call but he never did. I even took you back in for another exam, and the doctor hardly mentioned the EEG, brushing it off as if it were an afterthought. What a fiasco.

The doctor wrote a prescription for you for something called Ritalin. This new drug was supposed to help you to focus and settle down. He never mentioned any side effects or long-term effects. Three weeks later we sat down for dinner and you began to cry. Don asked you what was wrong, and you said part of your Brussels sprouts was not warm, then you hung your head and had a meltdown. You sobbed over your vegetables even after I heated them up. You cried all the time or were listless, or over-the-top hyper. Your emotions were all over the place and you seemed frantic inside. Obviously this medicine was not the answer to your behavior issues. I called my grandmother for advice, then the doctor's office, and he took you off this medicine. In a short time you again became a very happy responsive little boy.

Jeff, when you had been in Kindergarten a few months, the teacher told me during our parent/teacher conference that you were showing signs of antisocial behavior. Apparently you would play but not interact with the other kids; you would play next to them doing your own game. That was exactly what your teacher in nursery school had said about you. Your kindergarten teacher went on to say she observed you hiding behind a tree then jumping out to scare the kids, but the kids were on the swings or playing with a wagon and not paying attention. No one noticed that you had jumped out with arms up, gloves on your hands. I felt a twinge of doom as I realized you were not mainstreaming like other kids, and I had no answers.

I talked to your dad and Patty and yes, they would love to see you for the holidays. We decided to send you to visit them during Christmas vacation. My next-door neighbor Sherry's husband, Kent, the man in charge of the Palm Springs Airport, took care of all the details. You were thrilled when we told you you'd be on a plane. We put you on a non-stop flight with attendants in charge of watching you, and your daddy Gene and step-mom Patty picked you up in San Francisco. They took you to their ten-acre place on the Russian River, which included Patty's childhood horse Taffy, and a big dog with blue eyes named Tasha. I knew you were having a wonderful Christmas, and I had two weeks of peace and quiet with your six-week-old baby sister. You had a great holiday with your dad and grandparents, with total attention bestowed on you. Don and I stuck bows on a rubber tree plant, opened gifts, and I carried our new baby as we walked to the pool for a swim.

The following summer I remember going outside daily to get the mail and using a pot holder to open the scorching mailbox. I remember, too, that our car windshield had been sand-blasted from a drive through a sandstorm. The dry heat was so severe, Jeff, that you went to the emergency room for a bloody nose and had to have your nose cauterized. We weren't snow birds, that's for sure. Then Don and I began to argue more than usual, and we wanted to move back up north to be close to our family. With your new baby sister and your antics, we thought that being near family would bring you back down to a manageable level.

It took one long year, but finally we sold our home, packed up, and headed back home to Chico.

Mother Deaf

First grade began for you, and we were back in Chico. You were still being a clown in class, and the principal called me one rainy day to tell me that you were standing under the rainspout, fully clothed, pretending to take a shower to the roars of laughter from your classmates and a gathering crowd. I bundled up Dana who was then thirteen months old and drove the two blocks to the school, walked into the principal's office and retrieved you, my soaking wet six-year-old. I asked, "Why did you do that?"

You told me, "I don't know, but it was real funny."

A few years later, the school child psychologist tested you and called us in to discuss the results. Don was working so I went in with your three-year-old sister Dana, and your one-year-old brother Spencer. The psychologist said, "Jeff has a personality disorder known as *Cause and Effect*. This means that he does something and when he gets into trouble he is totally surprised. He doesn't think of the effects his actions will produce, or the pain this might inflict on others or to himself." Now I was beginning to get it; a small ray of light flickered in my mind. Yes, I agreed with her, and in my mixed bag of emotions felt a wave of relief along with a sinking feeling of sadness for you. She offered no suggestions on how to cope with *Cause and Effect* disorder. We were free-flying with no instructions. "Just know that he will continue to act out and he will be surprised with the results," the psychologist said.

Oh good grief, I thought.

Jeff, you then developed *Mother Deafness*; you tuned me out. I had warned you so many times to not do something, or to be careful, or to stop whatever it was you were doing, that you simply didn't hear me anymore. I clearly remember seeing the very familiar look on your face so many times when you were in trouble, or when Don would come home and be furious with you over your latest antics. The look of surprise and confusion across your face infuriated us, but still we continued to reason with you, lecture you, put you in your room, or sometimes even spank you in an attempt to get you to behave. You seem to understand (after the fact) but continued to act out without thinking of the effect. Now I feel so sorry that we were so angry and hard on you. I know now that we were the ones who didn't get it.

Our marriage was strained. Don kept his promise to love you as his own child—until I gave birth to his daughter and son, who became his shining glory. He was passionate about his little girl, whom he affectionately called Lolly, and his own bubbly son. You were there, too, but often went unnoticed unless you were in trouble. Tensions between Don and I were running high. I could see a clear difference in the way he loved his own little ones, and how he loved you.

During your childhood in the '70s, there were few labels. Autism was unheard of then, and we certainly weren't aware that there were levels of autism, slight to serious. We'd heard of ADD, attention deficit disorder, and thought you may have had a small case of ADD, but you were not hyper. You were quiet, and creative, and fearless. Bipolar was a recognized label for severe mood swings, but you stayed the same, day in day out. Quiet, silly, and busy. Savant was the label for one who was genius is some areas, and you were a genius in music, and also clever in the classroom and in some other situations. Prodigy? Maybe.

But back then, any child who had any of the above disorders was tagged unruly and simply needed a spanking or punishment of some sort or a good stiff talking-to. Very little information was available and few studies had been focused on childhood disorders. Medicine, such as Ritalin, only made you drop into a zombie state, or become a weeping child. Kids with personality disorders in the '70s and '80s, like you, were guinea pigs.

Don and I made an appointment with another child psychologist who was in private practice when you were going into fourth grade. We avoided going through the school system as we didn't want any paper trails to follow you. The psychologist's name was Janet. First she talked to the three of us, with Dana coloring next to me and Spencer bouncing on my knee; then she talked to you privately. Two months later, and after weekly appointments, she called us back in as a family. "Here is the plan," Janet suggested, "When Jeff is bad he sits in the corner for no more than ten minutes; if he sits longer, he'll forget why he is there. When he is good he gets a *ticket* (a square piece of colored paper with a star or dollar sign on it). A *ticket* for good behavior is worth money. He is in charge of keeping his *good tickets*. When he has a reasonable amount of good tickets, he can use them as money to buy whatever he wants (as long as it's appropriate). "Don't wait forever or he'll lose interest and the game will mean nothing," she warned.

Jeff, you eventually earned nine *good* tickets for excellent behavior so we had a meeting at our kitchen table with an audience of two little faces. Even your brother and sister sitting nearby sensed that their big brother was a good boy today. We asked, "What would you like to buy for yourself for being a good boy, Jeff? You just name it!"

Jeff, you put your finger up to your cheek and thought, *hmmm, well, let's see.* You asked about prices of record albums, then said, "If I have enough *tickets*, I would like the album *Grease.*" On Saturday I left the two little ones with their dad and you and I went off to Sundance Records and bought your album with money to spare. You began building a bank account. You were excited and you listened to Grease *Is the Word* many times. I still have your album today. Unfortunately, you thought you were one of the characters and wanted to flip your coat collar up at all times.

Jeff, you were proud and happy, and could see that good behavior brought good things your way. This plan lasted about a year, but with a two-year-old, a four-year-old, and nine-year-old you, this plan began to waver. I dropped the ball as I had no time to cut up squares and take you shopping. Besides, you knew how to work it to get a gift. You forgot about this game, too, though you continued to listen to your album and play with your Rubik's Cube, and speak into your new recorder. I felt I had gained control, and that we were a functional family. *Grease IS the word.*

In the meantime your friend Keith came over a lot. He already had five years of classical piano lessons. You sat next to Keith, watching him play, then I heard you ask to watch just one more time. Next thing I knew, you'd scooted him over, and you played Beethoven. In between your being outside making forts, building bicycle ramps for jumps, or swimming, you would run into the house to play the piano. Or while waiting for dinner, our home would be filled with the music of Bach or Beethoven or other classical composers that Keith had shown you. Sometimes you added a boogie-woogie song to mix it up. The rest of us played *Chopsticks*.

You and Spencer would sit for hours drawing dragons with many personality disorders. Some shooting flames out of their mouths, some dancing, and a large scared dragon is yelling, "Oh gad." Your dragon art designs are skillful and clever, and any mom would have saved them. I did, and now they're treasures. *Look out, it's a dragon!*

Then one day you came home from school and sat on the curb. I thought I heard a radio. It was you, Jeff, playing *Theme from Rocky* on a trumpet. My neighbor walked down the street, knocked on the door to tell me that her son had taken four years of trumpet lessons and still couldn't play that tune so well. I was stunned that it was you filling our neighborhood with *Theme from Rocky*. Over the years, you would play in many concerts at school, while Spencer took saxophone lessons, and Dana had piano lessons. We almost had a band.

Not all was going so well for you, though. You always had swollen eyes and sometimes you were listless, so off we went to an allergist. He made little pinpricks in your back that contained different solutions you might be allergic to. The test was positive when a tiny red welt showed up where the doctor had inserted the pin on your back. What a shocker to see so many welts on your back. You were allergic to weeds, pollen, dog and cat fur, dust, flowers, and the list continued; but the biggest welt of all showed you were allergic to wheat. I always was a health nut, even grew sprouts in the kitchen window, and I made sure my kids had plenty of wheat bread and wheat germ meal to sprinkle on their wheat cereal. I am so sorry I gave you wheat, wheat, and more wheat.

I also wish I'd known then that sugar can lead to behavioral problems. I made sure you had lots of Kool-aid (one package mixed with a whole cup of sugar!) in the summer, even filling ice-cube trays so you kids could suck on Kool-Aid popsicles. I know, this makes no sense. And even less sensible was the *healthy* drink called *Tang* (basically orange flavoring and sugar) that I'd mix with water, more sugar, and cinnamon. No wonder you kids were off the charts.

Confirmation

Mr. Wing, your fourth grade teacher, called our home one evening. I thought, oh dear, now what? To my surprise, he asked permission to submit your name to the gifted program.

He felt strongly that you were very smart, and needed to channel your intelligence. He jokingly said that Jeff is the only student he'd ever taught who learned through osmosis. He said you clowned around, made faces, and always sharpened your pencil to cause disruption in class. Then he went on to say that he would pass around a surprise pop quiz, and you would always get an A.

The names for the gifted program were submitted from all schools, and then the eliminations were posted. Sadly, you did not make it into this program, Jeff. I was so disappointed and let down, but you shrugged your shoulders and told me it was okay.

How Dare He

When your fifth grade teacher, Mr. Wetmore, talked to me at a parent/teacher conference, he chose his words carefully. He said he believed you had a learning disability and suggested that you receive special attention or work with a tutor. I found his remarks, which were opposite from what your previous teacher had expressed, insulting. I mentioned to him about the gifted program, and he shook his head no. Looking back on this, I should have swallowed my pride and listened carefully to what he said. I may have realized that you were a genius in some areas, but had trouble in others—for example, understanding a list of verbal chores and simple instructions. Also, the *Cause and Effect* personality disorder was an ongoing issue. I see now that Mr. Wetmore was right, too.

Jeff, you were confusing to me. In between your daily comic antics and playing outrageous classical tunes, you helped me with my mother. I recall you, walking slowly next to her and helping her with her walker as you led her into my car. You were very gentle and patient with Nana. But I had no idea who you were or when you would take another turn. Sometimes you and the younger kids would take Nana's walker and race with it up and down our street. And once I saw you, and I think it was Dana, pop a wheelie with the walker. We had to replace the wheels. Still, Nana was happy to be with us surrounded with all our household commotion.

None are so blind at those who won't see.
Author Unknown

THE TURNING POINT

SEVENTH GRADE—YOU'RE IN JUNIOR HIGH NOW! You tried out for the football team, and you made the grade. This was a major victory, and you were ecstatic. You went to practice every day in August and then after school. The big day arrived when you came home with a duffle bag and showed us your shoulder pads and helmet. Spencer ran around the house with your helmet on. Dana stood behind me watching, then she reached out and you let her touch your shoulder pads. You were beaming, and I couldn't remember the last time you were shining from within like that. Your excitement was contagious. You also worked out after school to prepare for the big game.

The next day your school counselor, Barbara, phoned to say you needed to bring back the equipment because you lacked two points due to a math grade and could not play on the team. I begged her to let you play, to give you a chance. I called the principal and explained your history, that you were on the threshold of getting into trouble and being on the team would turn your life into a positive, "I know how my son works," I said. No was the final answer, all the way to the Superintendent of Schools. It killed me to tell you the devastating news. You cried and became very angry and simply didn't understand. I drove you to school and went into the offices, handed the counselor the bag of gear and glared at her. She said something but my anger made me deaf.

Downhill

Jeffrey, you had been in the principal's office frequently and had missed school often. Still, being selected to be on the football team, only to have this snatched away, left you in a dark angry place. You acted out—meeting kids who stood across the street and smoked, and you stayed out until late into the night. I lost control, Keith lost a friend, and your music went silent.

The summer before your 8th grade year, you and a friend ran away from home. We put in a missing persons report, and five days later the police called. You kids were found inside a yacht that was parked behind a huge car dealership. The owner noticed the crank window was up on the top of his yacht, took a look inside, and found you boys, two girls, hamburger wrappers, candy wrappers, and boxes of his crackers and food all over the place. This gang of thieves had eaten all of the owner's peanuts and drank his Amaretto.

You were now in the system, following a pattern that was going to change the rest of your life. You were arrested four months later for holding the door open while your friends carried out a TV set, tape recorder, and cassettes from the Junior High School. I couldn't help but note that this was the same school that took away your football gear. I'm sure this created a deep-seated hatred in you, plus I suspect you had some level of enjoyment in getting even.

This petty crime landed you and your friends in Juvenile Hall for the weekend.

When you were a young teen we transferred you to a private Christian school, you pulled yourself together and were doing well, but you were very street-wise by then. I later discovered that many parents with kids who were on the edge of crime or out of control put them into this Christian school. While there, you made many contacts for smoking pot. You eventually told me that your class planted a garden at the school, and that you and your pal Vince cultivated your own pot. No one noticed or knew what it was.

One evening, you took a hot shower after dinner, I reminded you that you were grounded. I watched you put on your jacket, do one last check of your hair in the hall mirror, then walk out the front door. I ran to the door and yelled, "Come back here! You are grounded, mister!" You turned slowly back to me, smiled ever so sweetly and calmly said, "I'll see you tonight." I stood watching from the door, with your brother and sister peeking around my legs, as you walked away. It was a hopeless feeling, knowing I'd lost the war.

Dana and Spencer never asked me what you had done or why you were in trouble. They just watched, said nothing, asked no questions, and continued to love you wholeheartedly. And your love for me and the kids was ever-present and never wavered, but you were headed down the wrong road.

On a warm summer night you were headed home, riding your Schwinn bicycle, when you cut down Fourth Street; but instead of turning left onto Wall Street, you kept on going to avoid the traffic. You were taking the shortcut through the park when you were stopped by the police. They gave you a ticket for going the wrong way on a one-way street for one block. You tried to explain but took the ticket and rode home.

The next year you were driving south on Highway 99 in your Datsun pickup and were pulled over for having a broken tail light. The police checked your license and found that you had an unpaid ticket for going the wrong way on a one-way street on a bicycle. You were arrested and taken to Juvenile Hall.

I retrieved you, paid the ticket, and we went home. We talked repeatedly about this, but you felt targeted and eventually lost your job and let your petty arrests build up. Granted, you were going the wrong way for only one block, and you didn't know your tail light was out, but these incidents helped put you deeper into the system. We talked about it and decided you needed to go to Right Way Homes and get your life straightened out. You wanted to leave town so agreed to go. My friend Shawn helped with this move.

The probation officer, with Shawn's input, sent you to Westwood, California, a small town close to Lake Almanor, about a two and one-half hour drive over a mountain range north of Chico. You were enrolled into high school there for your junior year; you had a strict curfew, homework, and chores. You excelled with these clear boundaries and no outside influences.

A Star Is Born

Your life was about to change for the better, Jeff. You were the new kid in town. You stood out in this small school, which most students had attended since kindergarten. You were noticed, and all the girls liked you. Your wavy golden brown hair had grown longer than ever before. You met a cheerleader named Lisa, who was born and raised in Westwood along with four brothers and a sister. You joined the drama club, dated Lisa, and seemed happier than ever.

Not once did I visit you during your school year. I felt you needed to get your life straightened out, and that to see us would be stepping backwards. I thought you would be homesick and might slip back into old habits. You phoned us frequently and I'd listen to you, and could hear the happiness in your voice when you talked about this girl called Lisa. Lisa's family welcomed you into their home and you frequently got the okay from Right Way Homes to stay at Lisa's for dinner. You also became friends with a couple of Lisa's brothers, and everyone knew her mom because she owned the only video store in town. Then, your little brother and sister would say hello and tell you a story. You had to check in and out of Right Way Homes and have good points to get time away from the home. But Jeff, you knew this game of *good tickets* from our home, and your *Grease album good points* were now cashed in for time with Lisa.

Once you wanted to watch a baseball game on the field behind your new home, but for unknown reasons you could not leave the grounds. Lisa said you climbed up a telephone pole on the edge of the property and sat there and watched the game from this high vantage point. You were still a climber. Lisa told me you asked her to the prom, but she had promised her best friend from kindergarten they'd go together one day. She kept her word and said you asked someone else. You and Lisa managed to dance and have your photo taken together under the decorated arbor.

I could tell how much you loved being in Westwood; but when school was out for the summer, to our horror you were pulled out of there and sent to a foster home. The plan was that they had to slowly integrate you back home, so you were moved to Palermo, a town about thirty minutes from us. It's a wide spot in the road with scattered old homes, weeds, and trailers.

You never told me how it felt to say goodbye to Lisa and your friends, or just how frightening it was to be sent to this hell hole. You just phoned home and sounded very intimidated and worried. You told me you were living in a large dirty house, sharing a room with a thug, and that your roommate had already taken some of your money and clothes. After he threatened you with his fists and roughed you up a couple of times, you were scared out of your mind. Do you recall pleading with me to help you get out of this dangerous holding home? I called my attorney friend Shawn, and we drove to Palermo where you met us at the corner market as planned. Shawn and I picked up a double cheeseburger, fries, and a soda for you, which you loved. We hugged, but you were on a time clock so we got down to business quickly. Shawn told you that he had talked to your probation office and you would be returning home within days. Hang tight, my boy!

It was a bittersweet reunion when you returned to our family. You and the kids were overjoyed, but I was worried. Jeffrey, you were happy to be home, told me about dating Lisa, getting good grades at school, and performing at the Lassen County Fair with your drama class. Apparently your class put on a concert where you each did a lip sync—you performed *Hotel California*—the class was asked to return the next day. Your brother and sister listened to your stories in awe.

Slowly things would begin to change, Jeff. You met a guy whose parents lived by the river. You felt sorry for him, and asked if he could stay with us for a month. At first I said no, then I changed my mind and said, "Well, okay, maybe for a week or so." Your friend was nice, so I assumed he was a good kid and just needed a break in life. You two watched TV, raked the lawn; and—this guy could cook—he would make us amazing breakfasts. Still, I was uneasy and on the verge of asking him to move out when I came home from shopping and saw two police cars, one in front of our driveway and the other on our lawn. I would soon learn that your friend had a record, and that you boys were caught stealing a case of frozen corn dogs out of the back of a delivery truck. You were arrested and sent to Juvenile Hall, where you had to stay for five months—until your eighteenth birthday. Your friend was twenty so he was sent to in jail.

When you were away at Right Way Homes, I separated from Don in October. I was still thinking that with counseling Don and I could work out our differences. On Thanksgiving Day we all went to Don's new apartment and put a bird in the oven; and while the turkey cooked, we all went for a walk through the park. Dana, Spencer and you ran ahead. Don told me he'd met someone and was thinking of marrying her. I listened and kept quiet. We walked and talked then went back and had a great Thanksgiving meal as a family, I knew it might be the last holiday we would spend together. I told Dana and Spencer, and they were very upset. I told you, and you were furious

with me for divorcing both of your dads. Don would marry Carolyn
the day after our divorce was final.

Twenty-seven months later, I met John while attending a Chamber of
Commerce barbecue. He was casual with messy curly black hair, and
a nose too big for his face. He was short, with a dark complexion, part
Sicilian and part Lithuanian. We danced and talked that evening, then
dated and became a couple for the next seven years.

One day John suggested I ask for a day pass for you, he wanted to take
us as a family for an outing. Three weeks later, on Mother's Day, I
picked you up and it was so wonderful be with you away from watchful eyes. We drove to Lime Saddle Marina on Lake Oroville to meet
John, who told us to jump on the shuttle and we'd be delivered to his
houseboat. You seemed quiet and didn't seem to know how to mix
with us. We sensed you needed time to adjust, and that this outing
was a bit awkward for you. John had suggested we jump into his
Zodiac, and off we went around the lake to explore the shores and
waterfalls and rock formations. He found a great spot for us to get
out and play, and soon we were all swimming. You and your brother
especially were jumping off rocks and sliding down the short waterfall. You were a kid again, Jeff. It was a wonderful day as we buzzed
around the lake with the wind in our hair, and you came alive again.
I took your picture as we headed across the lake. You were looking
ahead and seemed to have new depth as you were taking in and loving your one day of freedom. You tried wind surfing, and you three

kids played on air mattresses as John and I fixed an early dinner since you had to return and check in by 6:00 P.M. It was wonderful to be with you on Mother's Day and for you to be able to play with us and relax. When you returned that night, you had two months left on your sentence. I know it was terrible for you, but I felt this was my last hope—that you would have time to think and learn and reflect on your life and turn it around.

Seriously, Jeff, frozen corn dogs?

I visited you on a regular basis. We talked and I'd tell you about your brother and sister and their lives. Jeff, you hung your head and cried when I went to visit. I remember how the tears soaked the thighs on your blue jeans. You were scared and sorry. *Cause and Effect*, understood after the fact. Son, I kept thinking, you have to get your life on track. You are eighteen, I'd remind you, and this ongoing nonsense, if continued, will land you in prison. The crimes you'd committed were petty, but it was stealing and against the law and this adds up. I slammed it home, reminding you to never ever go to prison. For once I could see that you understood. Well, I did get a little graphic. We decided you needed to move away because of your contacts in town, and the unsavory friends who waited for your return.

You were home with us for a few months, but the kids were gone all day at school and you seemed lost and bored. So Uncle George helped move you to Lakeport, a two-hour drive to the west. Then, if you wanted to go to the ocean, it was only forty-five more minutes to Fort Bragg or Mendocino.

Jeff, you moved into a duplex right on the lake, with long docks and a great view from your front window. Your dad and Patty lived just twenty minutes away, and they came over to visit or took you to lunch with their little girl Sarah. Your dad worked in the three-story court building in town and saw you often.

Your brother, sister, and I visited you in your one room, and we all stayed there with you for three days. It was the Lakeport Centennial celebration and we had a great weekend, but not necessarily at the celebration; we had fun being together, just the four of us. You and I went shopping and filled your cabinets and refrigerator with food. I gave you a perm in your tiny kitchen so you had this super curly hair for awhile.

We had showed up at your place with another surprise, too. Just before the kids and I drove over to see you, John had been clearing off some downed trees and underbrush when he found three kittens, their feet still webbed. He'd also found the mother cat, but she had been killed. So he'd brought the kittens to my house in a bucket, and Dana and Spencer had gone into rescue mode. We packed the newborn kittens into a basket and the kids had been taking turns giving them milk from syringes. That weekend in Lakeport, we cooked a great meal, and then each of you three kids filled a syringe with warm milk, picked up a kitten and fed it. I regret I didn't get a good picture of all of you holding and feeding those tiny kittens. Our family was complete that weekend, and how I wished I'd been able to bring you home; but I knew you would meet up with the wrong crowd again.

We watched a video of a song I'd never heard, and I recall being mesmerized by Tracy Chapman singing *Fast Car*. Jeff, you brought me up to date about her, and we listened together. You were also working at Roundtable Pizza at the time, but I'm sure you were lonely when we left. I confess, I didn't know what to do. Looking back, I should have had you come back home with us. It was apparent that you needed guidance.

Towards the End

A few weeks later, your Uncle George flew you home in his small Cessna. I took a video of the plane coming in and landing, which I've watched many times and enjoy so much. How naïve I was to think a mini-vacation and a fun meal with us would somehow help you stay on track. You were so happy to be back home. You thanked Uncle George, then you and I waved goodbye before heading home to Durham where your brother and sister eagerly waited for you. After a brief reunion, I gave you a haircut and then we packed the car and headed south to visit your cousin Tammy and her family's home. It was a delightful road trip with good music and lots of chatter among the four of us, together again.

It was one of those trips that you never forget. Tammy had a large backyard and swimming pool. You three kids, Tammy's husband Jerry, and your cousin Roger all jumped into the water and had a fierce water fight. Jeff, ha, too funny, you put water wings on your ankles and kept jumping off the diving board. I continued to tape the action. Then we took you kids to a huge water slide, and then to a snake museum—which was a huge mistake, as it stunk so bad.

Then we drove from the central valley to the ocean where I spent the day lying on the beach and watching my kids playing in the surf. Spencer and Dana had their brother back, and the chatter, the jokes, the mimicking never stopped.

One cold winter day not long after, you were on your way to the local junior college for an appointment with a career counselor, when your Datsun pickup began to spew black smoke. You pulled over and walked home. I was working late the next two evenings and it was two days before we could get back out to see the pickup and have it towed to a garage. By that time it had been vandalized, so instead of taking your truck for repairs, we had it towed to a junkyard. This was a terrible blow because now you had no transportation. Jeff, you were hiking into town from our house, about ten miles away. Then suddenly, I didn't or hear from you for a month. You later told me a girl named Vicky had picked you up and taken you home. When you did return home, at 1:00 A.M. one night, your eyes were dilated and your conversation was exceptionally fast. Vicky was in the driveway, sitting in her car honking while you, Jeff, were trying frantically to gather your belongings. I told you to tell her that if she honked her car horn one more time, I'd call the police. Silence. She stopped making a racket after you talked to her, and then you ran back in the house, grabbed some clothes, and left.

Jeff, you were twenty years old by that time so I couldn't say much, but now I can see this was the beginning of the end. When I finally saw you again, I asked where you were living, and you told me, "At

Vicky's." You also told me that Vicky had taken some of your things, including your bicycle. I ordered you to get in the truck, which you did, and we drove to her apartment. I told you to go up there and retrieve your belongings or I would notify the police. I felt sure Vicky would do as I said, as I suspected she was doing drugs and wanted no part of my threats. Older than you, I saw Miss Vicky as the culprit. I knew that I needed to nix this relationship but fast. We loaded your belongings into John's truck and headed home.

Jeffrey, my son, you had become so thin. You took a hot shower as I cooked dinner. I was still trying to fix you, on one of my only days off. But it was apparent that something was very wrong. You are so quiet and sad, and when you sat down after a shower I rubbed the back of your neck and you quietly said, "Thank you, Mom." Jeffrey, you went on to tell me that this person Vicky was *really mean,* and I could tell you were exhausted and maybe coming down from something you'd taken, some sort of drug. I never actually met Vicky and was so relieved to have you away from her. I reminded you to think back and remember happier times in Westwood and the nice girl you had once loved. But you weren't with me. You simply sat and stared out the window and seemed shell-shocked and exhausted, though safe and clean.

I made an appointment at the community college learning center for counseling. I picked you up in front of my salon and off we went. When I checked us in at the front desk, you walked outside. I followed to see what you were doing and you said you were claustrophobic and couldn't be in a room. So the counselor came outside, and we sat in the courtyard and had a session. It was very weird; I talked, telling the counselor all about your behavior, while you listened. When it was your turn to talk, you just said, "She's right." I was dumbfounded by your lack of interest. We never returned to that counselor.

Later we went to the county seat to see about getting you into a housing program and receiving a monthly check for food and expenses. You sat next to me in the office, and as I went over your needs with the social worker, you literally blew a cork. Jeff, you were so angry that you were red in the face. You cussed me out and pushed my chair away from you using your foot. This triggered an intervention in which some other social workers ran over and asked me if there was any adult abuse in our home. The social worker suggested I get protection for my safety, asking if you had ever hurt me. I assured them that I was fine and that you would be fine when you calmed down. The social worker recommended that I get protection and offered to have you taken away on a 5150. I said no thanks and we left. You did calm down and neither of us ever mentioned this explosive outburst again. I backed away and let you be for a time.

I did, however, make an appointment for you to be tested by Stewart Bedford, a psychiatrist I had taken you to for an evaluation five years prior, thinking that a re-evaluation might shed some light on your frustration and emotional state of mind.

Dr. Bedford talked to you privately, and then mailed a letter to me detailing his findings. He suspected you might be developing schizophrenia, and further down in the letter he wrote that you might also have suicidal tendencies. I read the schizophrenia part and was surprised at this word, which I'd become familiar with when my sister and brother-in-law had worked as technicians in a mental hospital. That word was not Jeff; it absolutely wasn't and couldn't be. Dr. Bedford's prognosis was worrisome and sad. I thought maybe you had used your imagination and clever wit to play a mind game with him. I have to admit that I dismissed the phrase *might have suicidal tendencies.* I wanted an evaluation, but when I read it, I refused to accept it. I see now that denial can be a lethal weapon. But then I still had very high hopes for you, dear son. Now I must take full blame for living in to the fantasy that you were still the bright son who narrowly missed getting into the gifted program, the son who was gentle and sensitive, the son who kept our family laughing. I'd brainwashed myself: My son, who plays classical music, cannot be suicidal. I also didn't exactly understand what schizophrenia meant—just something about two personalities, and something about being unstable. If I thought I was ill-equipped to handle my son and his ongoing battle to mainstream, this new word sent me into denial like never before.

I still had a vision that you one day would own a modest home, have a wonderful wife and some children, and I could also see you caring for me when I grew old. I wore blinders regarding your future. I am so sorry, Jeff.

One day, when you were about fourteen, I was so frustrated with something you'd said or done, which has now faded away like so many other scenes. I looked at you and said, "Jeffrey Paul, please stop this! I have two other children to raise, and you are sucking all of my energy!" You looked at me with the most hurt look on your face, your eyebrows deeply furrowed; and worse of all, you said nothing except, "I'm sorry." I said I was sorry, too, but I needed to pay attention and raise Dana and Spencer. As I recall, you did cease fire and seemed to understand. The kids were always happy and busy with games or friends, but I felt I wasn't paying any attention to them. You did make me crazy, and I didn't know how to fix you.

I sat on the couch sipping my morning coffee one Saturday morning, and was thinking back to the summer when you came home with us from my sister's house after I'd called relatives to step up and help me with you. Only my sister and her husband came forward. After you'd spent the summer with Bobbie's family, you, your sister, your brother, and I had a glorious ride home on the Amtrak. I remember heading home on the train, knowing you were so happy to be with us again. It seemed clear then that we were your anchor, your home base. Life was good when we were all together. I actually thought I had regained control and had you back forever, but you continued to slip through my fingers. I put my coffee cup down and stared into the orchard, thinking what am I going to do with you? What?

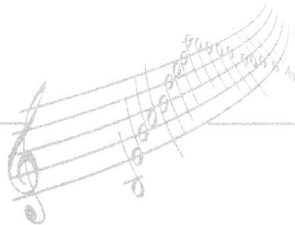

The Totem pole was never an object of worship. Some represent clan, some are simply artistic expression.
The association with the idea of idol worship was an idea from the local Christian missionaries of the nineteenth century, who considered their association with Shamanism an occult practice.
Wikipedia

TOTEM POLE

AFTER YOUR DEATH, ANGER BEGAN TO WELL UP inside of me towards you for being so incredibly selfish. Could you not have waited one minute, stopped and waited, and thought about this final decision and the long-term effects on others? Did you think about your brother and sister? Your dad and Patty, and Sarah? Did you think of me, and of the horror and shock this violent act would bring to each of us?

I've come to realize through the passing years, and through many soul-searching bouts of retrospect, that when people are in a state of mind to take their life, they are in so much pain and want so badly to end it, to find peace for themselves, that there's simply no room to consider others. I understand this now, Jeff, and I try in vain to forgive you and understand, but I don't think that will ever be the case. I also realize that I can never entirely forgive myself for not understanding your deep pain, for not seeing the darkness that led you to end your life. Never will I live in complete peace, knowing that I was the person in charge of raising you and you became so miserable that the only escape you could find was death.

I've been told many times not to beat myself up, and not to carry the guilt. This is an easy cliché for counselors and well-meaning friends, but no one knows how a mother or father feels deep inside—knowing we missed something, feeling that someone or something could have saved you.

Before your death, I was desperate for help; as a working mother and business owner, time was precious. Your lack of respect for authority, and your ever-present quest for excitement was becoming a larger and more critical situation than before, and I was not equipped to handle you alone. This was when you were about fourteen, almost fifteen—not long after that painful day when they pulled you off the Junior High School football team and you had to return your football gear. I understood your anger with the school, and admit that I felt what they did to you was inexcusable. I suspected that incident would change the course of your life, but didn't realize just how much. It seemed that you were never again the innocent and hopeful child I once knew, and I realized I needed intervention for you. I had to get you out of town, far away from your scummy friends and drug use.

Maybe I had used up my plea for help cards. When I called your father
in Potter Valley, asking if he and Patty could take you for the summer,
they said no. They had taken you for the nine months during your
third grade year—why, I don't remember. Either they wanted you there,
or I was going stark raving mad with two little munchkins (Dana and
Spencer were twenty-four months apart) and I had begged for help at
the time. You obeyed and did well in their home, but felt isolated living
on ten acres and attending a small school; and you missed us terribly. We
saw you during Christmas break, and Dana and Spencer visited there during Easter break. You wrote long letters about how much you missed
and loved your brother and sister, and begged to come home. Your
dad and Patty said the separation when you returned to us after school
was very hard for them. They were very clear after third grade that
once you moved back you could never return because they didn't want
you going back and forth on a whim. So this time, my plea went to
deaf ears. Then I phoned your dad's brother in Vacaville, but he said
they all worked and it wasn't a good time as they had their own lives
and trials to deal with. I asked my step-brother George if you could
work in his furniture store on weekends and live there for the summer, but he didn't need any help and asked where would you live?

Then I turned to my sister for help. She was my last hope, and I was
delighted when she agreed to help. Her family lived 450 miles from us
in a beautiful town close to the ocean. Your aunt and uncle each had
been trained in counseling and worked in a state-run institution for the
criminally insane. They expanded on their ability to understand and

teach you because they were trained professionals. They said they would counsel you, and be family, take you to church (they had recently become born-again Christians in a fundamentalist church), and get you on the right path. In theory this seemed like the ideal opportunity for you to gather your thoughts and make new friends and return home with a stronger conviction to achieve great things. I confess I had no idea how tightly run their household was going to be. The rules were strict: you'd attend church twice on Sunday, Bible classes on Wednesday, and a Christian youth group where you would meet friends your own age. I do thank them for stepping up and helping. However, I was to become aware that their child-to-parent relationship was learned while working at mental institutions as technicians: rules are not to be broken; you will not miss school; you will mind; you will do chores; you will attend church.

Jeff, you were a great kid when given reasonable boundaries, though sometimes you'd just smile at me and do whatever you wanted. But you never responded well to a highly regimented program and a finger pointing at you, which is what you faced when living with your aunt and uncle. Your experience there taught you to appreciate your family, our lifestyle, and our more flexible rules when you returned.

Jeff, dear boy, you packed your totem pole and took it with you—the totem pole you brought home after your month-long visit with our friend Roger in Alaska at age twelve. Now, as a young teen, you'd prepared to nestle into your new home with your aunt and uncle. Your clean room was waiting for you, and you began to put your belongings away and decorate your new space with your personal things. You placed your prized possession—a seven-inch-tall totem pole tinted golden brown—on a nightstand at the foot of your bed in front of a window. You told me that your aunt came into your room to check on you, and when she saw the totem pole she demanded that you throw it away. You refused and told her you'd bought it while in Alaska. She said a totem pole is evil, devil-worshipping, and that you had to remove it. I can only imagine the look on your face and the argument that transpired.

You also told me you were in lying on your bed one evening when your aunt came in with some of her church friends. They opened the window, gathered in a semi-circle around the small end table that held the totem pole, held hands and began to pray. She told you that the prayer and hand-holding was a show of unity and strength in their faith, and the results were to let the evil spirits escape out the window. Your aunt told you to leave the window open all night to make sure the last of the spirits got out. These church friends were in and out like the Navy Seals, but supposedly under the command of Jesus who dispatched them to clean out and disperse spirits into the night. But now, I couldn't help but think after I heard the story, the evil spirits are free to fly around and slip into someone else's home.

I answered the phone and heard you whisper, "Mom, they're crazy! Please get me out of here." I didn't drop everything and get you, as you requested. I wasn't sure what was going on and you had only been there a few days. So instead I calmed you down and told you that this is their belief and to go along with it until I can make arrangements for you to come home. It sounded like this thought process of letting evil spirits loose was too *out there* for a boy who was already getting shuffled around. I said, "When you come home we will get counseling, and live harmoniously, and get you back in school, and you'll be a good boy, right?" You agreed.

Little did I know that you took it to heart to join in the program. My sister phoned one Sunday afternoon to happily tell me that during the church service you took the altar walk and accepted Jesus as your Savior. They were so proud of you. Then after another Sunday service, my sister told me how you had stood up in church and spoken in tongues. Speaking in tongues had always been one of my biggest fears. Having been raised in the Assembly of God church, I'd watched my mother, grandmother, aunt, and sister do this. I vowed to myself, as a five-year-old child, to always have control of my tongue. My cousin Fair told me that speaking in tongues is like frosting on the cake; it is the language only God can understand, and the devil can't decipher it. Fair and I had been close playmates, but I decided to stay mum and never speak such gibberish, frosting or no frosting.

If you were being true to yourself, and if you were indeed filled with the Holy Spirit, I guess I was happy for you. But it seemed to me that your pendulum had swung way too far to the right.

Dana, Spencer, and I visited you for a weekend. It was a long drive for me and the kids but was pure joy to see you and be with you. We spent

Saturday at the beach. On Sunday we all went to church with my sister and brother-in-law. The preacher was delivering a stunningly powerful spirit-filled sermon when you abruptly stood up and began to speak in tongues. I looked up at you in amazement as you raised your hands skyward. When you sat back down next to me, I looked at you to see if you were the same person. You returned my gaze with a wink. Later I asked if you still wanted to come home with us or were feeling comfortable in your inland beach town, with your new church, family, and friends. Jeff, you looked me straight in the eye, leaned towards my face, and I'll never forget your low whisper, "Take me home, please."

Once I got back home, I made arrangements and bought three Amtrak tickets. When the kids were out of school, we prepared for our first-ever train trip to collect you.

The Amtrak ride south with your sister and brother was a visual candy ride, as we were seeing our coastline and the inner city including ghetto areas from a safe distance as the train chugged along. All I could think about was you, Jeff, and I was hopeful that you had cleaned up, hopeful that you were ready to reclaim your life and move forward. The Amtrak seemed to be the answer; to travel back home and start fresh.

Riding down on the train was an amazing trip; the scenery was wonderful as we headed along the western part of California inland and parts of the coastline. Dana and Spencer were anxious to see you and bring you home and resume our life as a close-knit family that entertained one another. I noticed that neither child ever asked why you were living with my sister, or why you went to school in Potter Valley that year, or why you had so many doctor appointments. They loved you and they didn't really want to hear the reasons for the continual commotion in our home. What mattered to them was you, living with us again.

We zipped along, passing cities, and fields of flowers and lush landscapes. I looked out the window and the train ride lulled me to daydream about my life when my children were babies and little kids. Thinking back to when Spencer was just a little toddler, I recalled how your little brother couldn't pronounce the word Mom. He would call out to me, "Ham, Ham!" Jeff, you clever boy, you changed this name to *Hameartheous*– what a great name. Later, in the '80s, when I was flustered or short on patience, you kids would say "It's Hammer time!" and run. You kids certainly got a lot of mileage out of that nickname for me. Chugging along, I told some of the people riding south in our train car about you and this story of the nickname you kids had for me. Then Spencer and Dana said, "Ham, I'm cold." I reached around to my bags and pulled out two beach towels to wrap around their legs as we continued to head south. To our surprise, there was no heat on the train.

Reaching our train's destination, San Luis Obispo, meant we had to actually bypass my sister's house and continue on another ten miles to the station. I told the kids and some other passengers who were in on the scenario to look across the pastures towards a house with a porch. I told them to look for my son and sister, who would be standing on the porch, looking to the east, and waving their arms. Most people traveling with us were taking pleasure in helping us search for arms waving in the air. The plan was, after they waved, they would jump into her car and drive to San Luis Obispo, and wait for us at the depot as we continued south through emerald green rolling hills.

The long train passed the green fields and white rail fences, and as the train took the next curve, we began to search. With my forehead pressed against the window, I looked for you, my son, and Dana and Spencer eagerly searched for their brother. Then as we took a slight curve, you appeared. "I see him!" Dana and Spencer shouted. You were coming up quickly, standing next to the train tracks holding a long wooden sign across your chest. I yelled, "There he is, there he is!" And there you stood, erect and serious, facing the rows of train cars, holding your sign out in clear view. On it, painted in large red letters, was HAM TRAK.

Everyone on the train clapped and we laughed and watched as you leaped and ran across the tall grass with a long wooden sign under your arm, across the fields as fast as the wind, back to your aunt's house. It was a giggly time and I cherish this memory.

By the time we chugged up the grade, over long stretches of hillside and around curves, we could look back and see the end of the train and look forward and see the engine at the same time. The train was long and the sharp curve created the letter C. We finally heard the whistle and the squeal of breaks and the train slowly screeched to a stop. We repacked the beach towels and collected our suitcases, inched toward the exit, and there you stood. My sister was happy to see us, all smiles and warmth. We hugged you, she hugged us, and we walked quickly to her van and jumped in. I could hear the kids tell you they saw you holding up the Ham Trak sign; the chatter and giggles were infectious.

Bobbie had prepared a hearty meal for us and we visited with you, my long-lost son. Back at the station, you'd given me the impression that you'd rather nix the formality, forget the meal, and jump right back on the north-bound train with the rest of your family and wave goodbye to Bobbie. After we rested and spent a day at the beach, my sister drove us back to the train station and we headed home. This time we dressed in light sweaters and sweatpants.

Jeff, you were happy but quiet, and I watched you as you were deep in thought. We talked some, too, and you told me that the fair had come to town and your uncle had given you permission to go over and watch. You walked around and watched the booths being set up when you were distracted by the sound of music, the sound of guitars being tuned. You told us that you went inside this area, stood there and watched as the country music band *Alabama* practiced for their concert that night. With your musical skills, you must have thought this a huge treat.

You sat across the aisle from me with Dana and Spencer. We decided to walk through the cars and find the observation car with the huge windows and glass roof. We bought drinks and snacks and watched the coast and cities go by like a nature documentary. It was like watching the world fly by. I had high hopes for you as I realized how much you cherished your home. I felt sure we'd get your life squared away. I was rested mentally, felt strong physically, and your brother and sister were thrilled to have you back. You three shared many private jokes and childhood memories, and I listened to you mimic the characters and recite one-liners from the movies *Caddy Shack*, *Stripes*, and *Poltergeist*. This chatter was music to a mother's ears; it was, as always, an easy fit for the four of us. You didn't talk about the months away then; but when we were alone, you related stories to me.

Jeff, I only sent you away to save you from drug use, and to get you way from the influence of your friends. It was always a difficult decision but somehow seemed to make things better. When you came home, you were the best kid in the world ... for a while.

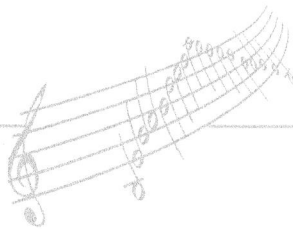

Friendship is unnecessary,
like philosophy, like art ... It has no survival value;
rather it is one of those things
that give value to survival.
C. S. Lewis

BEST FRIENDS

JEFF, YOU AND SEAN MET IN JUNIOR HIGH AND CLICKED. You were having problems getting along with your step-dad. Your real dad, Gene, was nice enough, but he didn't call much, nor did you see much of him. He worked, kept very busy, and now had a new young daughter, which changed his focus. Sean's dad was completely out of the picture so his life centered on his single working mom Betty, a distant older brother who lived out of town, bicycles, and girls. You spent a lot of time at Sean's house, where his mom let you do whatever you wanted, which included listening to loud music and working on car engines. Betty loved to cook and always put out plenty of food for you boys.

You and Sean were on the same level and had some of the same interests. One day I phoned Betty, then drove to her place across town to meet her, give her money for all the food you had consumed, and thank her for her generous hospitality. I told her how much you liked being at her place. Betty was a tiny woman and wore her hair in a short dark brown bubble, coloring and cutting it herself. This was the '80s and Betty was still living her life as she had in her heyday in the late 1950s. During the week she worked as a secretary for an architect, then did her food shopping every Friday night so you boys could snack all weekend. When she wasn't working, she was always home. If she wasn't cooking, she smoked a lot of cigarettes, watched TV, and read romance novels. Betty was organized, open, generous, and predictable.

Living without a man, her home and son were her life. She had built a nest of comfort and freedom for Sean, so he would stay home and be with her as much as possible, and it worked. I began to like her as much as you did. I even visited her at work a few times, since we both worked downtown, and we'd walk and talk about our sons.

You boys worked on bicycles together, Sean taught you how to tune up engines, change oil and sparkplugs, and do all sorts of mechanical things. Sean had natural talent in this area and shared his knowledge with you. Jeff, you picked it up quickly and thrived on learning what you should have been taught many years ago. You reciprocated by showing Sean how to play the guitar.

Sean was a strikingly handsome boy, with a muscular build and thick black wavy hair and dark brows. He could have been one of the boys in the movie Westside Story. When you boys went out together, you were chick magnets. You dressed the same—t-shirts, worn faded blue jeans, and tennis shoes—and had an air about you that screamed, *the boys are back in town.* I began to give Sean free haircuts and asked if he would consider being a model for my portfolio. He was surprised and happy with the idea of having a professional photo taken of himself. You thought it was a good idea, too. You guys continued to go out at night and meet girls, then you'd get together the next day to repair your bikes, and to play and record music. You had finally met someone who didn't judge you, and in return you respected Sean for his easygoing manner. There was no competition so you didn't have to act crazy, and Sean didn't have to explain where his dad was. You two were pals and life was good.

One day you didn't come home. You had always asked if it was alright to spend the night at Sean's, but this night you hadn't called, and I was worried. I called Sean's house but got no answer, then drove by his house but found no one at home. Not even a porch light lit the driveway. I peeked through the window next to the front door looking for the familiar amber glow of their night light. Nothing was on. I assumed all three of you were out to dinner or that a relative was in town. Nevertheless, I found it odd that you hadn't picked up a phone and called home, nor had Betty. Yes, you were hard to handle, a wild one at heart, but you generally checked in at some point.

The next day, nightfall was already creeping in when I heard you ride up and put your bicycle away. I went into your bedroom and there you sat on your bed exhausted, your head hanging down.

You didn't look up, just sat there. I began to harp on you for not calling and letting me know where ... then you slowly looked up, and I saw that your eyes were red and swollen, your face reflecting an inner sadness and worry lines I'd never seen before. You were full of despair.

Sean had been driving home for lunch the day before, and as usual took a shortcut along the dry creek bed called Lindo Channel, where he followed the winding road towards the turnoff to his house. He was speeding and overcorrected, hitting one of the massive sycamore trees that lined the creek. He totaled his car, hit his head, and suffered internal and external injuries. He was taken by ambulance to our local hospital, where he still lay in a coma. You told me about this accident while in a state of shock yourself. You went on to say you were sorry for not calling but had been by Sean's bedside, holding your friend's hand as he clung to life, with his mom on the other side of the bed. All night and day. I could feel your pain and relate to your helplessness as I'd stayed with my friend Rita after she was run off the road in her Austin Healy and lay in a coma for longer than I wanted to tell you. I knew how you felt—helpless and worried—as you held your friend's hand and encouraged him to survive. You told me that you and Betty took turns, and that now you had to go back.

Sean eventually did come out of his coma after over a month. He received much medical assistance, because as he recovered, his prognosis was not good. You and I had many heart-to-heart talks about Sean and my friend Rita. I knew you could imagine the long-term effects because you knew Rita, too. This accident brought us very close as you tended to your friend as I had mine. Sean was never the same mentally or physically. His hand curled inward, he walked with a lifelong limp, and his speech was slurred. He was not the same cool dude who had once graced our town. For a while, you worked with Sean at home, helping Betty with his physical and speech therapy.

Then Sean began to spend more time at the physical therapy clinic and started participating in bicycling events for endless miles. Your friend wanted to be alone. Sean's accident proved to be the second punch in the gut for you, the first being your rejection from Junior High football and returning your gear.

Sadness began to overwhelm you as the long-term effects of Sean's accident became obvious, and you and Sean went your separate ways, though you would eventually meet up again as downtowners. You grew more withdrawn and angry, not engaging or responding to my nagging and suggestions, and began to hang out with what I decided were thugs. You were unreachable for a long time.

Then, on your own, you pulled away from your low-life friends, got a job at the mall at Taco Time and came back to live with us in our new country home ten miles south of town. Then you landed a better job with the 3M Company and bought yourself a small motorcycle for transportation since your Datsun pickup had been vandalized. You got up early each day in the dead of winter and drove into town to work. For Christmas my boyfriend John gave you a high-tech face cover, usually used for snow climbing, to wear while riding to work those freezing December mornings. After the holidays were over, you were laid off along with many others, and began pondering college. Your dad suggested the military, which I thought was a great idea, but you balked at joining the service.

Then you had your own great idea: to train as a fire fighter. You prepared for your physical and your written exams, and I took you into town with the list of items you needed. We bought you your first steeltoed boots, above the ankle, along with everything else on your list. On the way home you struggled to put the boots on in the car, then asked me to stop and let you out so you could run home to prepare. No use arguing with you when you had an idea so I pulled over. Then you, new thick socks on and boots tied, said, as usual, "See ya later" I drove away and watched in my rearview mirror as my grown son began to run alongside the road to follow me home. It took a while, but eventually there you were, still jogging in those heavy boots down our long gravel road, and we stood on the porch and clapped. You then gulped water, took off your boots and asked for some band-aids, a hot shower, and dinner.

A week later I took you, dressed in cutoffs and a white t-shirt, to the local Junior College for tryouts. You were to run five miles in your boots. Jeff, you came in seventh out of sixty-five boys. I was so proud of you. You attended classes and physical endurance training each day, then you boys got on a bus with your gear for a week-long boot camp in Mendocino National Park, to learn how to actually put out fires. This was a happy time for us; we cheered you on and hoped for the best. I gave you a pep talk the night before you left. You came back with the good news that you had been asked to go a step further. You and a few others were selected to forge ahead during a forest fire and cut down trees and help with fire walls. You were shown how to cut the branches and down trees with chain saws so they would fall in a certain direction.

This particular summer proved safe from forest fires. But finally one day your pager beeped and you knew it was time to grab your gear, get to the designated area, and hop on the bus. I was at work so you gathered your gear and walked towards town. Fortunately, your uncle was visiting relatives about a mile down the road and saw you trudging past, so he drove you to the area and dropped you off. When you saw your name on the alternate list, along with five others, you had to walk, carrying all of your gear, the five miles back home. You were so tired and bummed that you hadn't even worked. I hoped that once the summer heat set in, the usual threatening fires all around our area and nearby mountain ranges would mean more calls, but not that summer. No fires. You waited, got another beep, but missed getting there. With no job and no money, you began to let your dark side take over. You eventually moved back into town, where your red fire pack was stolen, and after that you went downhill quickly.

Ironically, you and Sean were both downtown staples, each in separate space. You never mentioned seeing Sean, but must have since Chico consisted of a grid of just a few cross streets. Something was wrong with the connection between these boys who were once like brothers, but I couldn't put my finger on the situation. This seemed odd to me since you had witnessed my continuing affection and ongoing friendship with Rita after her car accident; I knew you could see how much I loved her no matter what.

Sean was riding his bike all the time and was entering events like the Wildflower Century ride, a 100-mile ride around the countryside to coincide with the spring blooms. My salon was also downtown and I worked upstairs, so now and then I would see Sean, always decked out in full bicycle gear, riding down the busy street next to cars. He occasionally came upstairs to visit so I gave him a free haircut now and then. We talked about you, and I asked if he would try and get you interested in enrolling in long-distance bicycle events. He said yes, he'd ask you. Sean looked strong and in great physical shape, even though he had difficulty speaking, walked with a limp, and had little use of his left hand.

The following week you popped in the salon steaming mad, telling me to stay out of your life and never to ask Sean to approach you in public ever again. You said you wanted nothing to do with him but wouldn't say why. We easily dropped back into one of our million arguments about life and socializing. I talked about how Sean had made something of himself, despite his physical disabilities, mental deficiencies, and speech impediment. He is a survivor, a positive force. You glared at me and left. I slowly backed away from Sean as you wanted me to.

Later in the year I was surprised when Sean was arrested for aggressive behavior. He was so cool and polite around me that I didn't realize he had developed an explosive violent temper, probably due to his head injury. Apparently his outbursts were well known to the locals, and to the police. He was released from jail and then arrested again for disturbing the peace and fighting. On the front page of our local paper was a photo of Sean being led out of court in handcuffs. The article reported that he bit the jailer on the arm, drawing blood. The paper further stated that because Sean had been diagnosed with AIDS, he was charged with attempted murder for knowingly and willfully passing on the virus and had been sent to a prison at the California Medical Facility in Vacaville for life. Now I understood why you wanted no relationship with Sean and didn't want me to ever mention his name again. You had clocked out on that part of your life. Still, I felt sorry for Sean and asked my attorney friend to get Sean's prison address. I wrote him a letter, I never heard back.

Three years later, at the grocery market one Friday evening, I would see Sean's mom by chance. She had retired, but looked thin and worn down. We stepped to the side with our shopping carts and discussed our sons—hers dying a slow death in prison, and you already dead for a year. Betty and I had a relationship focused on our handsome sons who held such promise, whom we loved so much. Who could have predicted your tragic ends?

Betty died a year later from lung cancer, and I never heard from Sean. I imagine he is near or has reached the end of his path with a terminal disease that was relatively unknown at the time. You boys would be forty-four years old today, and I can only imagine what you might have been as men.

I still think of you and Sean as young teen boys hanging out, learning the skills of car repair, camping, playing music, and meeting girls. All changed in the senseless and avoidable moment when Sean wrecked his car and suffered a brain injury. The photo session of Sean for my portfolio had been scheduled for the week after his car accident. This, of course, never happened, and it's too late now to capture that once handsome guy on film.

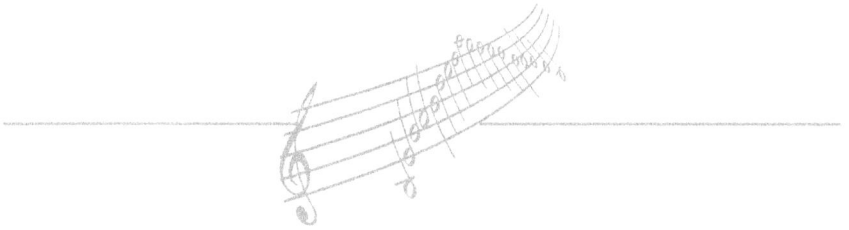

Lettin' the cat out of the bag is a whole lot easier
than puttin' it back in.
Will Rogers

A SCENT OF CINNAMON

I BELIEVE THAT EVERY ADULT WANTS TO CONFESS CHILDHOOD ANTICS. One reason is to watch the horror on the parent's face as the tale is told; the second reason is for the sheer joy of reliving it.

Jeffrey, you and Spencer finally confessed a harrowing story later in your life. When you were about ten-and-a-half years old, I'd asked you to stay with your brother and sister while I made a quick run to the grocery store for a few things. I told you to watch television, sit still, and I'd be back in a flash with a snack. Everything in place, I smiled, locked the front door, and drove the few blocks to the store to buy bread and milk. When I returned fifteen minutes later, you kids were still watching *Scooby-Doo*.

Years later, you boys told me that as I was backing out of the driveway, you would climb up the fence, hoist yourselves onto and over your fort, then climb up on our roof. You brothers then took turns jumping off the roof and doing cannonballs into the Jacuzzi. I listened in horror, picturing the concrete circle which held about four feet of water and was approximately five feet across. And let's not forget the concrete seating around the outer circle, which made the actual target just three feet in diameter. Now Jeff, seriously, you were old enough to know the dangers, but your little brother was only three and half years old! Either one of you could have broken your legs, or missed and hit your head and died. This was incredibly dangerous! And how did you boys dry off so fast? Of course, by the time of your confession, you were much older, and as I ranted and raved about the dangers, you boys laughed and did a high five.

I do remember asking you kids if you knew why the water level in the Jacuzzi had dropped. Had you jumped into the water, or maybe had a water fight? *Nope, you had no idea;* you boys were dry and calmly watching television as instructed. When Don came home from work, I showed him how low the water level was, so we went outside and looked at the return duct that went under the concrete and into the pool a few feet away. By then the water around the concrete had dried and the Jacuzzi level had gone up. We scratched our heads and speculated that we had a plug of leaves, cloth, or something. I remember Don saying that the Jacuzzi water comes from the pool so should stay consistently full of water. Never once did we suspect human bombs dropping from the sky. In the back of our minds was a financial worry, so we kept an eye on our pool and the water levels. This act stopped, as you knew we were on high water alert. Dana never told on her brothers.

I heard another confession from Spencer that when I worked on Saturdays, you kids would be on the couch watching cartoons when I'd say, "Goodbye, see you later this afternoon." Spencer told me that as I drove down the gravel road, you brothers would run into the garage and jam for hours—you playing guitar, Spencer banging his drum set. The neighbors confirmed this story. You kids were very good at acting calm with an agenda. I thank my lucky stars that our house was on an acre.

A few years later, one Saturday night on John's forty acres, a group of us built a bonfire and sat around staring into the embers and singing. We sang the theme song from *Flipper*, then the catchy little tune from *Gilligan's Island*. Towards the end of each song, we began to make up lyrics because no one knew all the words—except Dana, who knew every word of every chorus all the way to the end. I was sitting next to her on a log and asked how she knew all the words. She smiled and told me her childhood nightmare; "Mom," she snuggled closer and as the embers lit the sky and flickered and confessed, "sometimes when you had to make a run to the grocery store, you would tell us not to move, to watch our program, and you'd give us a snack when you got back in about twenty minutes." Yes, I remember. It was summer and you kids were home all the time, and taking three kids to the store was an expensive nightmare. Occasionally Don would bring groceries home, but sometimes I had to make a quick run to begin dinner. Dana continued, telling me that Jeff would drag the toy box in from her bedroom then make her crawl inside. He'd first punched a hole on the side for air. Then he and Spencer would sit on the lid and watch *Flipper* or *Gilligan's Island*, depending on the time of day. Dana couldn't see, but listened to the lyrics and memorized the songs. Dana never told on her brothers as she felt their retribution would be worse than being stuck in the toy box. I swear, Jeff, I can't believe you did that to your sister. And you, too, Spencer!

I still have the side of the toy box with all the stickers from the '70s, just because it's part of our history.

Dana confessed even more. "Mom, do you remember when you made homemade applesauce, with sprinkles of cinnamon on the top? You walked into the bedroom and served it to us still warm as we sat on the floor at the foot of your bed, with pillows propped up behind us."

"Yes, I remember this so well, Dana. Thank you for reminding me; this is so sweet of you. You kids were watching a kids' special in our bedroom, all cozy and warm, it was a great treat. I surprised you with three warm bowls of fresh homemade applesauce, carrying them in on a Mr. T tray, and handed each one of you a bowl, a spoon, and a napkin."

Dana went on, "Well Mom, after you left the room, I looked to Jeff for help," she smiled. "I didn't like the taste of fresh applesauce and didn't want to eat it, and I really hated the cinnamon. I asked Jeff for help and he solved my problem."

"Oh no, Dana, what did he do?"

Jeff, I was to learn that you showed both kids how to lift the grate up off our burnt orange shag carpet, then you showed Dana the vent that went under the house and told her to toss the food into the opening. You stood watch as Dana scooped her applesauce down the vent. I remember clearly, as if it were yesterday, climbing into bed and telling Don how much I loved the scent of cinnamon in the house. I knew nothing about this food toss until Dana's confession when she was in high school. I can only imagine what else is growing down there. That evening by the campfire, as the sky was dark and full of stars and the embers crackled, Dana had finally confessed and cleared her conscience about the applesauce dump. She looked at me and smiled again, reveling in the shocked look on my face, the look that all kids wait for when they are old enough to safely confess.

Jeffrey, I must confess that there is one scene that makes me cringe. You were twelve years old and preparing for the adventure of a lifetime. You were in your bedroom packing to go with us to San Francisco where you'd catch a plane and fly to Anchorage, Alaska, to spend a month with our former neighbor Roger, a good and trusted friend who had moved there in the spring. Roger, at twenty-six, was like a big brother to you kids. He was funny and caring and somehow an old soul but young at heart. He had an AA degree in Ichthyology (the study of fish).

Jeff, this story tells so well how I was always thinking the worst and ready for the next shoe to drop, and I do apologize.

You never liked me to help you with anything because you always believed you were the boss. I came in to your room and told you I wanted to check your suitcase before we left, go over your clothes and review your packing skills. A trip to Alaska for a young boy was a big deal. I began to sort through the layers of folded clothes, gloves, flannel shirts, flannel PJs, toothbrush, cassette tapes, and snacks. I suggested you pack heavier socks and a windbreaker. Then I spotted them, a bulge on the side pouch of your duffle bag, and I put my hand in and came up with one of about twenty packaged condoms you had stuffed away. I looked straight at your sweet twelve-year-old face and asked, "Jeffrey, where did you get these?" You responded with "at the gas station." I asked you if you planned on using them, and you answered matter-of-factly, "Yes." I then asked, "How many of these do you plan to use?" You shrugged your shoulders, thought about it, and replied, "All of them." My jaw dropped open and I sat down on your bed to gather my thoughts. But before I could say another word, you asked, "Mom, what do you think these are?" I looked at your face, puzzled by how nonchalant you were, took a closer look at the condom, and said, "I think they are, ah, well, they are..." I squinted to read the fine print, and in my investigation I could barely read the small letters on the corner of the packaging: *Handy Wipes.* I said, "Uh, well, err, I ..." Jeff, you began to smile, and you dropped your head and began to slowly sway it back and forth. And I heard, "Oh Mom."

One Halloween, Spencer dressed as *Zorro* in a large black hat and cape, and carried a long pointed knife sharpener. Dana was a fairy princess in a pink tutu, and we dressed you up as a Rubik's Cube head. I painted a cardboard box with squares and black lines, and then colored in all of the squares with primary colors. You wore a blue ski sweater with orange and yellow stripes around your chest, blue jeans, and tennis shoes. Then we put the box on your head, and ha! It was the coolest costume of all time. But, the next day while eating Halloween candy I was disappointed when you pulled your actual Rubik's Cube off your shelf to show me that you had put all of the colors together, and won. As I looked closer, I noticed some of the edges were curling up. Jeff, you had cheated by peeling off the plastic squares and placing them where you needed them to be. I felt sick that you didn't try to finish the honest way, by twisting and turning the multi-colored layers of the cube. I recall being irked by this, disappointed that you were a kid who cut corners.

Still, I want to thank you for a lifetime of memories, good and bad. You were a lively boy, I must say. I can still see us, and hear us, doubled over when you mimicked someone or something, or got off one of your famous one-liners. I can still picture Spencer, his head thrown back as he roared with laughter. Dana would giggle and bury her face in my skirt, while I rocked with joy. You could be funny whether you were cooking, raking leaves, or pestering others. I usually tried not to laugh at you too much because it egged you on. But I swear, Jeff, you needed to grow up and get on *Saturday Night Live.*

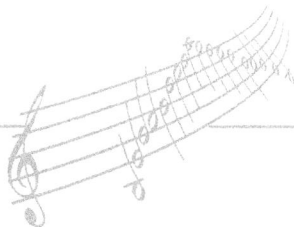

Words are the voice of the heart.
Confucius

LAST DAYS

YOU SEEMED TO HAVE IT LAID OUT IN YOUR MIND. I can understand this now, but I had to write a book about your suicide to begin to understand your walk.

Five days prior to you leaving for Lakeport, you and I went into town for lunch at a local deli. I had a feeling that today was going to be a positive time for us, and secretly I was hoping you were turning around, coming back to our family, connecting. We ordered custom-made sandwiches, a bag of chips, and drinks; you ordered a huge size of Dr. Pepper. When we sat down in a booth by the window, I was happy to be with you and felt the familiar mother-son connection we shared, stronger than ever. You took one bite of your sandwich and a sip of

soda, swallowed hard, and then you asked me if I could tell you anything about Charles Manson. My heart sank at this bizarre question.
I maintained my poker face as private thoughts about the summer of
'69 raced back into my head.

My due date was very close to that of actress Sharon Tate, and I was
hoping we would deliver on the same day. I remember thinking that
this would be too cool because of her beauty and status in Hollywood.
I gave birth to you on a hot summer's day in late July, my beautiful
healthy baby boy with strawberry blonde hair. Nine days after your
birth, Sharon Tate and her friends who were staying at her home were
all brutally murdered, or should I say massacred. Later the details were
disclosed on national and international news: Charles Manson had
sent drug-induced freaks out into the night to slaughter these innocent
people. A dark and frightening shadow seemed to smother everyone.
Sharon Tate's death is well documented so I won't go into detail, but this
and the death of her unborn baby boy weighed heavily on me, dampen-
ing the joy I was experiencing with your birth, and I felt the toxic fear she
must have faced.

After you asked about Charles Manson, I looked at you, sitting
across the table from me, chewing your sandwich and waiting for
an answer, and I wondered why in the world you cared about this
monster in prison. I cleared my throat, took a sip of soda, and explained to you that Charles Manson was a control freak, a manip-
ulator, and that he preyed upon the weak. He kept his pathetic
followers supplied with drugs, and he was a murderer even though

he didn't actually do it because he sent his people with instructions to kill. I told you I didn't want to spoil our lunch by talking about this; you said okay, no problem, and dropped the subject; but your interest lingers in my mind, and always will.

Our drive back home to Durham was uneventful except when, on our way out of Chico, we stopped at a red light at one of the busiest intersections in town: a four-way intersection that would lead each car towards home, shopping, schools, or the famous Bidwell Park. How could I have done this? I should have taken an alternate route home. We sat there, about six cars back from the light. Jeff, you rested your arm nonchalantly out the window, took a long last sip through your straw; and just as the light changed and I took off, you casually tossed this giant Styrofoam cup and the straw out the window into the middle of the intersection. I reacted with "Don't do that! Why did you do that? There's a fine for littering, and you should know better." I went on talking fast and furiously. "We need to keep our town clean." This was a one-sided conversation and quickly dwindled to nothing when I heard no response. Jeff, you just kept looking straight ahead with your arm resting on the open window, the wind blowing your hair, and said, "It's okay. Don't worry about it." Your flippant response made the hair on the back of my neck stand up, I was so mad at you for your disdain and lack of respect. There was no place to park, no chance of retrieving the discarded trash. You'd pushed my buttons and my built-up anger could not be disguised. I was livid, and embarrassed by all the people who saw your act of littering. But more than that, I was worried; your behavior was out of character for you. It was not how you were raised. Once again, I felt a sense of doom taking over. He is not well, he is not coming back, he is not connecting.

I headed south, taking not our usual freeway route but the long way home—down a two-lane paved road that led to the only four-way stop in our small farming community. We sped along under a pleasant ceiling of shade trees past beautiful ranches and well-groomed farmhouses, but I was on extreme high alert. You and I had always been connected by some kind of cosmic force, or mental telepathy. I sensed you might grab the wheel and pull us into a tree. I felt the tension and very slowly placed both hands on the steering wheel and held on tight. Within one minute you slowly and deliberately reached across towards me and touched the steering wheel with your finger, ever so lightly, a slight tap. I kept my cool and continued to look forward and just kept on driving, my face void of expression, trying hard to show no fear though my heart was racing. You knew what I was thinking and wanted to confirm it by reaching out and touching.

Once home, we walked into the house and your demeanor changed, like the snap of a finger. You seemed content as we waited for your brother and sister to come home from school. I suggested you take a hot shower and relax, and you did. After you got out of the shower and slipped into clean clothes, you sat down on the couch and leaned your head back. I went behind the couch situated between the back bedrooms and wood-burning stove and began to rub your scalp, then your neck and shoulders. We heard the bus come to a stop down the main road, and within minutes I could see the kids walking down the gravel road. I knew you always loved having the back of your head rubbed, and that it made you sleepy, so I kept rubbing. You dropped your head forward and moaned as I continued to massage your neck. The kids came in and suddenly our living room filled with chatter—Spencer always had a story to tell. Then he and Dana headed to their rooms. I moved toward the kitchen to get dinner ready, and heard you say, "Thanks, Mom." The kids came back out to the living room and Spencer flopped on the sofa to talk with you, while Dana turned on the television. They drank water and grabbed some chips while I cooked spaghetti and meatballs. Soon everyone filled their plates with spaghetti, sourdough bread, and salad. You and your brother continued to talk for awhile, and then you excused yourself and took your plate of food out to the garage.

When I peeked out there to see if you needed anything, there you were, sitting on the garage floor with a plastic garbage can next to you, sorting through your papers and personal things. Sammy, our sweet cocker spaniel, was with you. You rushed inside, headed straight down the hallway to my bedroom, and I heard you cursing angrily because the top drawer of our filing cabinet was jammed. Then after listening to you pulling and hitting the top, I heard a loud thump; you had hit the top of the metal cabinet with an object that subsequently left a dent. You then pulled the drawer open, filed some papers, and went back into the garage. This untamed temper was new to us, and I knew something was brewing inside you. You seemed busy, as if you were being timed, and you were extremely focused. You did bring your plate back into the house and put it in the sink, and I noticed it had been licked clean. I have always wondered if Sammy is the one who ate your dinner, and not you.

You stayed with your brother and watched TV. Then just before bedtime, you walked down the hall into Dana's bedroom, where she was on her bed reading. She told me later that you came in, stopped and looked all around her room. She had just finished an art project— thumb-tacked every card anyone had ever given her tightly together around the top of her bedroom wall just under the ceiling. She'd placed her greeting and birthday cards side by side so it appeared to be a wallpaper border. She pointed to the door and told you to get out of her room, as girls do to brothers. She said you chuckled, looked up and all around at her cards, and said, "Dana, you're a trip!" before you walked out.

The next morning Dana and Spencer got ready for school, ate breakfast, and Dana waited for her ride. Her girlfriend taxi driver always created dust when she wheeled in fast and squealed around our U-shaped driveway. I drove Spencer because he had to take his football gear. Just as he was gathering his books and bag, you asked if it would be okay if you went with us. Well, this was a surprise, but yes, of course, come on , jump in. You sat in the backseat directly behind Spencer as we buzzed down the long road, across the train tracks to the four-way stop, then on to the school. You leaned forward to ask Spencer what team Durham was playing that night. Spencer replied with one word: "Chester." Something about his answer set you off, and you belted out a laugh and continued laughing all the way to the high school parking lot. I remember Spencer looked towards me and raised his eyebrows; I looked back and watched you busting with laughter, but it wasn't that funny. In fact, it wasn't funny at all. You began to calm down as I maneuvered around cars to get Spencer to the front entrance. When Spencer got out of the car, you said, "Hey, Spencer, good luck at the game tonight, see ya, man." Spencer walked towards school, looked back, and waved goodbye. You then jumped into the front seat and waved again as he looked back once more. No one would suspect that this was the last time you brothers would see each other. The signs of impending suicide were so subtle—sorting papers, not eating (let's assume Sammy ate the spaghetti), and then saying goodbye to each of us, one by one.

Next you asked if you could ride into town with me. Absolutely! Let's have breakfast and get ready. First we went back home and had our morning *Café Francis* coffee drink, and ate something quick and easy. I went into my room, prepared for a day at the salon, and we left. You seemed content and we talked all the way into town about forest fires and my secret to cooking good tacos. I remember you mentioning the car I used to drive, a Datsun 510 that had a sun roof and a maroon racing stripe down the middle. You smiled as you spoke of that car. It was small talk, but friendly talk. You changed the radio station and I hit the button back to my station (oldies), and our fingers were dueling with the radio keys as always. You changed the station back to hard rock, but I wanted to listen to The *Bee Gees*. Our fingers did a dance as we pushed buttons—AC DC vs. *Bee Gees*, back and forth.

Your last goodbye was to me. I parked in the ten-hour meter parking lot, then we walked along Second Street together, you carrying my bags draped over your shoulder the three blocks to my salon and up the staircase. Then you said, "See ya later." I smiled and moved the heavy duffle bag into the salon. You returned about an hour later, with a new fresh haircut. I was shocked and asked where you went and why. Jeff, you stared at me with an unnerving look and said nothing. Your getting a haircut from someone other than me hurt my feelings. I was not comfortable with this, and your odd demeanor gave me a sour stomach. I now suspect that this particular act, having someone other than your hairdresser mother cut your hair, was a sign of disconnect or hostility. You had perplexed me most of your life, but now the signs were greater, the statements bolder. But, not bold enough to signal suicide. I took it as ongoing frustration with the path your life had taken.

Jeff, you returned to the salon later in the day to say goodbye again. You told me that you were going to leave, and that I wouldn't see you again for a long, long time. I took this as a threat but knew you were a homing pigeon and would be back sooner than you thought. But it was a worry that you said this, and I knew I'd need to talk to you about this later, when I wasn't so busy. As usual, I reminded you to please be careful. I had no idea this was my last chance to look at your face, ever again. The tension in the air was evident. You were interrupting me as I was cutting someone's hair to tell me you were going to the lake. I wondered why you didn't say this at home, or in the car. If you had plans to leave and for a lengthy amount of time, why wait until I am too busy to chat? That was a strange morning indeed.

I should have suspected more than a hint of trouble; but we had experienced a couple of great days together, except for the weird vibes when we were driving down the Midway. I was happy for you to be on the lake, as you had said, although I never asked you who your friend was who had a boat or exactly where you were going. You had just turned twenty-one, and I didn't feel the need to cross-examine you. Later, after your death, I heard that you were seen a few days earlier at Marigold Elementary school campus, where you'd been a student. Someone saw you go over to *tire mountain* by the kindergarten, first, and second grade classrooms and look around; and then you roamed the halls. You were also seen on Hillsboro Circle, the street where you were raised as a small boy until age seventeen. I guess you were revisiting your past, but how was I to know? Even if I had known about your visit to Marigold Elementary or Hillsboro Circle, would have I suspected suicide? Possibly. But I didn't know anything about suicide. No one in our family or in my life had done this.

The tension between us could be stifling. I could often feel your anger, brewing just under your skin, your eyes burrowing a hole in my heart. Yet you could smile, chuckle like you so often did, and say "Mom" in such a sweet way that it brought me back to happier times. You had become a mixed bag of emotions and crossed signals.

Even after I realized you were going downhill, I went on with my life with my other two children and my business. Oh how I wish I had enough insight and courage to step forward and take you into mental health again. I did have you picked up at our house in Durham twice on a 5150, but they kept you for only twenty hours each time. I begged the doctor to please not release you, as I felt you were a danger to yourself and others. I begged them; but Jeff, you were well over the legal age of eighteen years old, and the doctor could do nothing but release you. About a month before your death, you were very angry and yelled at me for moving so far away from town and for divorcing your dad (meaning step-dad Don). I walked into the kitchen explaining to you why I did what I did, why this happened, what had transpired in our marriage, and you fumed and followed me into the kitchen, yelling. I backed up to the stove while you said some very hurtful things, and then you reached around me and slammed the tea kettle down as hard as you could, and the hot water bounced out of the spout and burned my arm. I stayed calm as I stepped away from the stove and rubbed my arm, trying not to appear frightened or hurt, while you went back to the counter and sat down, still fuming. You said you were sorry the water burned me. I told you it was okay, that it didn't hurt (which was a lie).

A few weeks before that incident, the kids had come home from school, and you began to yell, and the kids looked scared of your explosive anger. I told Dana to run out the back door to the neighbors and have them call the police. She did, and the police arrived and took you to mental health on a 5150. This is when I talked to the doctor and begged him to keep you for observation and to evaluate you, at least for another forty-eight hours. They let you go again, and I was not happy with the local mental health rules, the red tape, and quite honestly, with their lack of interest. They told me they could do nothing unless you hurt someone. Let me understand this: nothing can be done until violence has happened? That is ridiculous. Jeff, you were so mad at me and about life in general that I felt you needed immediate attention and medication. The problem with taking pills for you was that you were on the fence—smart enough to think you didn't need medication and weak enough to recognize you needed testing. If I had medication for you, you would level out, be an easygoing, cool, sweet guy; and then your sedated, calm inner self would give you the illusion that you didn't need medication so you would cease taking the pills.

The dark kept secrets are seeping out of my mind, and my memory of you is apparently sinking into the depths. Now my book has taken on a life of its own; it has become my own tapestry of memories and thoughts of you. This is a very sad story of a talented, funny boy, who fell through the cracks, and right before my eyes.

My son, you seemed so hostile and explosive, whether with anger or laughter, that you'd think any mother would know their child is losing their grip on sanity. You became angry and antisocial towards most people the last few months of your life. Your highs and the lows began to get closer together as the rest of us went about our daily lives, expecting and waiting for you to do the same; waiting for you to snap out of it and get on with your life.

Our relationship had been a roller coaster of accumulating reactions that were dysfunctional but workable. Some unhealthy interactions between us happened so often that I began to turn a cheek. I see now that I was numb to abnormal behavior. I would sigh and let you be; that was easier than trying to mold you into the person I would have enjoyed more, or I should say, you would have enjoyed more. The crazy thing is that I did enjoy you, Jeff. You were sweet, sensitive, and the funniest person I have ever known. But you always were drawn towards the wilder type of friend, the type who lives on the edge—not necessarily a criminal or a thug, but someone who has lived and survived the pitfalls of life. You were very selective, having just a few friends; you preferred being a loner and were generally very quiet. You always looked cool and tough, but we knew you were gentle and lonely. Jeffrey, you were a potpourri of feelings on the inside. Meanwhile, I tried to help you find your way out of the hole you continued to dig for yourself, deeper and deeper. Nevertheless, you slipped through my fingers.

Wondering about you, I came home after work and maneuvered the top drawer open, felt the dent with my hand, sat down on the edge of my bed and opened your file. You'd saved your medical records and I slowly read the letters from different counselors, including the last one: Dr. Stewart Bedford, PhD. He'd run a series of tests on you, and the two of you talked at length, and you didn't seem to mind these appointments whatsoever. You even said he was a cool guy. The evaluation from him now seems crystal clear, but then, with the small window of time closing in on us, I didn't believe you were going into schizophrenia. I thought Dr. Bedford was old and using the same terms he used way back when he was a young doctor. I thought this was a big word to justify his time with you. You'd first gone to him when you were fifteen, and now you were back at age nineteen for a follow-up from your short mental health stay. I confess I dismissed it then, dismissed it until the last six months of your life when I was forced to pay attention and seek help once again. I began to open my eyes and became wide awake. But time was running out.

Schizophrenia. The word alone painted a negative dark picture, posted a huge warning sign in my mind that I refused to believe. I was afraid to believe it, as my sister had explained how dangerous schizophrenia can be and made me even more frightened. She was worried for our safety, which made me worry even more. She told me to be careful, and I was, but I just could not, would not grasp that my son could ever hurt anyone.

Looking back, I recall other events that I now recognize as signs. For example, during those last few months, you only wanted prepackaged foods, nothing from any kitchen. In mid-June we went out for breakfast late one morning while attending a family reunion out of town, and you took forever to order. Finally, after a very long time reading and scanning the menu, you ordered a small box of Rice Krispies, and you were very clear to the waitress: "Do not open the box." She looked at me, smiled, and nodded an acknowledgment; the kids and my mom were quiet as they ate their breakfast. I suspected paranoia and confusion.

The family reunion was a lot of fun, and there was a parade in Placerville that day, but you kept to yourself. After breakfast we stood together on the sidewalk—your grandmother in a wheelchair and me with my brood—watching the parade go by. I really enjoyed the waitresses and bartenders running and balancing glasses full of water on a tray. I spotted a vender and bought two puppets that had boxing gloves on—one for you, Jeff, and one for Spencer. You put your hand under the material and maneuvered the two levers that moved the arms back and forth, making your puppet spar with the big fat mitts he was wearing. Spencer took the boxing nun, and made her box the famous Mr. T, which was your man, Jeff. This is the only time all weekend I observed you laughing and playing like a kid with your brother. On our way home, you boys boxed each other and I could hear you laughing and making moaning sounds from a knockout. I kept those crazy boxing puppets for years.

The family reunion in Placerville, held in mid-June, just three months before you took your life, has become a gauge for your odd behavior, Jeff. Then when you turned twenty-one the end of July, we went to Lakeport to celebrate with family. As we walked to the movie theater with your brother, sister, my friend Jan, and her son Mike, you walked one block ahead of us. We called for you to wait for us, but you continued to walk ahead and never looked back. When we got there, you had already bought a ticket and gone inside. There were two movies playing and we had no idea which one you'd chosen, so we watched *Die Hard* with Bruce Willis. You watched *The Terminator* with Arnold Schwarzenegger.

In August Dana, Spencer, and I took my dad to the ocean, and you stayed back home as you'd found work with a landscaper. Life continued to move forward and we had no idea we had only a few brief weeks left of normalcy. In September everything would change to black.

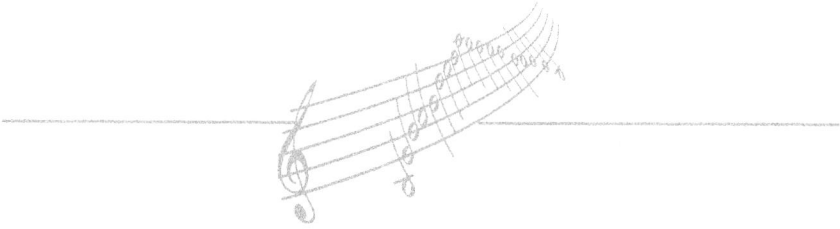

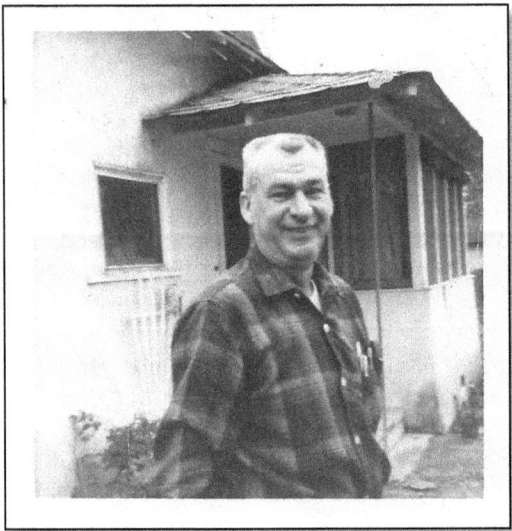

Four things come not back-the spoken word, the sped arrow,
the past life, and the neglected opportunity.
Arabian Proverb

GRANDPA'S JOURNEY

DEAR JEFF, your grandpa came home from the local Lakeport hospital only ten days after he'd been shot. His release was too soon for his age and type of wound. Marion wanted him to return home as if he had received only a flesh wound, instead of a bullet through his lung, and the small town doctors released him. I phoned my sister Bobbie and we agreed that Dad's release was too soon. So we balked, only to be rebutted by Marion, who reminded us that she was in charge and the doctor agreed with her.

Within a week after being released, your grandpa developed bleeding in his stomach due to an undiagnosed ulcer. I happened to be there when Dad felt sick so I drove him back to the hospital, and waited with him in a holding room across from the emergency room desk. Dad lay on the examining table far longer than I imagined he should have without being checked in. I summoned a nurse after he told me he had to go to the bathroom, but no one responded. After twenty minutes of being totally ignored, I sat him up, put his arm around my neck, and we walked to the bathroom across the room, where I placed him on the toilet. I could hear him urinating for longer than it should have taken. Oh, if you knew my proud German father as well as I did, you'd know how hard it was for me to take the initiative to gently push him forward and look into the toilet to see what was happening. What I saw was bright red blood; he was bleeding internally, not urinating. I went into the doorway across from the desk, looked at the station of medical staff members who had their heads down and at those walking back and forth, all oblivious to me. I transformed into an assertive monster-daughter and screamed, "Get in this room NOW!"

They gave him something to help coagulate the blood and scheduled surgery for the next day even though the doctor said Dad probably wouldn't survive it. My sister and her husband returned, and Marion came to the hospital. The doctor's negative attitude perplexed all of us, but what else could we do? Dad was gravely ill from lack of blood. I wanted to have him air-lifted to a larger hospital in Santa Rosa for this surgery, but Marion wanted him to stay in Lakeport. She was adamant. He survived the surgery but his recovery was very slow. I drove over every other day and held his hand or suctioned his throat and lungs while the nurses stayed behind the desk. He asked me to untie his wrists from the bed rails. I told him I couldn't do that, the first time

I'd ever said no to my father. When he asked me again, I thought back to when my ex-husband Don's father had developed an infection in his intestine. He had been pulling out his tubing, so the hospital employees had tied his wrists to the bed rails. Don told me early in our marriage that his dad had asked Don to untie him, but Don explained the rules to his father and didn't untie the restraints. This has been a lifelong regret for him, as his father died with his wrists tied to the rails.

I leaned close to my father and whispered, "If I untie you, you must promise you won't grab at your tubes or tracheotomy." He looked up at me with his ice blue eyes, and his head moved up and down. I looked back at the nurses' station and quickly undid the knots. Dad slowly took his hands and folded his fingers together; then he rubbed his wrists, and began to rub his chest hair and move around a little. He then put his hand under the small sheet covering his privates and rubbed his groin, and then he tossed the sheet off his privates. I saw more than I needed to see and said, "Now mister, let's keep you covered up." He smiled while I put the sheet back. He gave himself another sweep of his chest then he submitted his hands back to the rails and I retied the knots. He mouthed, "Thank you."

Jeff, your grandpa passed away six weeks after you did. It was 6:15 A.M. and I was asleep when my cat Marvin woke me up by galloping down the hall and jumping on my bed at the same time the phone rang. It was Shari, George's wife, who simply said, "He's gone," and I responded with, "I know."

I walked down the hall and sat on the couch. No crying, just acceptance mixed with a numbness that comes with denial. My dad had given me a Victorian black tea cup and matching saucer for my birthday to go with a small collection I had started. I heard a crash and ran to the kitchen where my four sets of Victorian cups and saucers were. The black set from my dad had fallen over and cracked into pieces. I just sighed and thought, Yes, I know, Dad. I swept up the chips and half of the cup and set it aside, thinking I could glue it one day, but that day has never happened.

Your grandpa's funeral was a blur of *Masons* and *Shriners*, long-time friends, and local business people. There were sympathy cards from the governor, and from all the agriculture commissioners in the state of California. A huge bouquet of flowers arrived from his secretary, Thelma.

I don't recall the music, but I think it was *The Garden Alone.* We slowly passed by his casket for one last goodbye. I do recall feeling terribly guilty that he died, at least indirectly, at the hands of my son, and I couldn't help but notice that not one person came up to me or my sister with condolences.

Jeff, before your grandfather died, while he was back at home resting, he asked what exactly had transpired. When he asked me if you were in any trouble, I had to softly tell him that you had died. Tears filled his eyes and he stared out the bedroom window. I could see his wheels in motion as he was thinking of more questions. He was sorting through his shock and gathering information, and he had to absorb the tragedy that had happened on his turf.

I had to tell him that the gun went off from your lap, Jeff, and that the bullet had pierced his lung. I told him the facts; he deserved as much. He turned towards me with furrowed brows as I told him your fate. He looked out the window and asked me if you had a funeral. "Yes, Dad, the funeral was across the street, at the Episcopal Church." Your grandfather continued to lie on his bed asking for more details, and he also expressed a bit of irritation that no one had mentioned you and your death while he had been visited by so many friends and family members.

In the next room, Grandma Marion and her sister Harriett continued to puff away, seemingly oblivious to the fact that Grandpa was in the next room trying to heal from a punctured lung. I walked into the smoke-filled room and told them to open a window, and announced that I'd be bringing an air purifier with me in a day or so. Marion said this was her home and no one will be putting in an air purifier, and she will smoke if she wants to. She was hostile towards me because your action led to your grandfather's injury, and since you were no longer around to blame, somehow your actions became my fault. So now Marion is going to torture her husband with second-hand cigarette smoke, I thought. The sisters continued to smoke a pack of cigarettes, while my dad struggled to breathe. As a girl who was taught to respect elders, I had to restrain myself from saying much, though I felt the hairs on the back of my neck stand up from anger.

Your grandpa then asked me why you did this to yourself, and why you did this to him. I told him it was an accident. Then grandpa said, "I think Jeff wanted me to go with him on his journey." I was speechless.

After taking a deep breath, I pressed on, saying, "Dad, Jeff didn't mean to kill himself; he shot himself after he thought he'd killed you. The gun went off from his lap. The police told me that when someone shoots someone, the shooter points with an outstretched arm. The police said you probably startled him when you walked into the garage and waved hello."

Dear boy, what were you doing with your grandfather's gun anyway? Why were you in his garage sitting on a box holding his gun? Please don't let me think for a second that you wanted to leave this earth. Yet there is a part of me that thinks you were considering this and maybe building up your courage, and were too deep in thought to know what you were doing. I don't know, nor can I believe you would have gone through with it if you hadn't thought you'd killed your grandpa, but a small spot in my brain tells me you would have.

I took the cardboard box you had been sitting on when you died, and I still I have it. The box, which came from Florida, had bold green printing on the side: *JEFF Cantaloupes.* Did you know this, or was it another random thing? What are the chances of this box having your name on the side? I took it home and packed most of your belongings in it. Years later, when transferring your personal items to a plastic container with a lid, I folded up the box and kept it.

Returning three days later, after our argument, I walked into Marion's house, past the thick smoke-filled room, carrying your grandfather's new air purifier. The instructions read to adjust a window by opening it just a crack, then turn on the filter. Dad looked up at me and whispered, "Thank you." I so hated to leave him there alone. No one was really taking care of him and well, he needed fresh air. Maybe you know all of this, Jeff. Were you hovering nearby, waiting for a companion to take along on your journey? Dad lived only three weeks after this visit.

The Aftermath

Well, sonny boy, these are some of the happenings we dealt with after you died. Many other things transpired after your sudden death; personalities and lifestyles changed, and relationships changed.

Dana became more assertive and somewhat daring. She jumped off the highest bungee jump in the world in New Zealand, and she became a fearless world traveler. I don't think she would have been a seeker of travel and experiences if you, we, had continued in the same vein. Dana is now an astute businesswoman and a very successful hairstylist and owner of a respected salon. She also has a select set of close friends.

Spencer found his footing as a young teen and surrounded himself mostly with friends from grammar school, and lifelong friends from high school. He went on to become a successful teacher of sciences and math. He's a wonderful teacher and can spot a student with troubles very quickly and knows how to handle the situation. Spencer also developed a fearless attitude, which served him well when he was a mountain guide and traveled the world. Your brother and sister live with a dark memory, but their friends and family provide them with a net of security. Both your sister and brother married spouses who are grounded, honest, and understanding, and I know they will be with them for life no matter what comes their way.

I dug into our box of memories, saved for many years. While looking through your medical records, I came across the letter from Dr. Bedford PhD. When I reopened the envelope, I realized this was a letter I had never seen. I don't know if you intercepted it, or if I glanced and decided it was the same as all the rest. This letter, on page three, included test results for your IQ tests. I was surprised you had this letter, but not surprised when I looked at the numbers and Dr. Bedford's analysis. He wrote that you scored on a superior level for motor skills, and that for verbal communication you were slightly lower than average. I knew this, or strongly suspected it, and seeing these test results confirmed what I felt to be true. If only we could have tapped into that superior part of your mind, I found myself thinking. Dr. Bedford wrote that he believed you were in a lower level for communication due to lack of confidence and low self-esteem. He wrote that he believed this began at a very early age. Still, I loved seeing the word *superior* that day. It confirmed my thoughts about your motor skills, and I felt so proud of you. It also caused me to be sick with regret.

I still live with lifelong guilt as the one who let you slip into obscurity. Recapping your life makes me feel as though I am walking uphill carrying sand in both my hands, and when I reach the top, all the grains have leaked through my fingers and all I had left is dust.

I keep going back to your teen and early adult years, especially to the last year of your life. In my struggle to come forward and take ownership of your downfall, I was going full throttle with *Tough Love.* This fad, which required family members to turn their backs on a loved one rather than support destructive behavior, seemed to be my last hope. I was determined to not be a co-dependent, to not be an enabler so that your destructive cycle would not continue. It is often expected that the child will mimic the parent in wants and needs. With everything inside of me, I assumed you would pull out of your dilemma, return home, regroup, enroll into a college program, and go on with the art of living and prospering as I have always done. What you needed, though, was your family. I see now that you were too fragile to survive *Tough Love.* I know now that I am a survivor, but you were not.

When I didn't intervene, you became homeless. I heard you were sleeping in an abandoned house, and you told me that someone stole your large new backpack full of clothes. You told me you used to go to the University gymnasium and shower. I'd see you downtown and you looked the same, except for an angry expression I hadn't seen before. I can still see you, sitting on the steps of a business, writing in a notebook. You carried this small note pad everywhere and seemed to be constantly scribbling something—thoughts? notes? After your funeral I found your notebook and later, after I'd returned home and took a day for myself, I opened it. It was gibberish to me, the worst sight I could imagine. Nothing made any sense, except that you were clearly frustrated, confused, and jotting down a hodge-podge of memories and sights. Spencer wanted to read it, too, but I didn't allow him to see the contents for eight years. Then one day he said he was ready to look through your box of personal items and asked to see the notebook. Reality can be brutal.

You and I were in a power struggle those last few months. We argued, and our home became a disruptive place for the other kids, who deserved a calm warm household to live in. I remember when I told the child psychologist on my first visit, "I won't have a child who disobeys me." She smiled and said, "You might win the battle, but you'll lose the war."

Well, she was correct. I did lose the war. I did relax and let up on you after your return from Right Way Homes in Westwood. You were happy and seemed to be sincere about putting your life in order, and you had missed us so much. You missed my cooking, which every mother wants to hear, and the banter with your brother and sister was wonderful background music. I got such a warm feeling listening to you kids laugh while I prepared a meal. The chatter at the dinner table, with your stories and interpretations of people you'd met along the way, was so entertaining. It killed me to see you slide downhill and pull away from us and from society. But then sometimes you'd return to us, be kind and thankful, and once again things were back like they used to be, a house full of kids and laughter. I swear, I had no idea how fragile you'd become. I didn't know what to do, or what decisions to make. It was as if I was lost without a compass and all of the roads looked the same. I just wanted you to heal, to mend, and to be happy. If I were to get an award for anything concerning motherhood, it would be for denial.

The Burying My Head in the Sand Award goes to—Jeff's mother.

Goodnight Jeff, goodnight Dad.

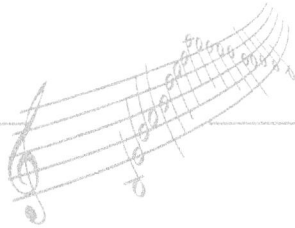

I calmed down after your passing and retraced your steps.
I felt you had left the answers for me to find.
Mom

EVERY DAY IS SEPTEMBER

I CONCENTRATED ON REMEMBERING your last evening with us. You seemed content, but you also seemed anxious. Looking back, you were trying to be calm, but you also had an agenda. Something was pushing you to complete your task of sorting papers. You were gentle when you petted our dog, and visited with Spencer as you two sat on the couch, then you dashed into the garage. My memory of you sitting on the floor, going over your personal papers only led me to think in an instant that you were getting organized, which any mom wants to see. You certainly didn't appear to be sad or melancholy.

When I returned home from your funeral, I went into the garage and peered into our new garbage can, there I saw a few things lying on the bottom; a photo of your grandparents, a photo of your dad and you, a photo of us camping, and a few papers from school.

I ran to my bedroom and looked in the file cabinet where I remembered you'd put some things the last evening you were home. Inside a file, I found your prom photo, poems and music lyrics, and photos of us as a family. You'd put in your medical papers as well. I sat down on the bed, stared at you dressed in a black tuxedo on your way to the prom, and cried for the loss of a life worth living.

Then, as if it were a tape of your voice inside my head, I heard, "Look in Spencer's room, in the wastebasket." I ran into your brother's room and spotted a small trash can next to his desk. It was empty, except for one small thing sitting on the bottom: your little black book that I had given you for Christmas when you were sixteen years old. My heart was pounding as I sat on your brother's bed and opened the book. You had listed girls and rated each girl on a scale from 1 to 10, which struck me as funny. Then I remembered you calling from Westwood and telling me all about a girl—I seemed to remember her name was Lisa. I recalled you telling me she was pretty, sweet, a cheerleader, and that you really liked her and her family. I wondered whether you had included her, so I thumbed through your black book pages and came across a Lisa under the Ms. I also noticed you'd rated her a *10* and had written that she is *nurturing, patient, and sensitive.* The phone number was in Westwood, so I felt certain it was her. It also came to me that you'd mentioned that her mom owned a video store, the only one in Westwood. Oh dear, do I dare phone them?

With shaking hands, I began to dial the number you had written on the bottom of her page. All the while I was telling myself, *Breathe deep, Judi girl, and stay calm.* I heard the phone ringing, then a young high-pitched happy voice said "Hello." I swallowed hard then said, "Hello Lisa, my name is Judi, and I think you used to date my son, Jeff." She was surprised but clearly wanted to talk. She quickly said she had heard rumors going around town about you and was wondering if it was true. Neither of us mentioned the word death, just "rumors." I waited a moment before I softly said, "Yes, it's true, Lisa." Next I heard a clunk; she'd dropped the phone and I could hear her sobs. This started a chain reaction, making me cry too; then she finally picked up the phone and we cried together for awhile, somehow talking through wails and sobs. I have no idea how we settled on anything, as it was an incoherent conversation. I told her that you had died two weeks before, in Lakeport, where you had gone on your way to Eureka to find a girl named Lisa. "Yes," she choked out, "that was me."

Every September I always think about how beautiful our town and the rest of Northern California is, when we have the most amazing weather known as an *Indian summer*. There is usually a light breeze rustling the leaves, and the evenings cool off, a welcome change from our hot, dry summers. Every September I can't help but wonder who would want to die on such a beautiful day. It still astounds me that you did.

I called Lisa again, about a week after that first phone call, and we talked about you, Jeff, and the relationship you two had. The more I got to know Lisa, the more I learned about you. Within weeks she drove the winding roads down the mountains that led from Lake Almanor, her hometown, to our town. Because Lisa had no idea where we lived or the layout of our town, we decided it was best to meet at a large gas station near where she would be driving into town. "Meet us at the Shell station next to the freeway between 8th and 9th Streets. You can't miss it!"

Spencer didn't get involved in this meeting and didn't seem interested. I suspect Lisa was too much of a reminder of you. But Dana asked if she could ride with me to meet Lisa. It has been just weeks since we said our goodbyes to you, Jeff, and now it was time to meet your Lisa. The drive to the gas station was only five miles, but our anticipation made the ride seem longer. I was nervous and excited to meet the girl you had loved. Dana sat quietly in the passenger seat.

We pulled into the parking lot and waited less than ten minutes when I saw her pull in. I first noticed her long curly brown hair. Suddenly I felt totally embarrassed, intimidated by the thought that she'd expect me to lead the pack; in reality, I was just a big kid full of questions myself. She opened her arms and we hugged. I introduced Dana as "Jeff's sister," which Dana promptly corrected with "Hi, I'm Dana." The girls hugged, then stepped back, creating an uncomfortable pregnant pause before we all giggled and said, "It's great to meet you." Finally I suggested Lisa follow us back to Durham so we could visit and get acquainted. I went to my car, sat down, and to my surprise Dana (that dirty double-crosser) jumped into Lisa's car. Off we went back to our house for what soon became a surreal meeting.

Back at the house, I introduced Lisa to Spencer without mentioning your name. He was nice to her but kept to himself. Later, when Spencer and I had a moment alone while I was fixing lunch and the girls were sunbathing on our deck, he asked me why Lisa had come. I explained that she had been your girlfriend during your year in Westwood. I could tell he was bothered by her visit so I told him, "We need to know her; she is the one Jeff wanted to find." But I don't think my answer satisfied him at that time.

We sat on the sectional couch and began to give each other gifts. Lisa had made a tape of your favorite songs for us. She also gave us copies of a video and still photos of you two at the prom, standing under an arbor in your formal attire. I'd never seen these photos so they completely took me by surprise. I was grateful that Lisa had gone to so much trouble to show us your world while you lived in Westwood. When I showed her the prom picture you had put in my filing cabinet, she smiled and said, "Oh yeah, he wanted to take me but I had made commitment with a friend from back in Kindergarten." Then she laughed and said, "Look at his face; he looks so mad!" We laughed as she nailed your expression.

I gave Lisa some of your clothes and copies of your poems, telling her, "The poem titled *Beautiful* is about you, Lisa." That made her cry, which opened my flood gates, and we were both out of control for awhile. She shared many things about your life and how much you and she liked each other. She then showed me a letter you'd sent her. I particularly loved hearing one line: "My mom is so cool, you would really like her." This was a shocker to me because I'd never once heard you describe me as cool.

We had been invited to a wedding reception the next day and took Lisa with us. Then I asked John if he'd mind if I invited Lisa to come along on our planned family vacation to Cozumel in July—even though Dana had already asked her friend Denise and Spencer had invited his friend Chris. John answered by telling Lisa she'd need a passport and would have to get medical papers together. She thought it all sounded like a great time.

Closer to our departure date, Spencer asked why I had invited Lisa. "Now who is she exactly, and why is she coming with us?" was his concern. He had never in his life been negative so I assume he linked Lisa to you, Jeff, and didn't understand the connection to us. I showed him the photos Lisa had given us and we played the tape she'd recorded for us, but he was still not impressed. Even when we heard your favorite *Here I Go Again* by Whitesnake, or *Livin' on a Prayer* by Bon Jovi, Spencer stayed neutral.

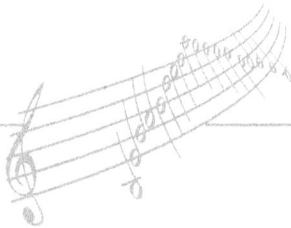

I would rather have a mind open by wonder,
than one closed by beliefs.
Author Unknown

HEALING

ON A DAY IN MID-SEPTEMBER, A YEAR AFTER WE LOST YOU, Jeff, and my dad a few weeks later in October, I was preparing for another year. I decided to make some changes, namely get my life in order, put my salon up for sale, and regroup. Blindsided by the fact that everyone had left me, I had to dig deep inside for a grip on sanity. I did my usual routine when stressed, or overwhelmed. I considered this method a sure cure for this comeback kid. I took a hot shower, pulled my hair back into a towel, put a deep moistening conditioner on my hair with a plastic bag over that, patted a cream facial mask all over my face and onto my neck and chest, and lathered my body with lotion. I tweezed my eyebrows, brushed my teeth, and painted my toenails while all of the goop was on my body. Then I rinsed off my lotions, face cream, and hair products, put on a robe, stared back at my image in the mirror, and thought, Oh crap, it didn't work.

I did make one significant change. After my dad's death I legally changed my last name to Loren, which is my father's middle name. I went into town to order new checks for a name change, and then went directly to the DMV. That afternoon I drove back to Durham, sat down at my desk to clean up papers, get organized, and get a grip on my life. I was shuffling, tossing, and putting papers in files when I noticed something hiding in the very back of my desk. Behind a picture was an unopened envelope from my dad's attorney. I tore into the letter, and there was a check left to me from my dad's estate. It had been there, uncashed, for three months. I felt that Dad's spirit was telling me thank you, and that he liked the fact that I changed my last name. Finding that check seemed a huge good omen that I had done the right thing.

Dear Jeff, Five months after your death, on a cold winter's day, I began to see a counselor. I had too many questions and my mind could not find a peaceful spot of acceptance. I needed to understand your actions and comprehend what you had done. I had to walk in your shoes to clarify your thought process. Your childhood doctor, Dr. Wood, gave me the name of a counselor who was a friend of his, and I highly regarded and trusted this recommendation because of my past connection with our pediatrician.

Dale greeted me with a handshake, and he seemed to emanate peace and understanding before I even had a chance to open my mouth, and in no time the flood gates opened as I began the tale of your death. Dale was quiet, compassionate, and thoughtful. His first response, after my long speech was, "I'm sorry your son fell through the cracks." *Ooh, that stung.* He went on to say he could have helped. He said he worked very closely with this type of behavior and knew of a place in a nearby town where you could have stayed and had therapy. And he would have worked with you, too, Jeff. Before he asked me to tell him about your life and death, he again said he was sorry and continued to say he wished we had connected sooner. This was not a comforting thought, that your death happened because you got missed by the system and that you could have been saved and alive today, if only. Your life could have turned around, if only. This revelation caused my heart to tumble to my feet.

Dale listened to my heartache, referring to me as a lovely lady who had experienced a terrible tragedy. His words touched my heart like no other comment I'd heard; finally I'd received the verbal confirmation I longed for. Most people were sorry for you, Jeffrey. Others were mad at you for doing this to yourself and for including my father in your dark journey. Some of the population didn't dwell on the sadness of your death; in fact, I was surprised at the amount of people who avoided me, and changed this topic altogether. Your name is rarely mentioned even today. But for some reason, no one acknowledged that I was suffering and my surviving children were suffering as well. Dale, with his gentle manner justified that I had walked into hell and was still there. He had asked during our pre-appointment phone conversation that I bring in a photo and any letters from you so he could get a feel for our relationship. On this appointment, I carried with me a letter you had written when you were eighteen years old about your hopes and dreams. Your letter is well-written, insightful, hopeful, and it was you. I could hear your voice as I read it. I cherish it because your sweet nature comes through and you so eloquently shared your dreams before you began your downward spiral.

I carefully opened the envelope, unfolded the worn edges, and began to read your words to Dale in hopes that he'd understand your sweet, gentle nature, and pick up on your comedic timing to better understand us. Aloud, I read one paragraph, then got to the words, "and go for drives with my girlfriend and Sheba." I began to cry and gasp for breath. I needed a Kleenex, and Dale graciously handed me the box. This crying and mournful sobbing slowly grew out of control from the depths of this mother's heart and continued for a long time. If I hadn't been so strapped for money, I might have cried the entire hour. I collected my emotions and regained my composure. Dale waited patiently as I released more built-up grief, then he asked in his soft voice, "Who is Sheba?" Through grunts and tears and a swollen red nose, out came a little girl's whisper: "Our dog." Then a flood of tears began to flow again. I'm sure Dale wanted to smile. Here I was in his office, paying by the hour, and crying over Sheba. It just hit me like a lightning bolt of grief, the finality of your life. Your shattered dreams , your future forever gone. And Sheba, our black border collie, proved to be the trigger point. Jeff, this was my first of four appointments, four long appointments. Dale must have sensed I was in a financial bind, and he suggested I pay off my tab by cutting his son's and his son's girlfriend's hair. I was so thankful for his insightfulness.

He continued to listen and slowly my voice began to sound like an adult's; the healing process had begun and my aching heart was not the focal point of my body. He worked on the guilt every parent carries, especially those whose children commit suicide. A child, your child, killing himself is a direct reflection on the parent, or so I thought. He explained that all types of kids and adults take their lives. Dale kindly explained that suicide is the cause of death for kids of privilege, from good solid homes, with loving parents, both wealthy and poor, and also kids raised in faith—all dominations included. Many factors that enhance the design of one's life could also lead to the desire to commit suicide. Death to some seems an easy way out, or is perceived as the only way out. Some studies even suggest that suicide can be contagious.

This made me remember back to incidents I'd forgotten, or suppressed. Our paperboy was a nice kid, polite and raised in a solid Mormon family with many brothers and sisters. I was surprised when I heard he committed suicide his senior year of high school. Also our neighbor, whose name I can't recall, took his own life. He was a late-in-life child, and his parents dressed him like a miniature adult. His clothes were always the same: bold striped long-sleeved polo shirts with a white collar, tucked in with a belt holding up his Dockers. It was the late '80s, when rock and roll was at the top of the charts, and he was dressed like a golf pro. He used to hang out with you and Keith when his parents permitted it, and the two of you made fun of his high-pitched voice when he yelled for you to come over and play. He wasn't allowed to come into our home; he could only stand on our lawn. His parents were very strict and kept a watchful eye on their pride and joy, and I felt this poor boy had no room to breathe. He committed suicide soon after you did, Jeffrey. They found his body at the Five Mile picnic area in a dry creek bed by the large chunks of concrete blocks that had been put there for a promised bridge. That poor kid never fit in, and I am sure he had other issues to deal with too. Back then we didn't talk about bullying, but I suspect this might have played a part in his demise. It was very hard for Keith to process his two childhood pals taking their lives—the one with obvious problems, and the street-smart, funny guy, who got caught in an undercurrent.

Dale focused on something I'd said and asked, "Can you explain why you didn't see Jeff in the hospital or at the funeral home?" I swallowed hard and told him that on a Saturday morning, directly after the shooting, you had been transported to Santa Rosa by helicopter and had been kept alive my machines so you could become a donor. I was out of town and didn't find out about your death until late Sunday evening, and time was closing in. I had to give my permission to harvest your organs over the phone, directly after I heard the news. Later, when you were delivered back to Lakeport to the funeral home, the director discouraged me from looking at your body because of your injuries and the harvesting. I didn't argue with anyone. I never laid eyes on you since the day you stopped by my work and said goodbye.

Dale suggested this homework assignment: I was to write a letter, as if I was sitting next to your hospital bed holding your hand. He told me this is called closure, and that this is what I should have done and will do now. He told me to speak to you and to say my goodbyes.

I have saved this letter, written with pencil on yellow legal lined paper. I have only read it once in all this time. After twenty-four years, it's a bit wrinkled and the edges are worn, but here it is, unedited:

Dear Jeff,

If I could have talked with you before you left for Lakeport, knowing it would be my last chance, or if I had been able to talk with you in the hospital and sit by your bed and hold your hand, I would have told you many things.

I love the color of your hair, I like your graceful walk, your athletic abilities and the way you run and you never fall or stumble. You are sure footed, not like me. You never make mistakes, and you are so handsome. I love your sense of humor, I like to hear you laugh. I love our morning coffee conversations too. Your piano playing is a gift and I love it.

I'm so sorry I didn't realize you were ready to leave this earth, and us. I'm sick to my stomach I was in San Francisco as you lay dying. I would have held your hand and whispered as I am whispering to you now: "I love you Jeff, please hang on, Jeff, and please don't leave me."

But I wasn't there for you. I had no idea. Knowing you had donated your skin and femur bones and your beautiful green eyes made it impossible for me to look at you under the sheet and say goodbye properly. I wish I had anyway and not listened to the funeral director. Just to have touched your hair one last time.

Today I will say goodbye. Let you go to a more peaceful place. I hope you are at peace now, resting and watching and smiling down at us.

I will remember you with fondness. You know my regrets. I have many. You know my frustrations and my tolerance level. I was pushed to my wits end with you. You never let up and you continued to be stubborn. You didn't bend or try to help yourself. You turned down housing aid, counseling, and all medical check-ups; counseling at the local college for skills and career best suited for you—you closed all avenues. You knew where you wanted to be, in the heavens.

So, in the clouds you are, waiting for us as we stumble through life, and you, shaking your head.

Goodbye my golden-haired boy. I have your picture framed.

I love me mom; I love me boy.

Dale suggested I keep my letter and read it when I needed more closure.

I began to improve after four appointments with Dale, but I still needed his guidance to help cope and understand. I called for another appointment, but he didn't return my calls. Then my life became full and busy and I let it slide for a few weeks. Finally I phoned the front desk in the three-story building where his office was located. The receptionist answered and I told her I was a patient of Dale's, and that I thought he must have changed his cell phone number or moved out of the building because I hadn't been able to reach him. With hesitation she told me that Dale had died. I did some research to find out what happened and finally got a call from Dr. Wood, who had originally recommended Dale as a counselor. When he told me that Dale had committed suicide, my face went numb and I couldn't swallow. I asked no questions.

Yes indeed, this journey has been very bumpy. It took me years to recover from this news, even though I took it in stride, making sure not to tell my children about my counselor. Dale deserved his privacy, and out of respect for him, I did not dig for answers, and I didn't open up about my feelings for a decade. Then one day, early in the spring, when I was home alone for the weekend, I began to think back to my last session with him, to remember his last bit of advice, and his homework assignment. I had a refreshed memory of the last time I actually saw you. Jeff, I have relived this a thousand times. The look and the pause, this is what I remember and still do in vivid detail. You stood at the front door with your hand on the doorknob, I heard, "Mom," turned and looked towards you, there you stood, watching me; it is this still moment I recall, the two of us looking at each other, then you saying, "bye mom."

This led to another important memory; my dad called the salon the next morning, Friday, to tell me, "Jeff arrived at our place about midnight." Dad asked if he should be worried and I told him "no, Jeff's getting his life back in order." Dad told of his concerns about finding pawn tickets in his wastebasket in the bathroom, which set off a red flag. Jeff, you pawned your leather jacket and much loved red electric guitar? He said they were a hold ticket, not a sale. Dad thanked me for easing his worries and he then apologized for disrupting my work, and ended his call with, "see ya doll."

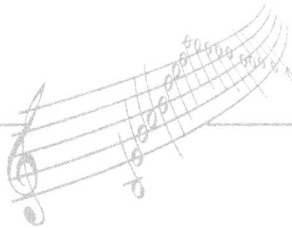

This Chapter is dedicated to Dale Wallen

The ocean stirs the heart, inspires the imagination,
and brings eternal joy to the soul.
Wyland–The Artist

COZUMEL

JOHN AND I PLANNED A TRIP WITH THE KIDS TO COZUMEL, it had been ten months since you left us. Once in awhile I would collect your clothes and bury my face to smell your scent. All of us wounded still, this vacation was to be a trip to remember, a getaway that would heal our hearts so we could move forward.

Lisa, with her paperwork in order prepared to join us. Dana invited Denise, and Spencer asked a friend. We had six months to prepare. We also got the low-down on Denise and her allergy to bees so John looked up the location of the nearest hospital just in case she got stung.

This was a much-needed vacation and we spared no expense on our hotel, the kids' rooms, and activities. John and I had our hands full with five teenagers, and this band of four young teens and one young adult wanted to play and party. John had found a great hotel two miles out of Cozumel, so there was no walking into the town. We ate well and relaxed on the beach, or cooled off in the large pool. John also rented a red jeep with a rag top that we took on many excursions. One day while in the center of town we went to the city plaza and danced. I saw a small white stucco church across the street, and walked towards it. The service was just starting so I went inside and sat down next to a Mayan woman who was about nine months pregnant. As I looked at the cross of Jesus and some white stucco sculptured doves, I began to weep, and then stood up with all of the other short darker-skinned church goers to take communion. I was about two feet taller than everyone in the church. No matter, they simply watched me with curiosity as I took the wafer into my mouth, drank the blood of Jesus (wine), and wiped my eyes. I walked out into the sun, squinting to see my kids and boyfriend waiting in the plaza.

Another day we drove around the island, stopping along a deserted beach and combing through driftwood. The kids played volleyball and found shelter from the sun under a thatched roof on the beach. John spotted some construction, checked out the foundation, and asked me to take a picture of the work, which left him shaking his head in wonder.

John also reserved a fishing and dive boat for a day, and the drivers took us out to a secluded bay with dark turquoise water. We snorkeled for hours and then, about noontime, the boat brought us in and dropped us off at a sandy beach where Mexican women were cooking over an open concrete fire pit. Our lunch was an amazing mix of Mexican foods with many dishes to choose from. Then the five kids played volleyball again, while John and I rested in the sun.

Later, after we were rested and digested, we went back out to the bay to continue our snorkeling experience. I stayed with Spencer, and as we swam close together looking down at the wonder below the surface, he pointed straight down underwater for me to look at a large school of fish. We then looked at each other with our arms outstretched, pointing and nodding our heads up and down. Then Spencer dropped a large shell on top of the hundreds of fish, which quickly dispersed in all directions. To our surprise, they had been on top of the huge mother fish. She looked like a motor home lying on the ocean floor. Spencer and I shot up out of the water and yelled "Swim!" We put our heads down and swam as fast as we could back to the boat, which was now quite a distance away as your brother and I had managed to drift way out with the current. I think the Mexican boat drivers had forgotten about us. This was a scary moment for me, but your little brother loved it.

John and I pushed for more tours around the island, even though the kids didn't look so well in the mornings, probably because they stayed up all night. John and I would tell them, "If you can't run with the big dogs, then stay on the porch," and we'd laugh out loud. This only irritated the worn-out partiers.

Each morning, John got the jeep ready while I banged on the sliding-glass door to wake up the island partiers who would slowly emerge and pile into the red jeep convertible for a torturous ride around the island. I have some great photos of them in the back and rumble seats, all five looking sleepy and somewhat ill. I also snapped photos of their room, saying "evidence." I'm sure we bugged them to no end.

The kids danced at night at the popular *Carlos and Charlie's*, a bar and restaurant smack downtown Cozumel. We tried to keep a watchful eye on them, but these renegades were very clever and we hardly knew where they were or how late they stayed up at night. We always made sure they had money for a taxi. All we could do was catch a glimpse of them across a sea of young teens on a crowded dance floor, when by chance we'd spot Lisa's or Denise's long curly hair flying through the air, flipping back and forth. I remember saying that I thought the dance was called *head banging*. Then I'd see that long-legged Dana jumping up and down next to her friends and wondered how I'd missed seeing her at first, as tall as she is. I was happy to see all of them having so much fun. Lisa and Dana bonded, and Denise was a great companion and friend because she never said exactly what the others were up to.

Of course, Spencer had his share of fun, too. When we were checking out of our hotel, John looked over the bill, and I could see the shock on his face. A large amount of liquor had been charged to our room number. All receipts bore your brother's signature. Spencer, age fifteen, didn't know that we would see everything he ordered with his room number and signature on it. And guess what, we saw right away that he had run up a pretty hefty bar bill. I had noticed throughout the week, and had pointed out to John, that Spencer sure was a popular guy around the place. For instance, while he was in the lounge watching TV or on the beach, everyone would yell, "Hey Amigo" and wave. Once we got back home, Spencer spent many hours at John's house cutting firewood, helping around the house, and weed-eating my property to pay off his bar tab. It was easier for me to forgive your brother because I'd also noticed that *all* the kids had such a great time. They formed volleyball games, made sand sculptures, snorkeled, and of course partied together.

On the flight home, during takeoff we leaned back with the powerful surge from the plane. The restroom sign fell off the wall onto the carpet, leaving a trail of wires dangling from where the sign once illumined. John and I sat in the front seats, the carpeted wall directly in front of us, and were unnerved by the swinging sign and wires. When the lights overhead blinked to show it was okay to remove seatbelts, John stood up, balanced on his seat, reached up and stuffed the wires back inside the slot, and then hit the sign with his hand to secure it. Everyone on the plane applauded.

Later, when the stewardess served our meal, I heard Spencer yell from about six rows behind us, "Mom, mom, hey mom!"

"What Spencer?"

"Is this chicken?"

I turned back and yelled to him, "I'm not sure."

Again the plane erupted into laughter. I thought for sure that our life had taken a turn for the better. Lisa was just what our family needed, a direct link to keep your memory alive. She is a wonderful girl and shared many touching stories about you, Jeff—you little *Don Juan.* I couldn't help but wish you'd been with us, and thinking how this vacation might have turned out with you around. But for now, today, we survivors were all tan and happy.

Besides a wonderful getaway to an island, everything went right back into place, which was out of place. I felt guilty for having so much fun, and realized I was a fool to think a special vacation would heal us. I had no idea grief was a life sentence. Back home, I tried to remember your voice and continue on without you. I had no forewarning that everyone was about to scatter in all directions.

We made it through this first year without you, Jeff, but the void in our home was ever-present. We missed your being there, missed anticipating your coming in or leaving, missed the sounds of you cooking then quietly walking into the living room to tell us that you made enough for everyone. We had experienced a wonderful vacation, and getting to know Lisa was gift all its own. But the vacation was just a band-aid on a deep wound. It helped for the days we were gone; but once we returned, we continued to stumble through the following year.

Then, after you have been gone for twenty-six months, the other shoe hit the floor. John took me to dinner and seemed nervous, then he confessed that he'd met someone. Through most of December he and I were seeing a counselor to help us mend our relationship; but as I discovered later, this was John's way of easing out because of my fragile mental state. He broke off our seven-year relationship on Christmas day.

John and his new girlfriend gave me a Christmas present. Seriously they did! I opened that Christmas gift as a robot with no emotion. They gave me a year's membership to an all-women's gym and a juicer. I gave the juicer away, but joined the gym and went each morning. My photo on the identification card looks like a serial killer, which says a lot about my mental state at the time. I ran on the treadmill with a vengeance, crying with every step, and no one spoke to me. This time of my life was bleak, or I should say bleaker. The bright spot was having Spencer living back under my roof. Each morning I dropped him off at the high school at 7:45, went to the gym for a workout, and began my day at the salon by 9:30. Order gave us some control.

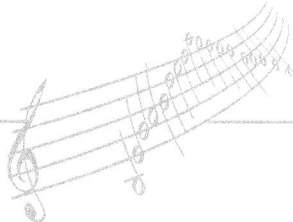

A woman's life can really be a succession of lives, each revolving around some emotionally compelling situation or challenge, and each marked off by some intense experience.
Wallis Simpson

THE REVOLVING DOOR

Many days Jeff, you had walked up the stairs to my salon. Now, the sound of the heavy front door opening and closing, knowing you wouldn't ever be coming in, is the worst sound of all.

Solemn faces were the only ones that looked my way. Acquaintances walked towards me with condolences. I was still in shock and the deep wounds of grief hadn't prepared me for a proper comeback. Thank you just didn't seem enough. Money was dwindling so I returned to work one week after your funeral. My dad lay in critical condition in ICU in Lakeport, a two-hour drive through winding mountain roads, and I had two grieving teenagers at home and back in school to add to the balancing act. Only one week after your death, when our heads were still filled with a slow-motion collage of memories and disbelief, we waded through this period of crisis and loss knowing that one single element was on our side: *time*. Time does heal, but we were to be left with deep scars, and mountains of debris in our hearts.

There was a hairdresser who worked in my salon, a handsome man, divorced with two children. He was also a Life Coach, or as I call them, a *self-proclaimed counselor*. When I came back to work after being out for a week, it was a pleasure to see him in early too. He was putting his station together for an appointment who'd be arriving soon. But for a time, the salon was empty except for the two of us. He hugged me for about five minutes, and I so appreciated his strong embrace. As our heavy door creaked open, we looked at each other, put on our professional faces, and began our day.

I managed to operate on auto-pilot, relying on years of well-rehearsed dialogue. The first people I had to face were a college couple who came in for a haircut. The girl was my client, and our relationship was as close as a client-hairdresser relationship could be after two-years. She brought in her boyfriend, whom I had never met before, for a small makeover. To explain my absence and state of mind, I told them my son, who was their age, had just died last week. Her boyfriend sat down on the hydraulic chair as I continued. Both were surprised and saddened by this news. "Oh, we're so sorry! That's terrible news. Are you sure you are okay to work?" I nodded though I was thinking, *breathe, Judi, breathe.* Then she asked me, "Do you think Chad should change his part? He has always parted his hair on the left, but I think he'd look better with his hair parted on the right since his hairline is thinning on the left side and that way would look better. What do you think, right or left?" Without a second to think, I spit out "The right" because I didn't care and wasn't ready for this quick change of atmosphere. I was tempted to buzz his hair off right down the middle, problem solved.

Then, later in the day, after a few other clients came in and left without knowing what I had been through, a client, Robin came in with her special needs son, David. We'd met in parent participation when she lived around the block from where I raised the kids. Spencer had developed a life-time friendship with David, and later took over as David's aide when Robin and her husband were out of town. I could tell Robin was very upset, but I knew time was of the essence because David, who has autism, can be impatient when he is in an uncomfortable situation. He sat down and I began to drape him when Robin quietly said how very sorry she was about you, Jeff. She wanted me to know how she felt, as over the years she and I had many talks about David's treatment and life in general. The entire time I spent cutting her son's hair, tears flowed down Robin's face and onto her blouse, and she made no attempt to wipe away her grief. I had to keep my mind in another place so I could be professional and not upset her son. David looked at my reflection in the mirror and said he, too, was sorry about you. This was huge. I realized that David knew and understood, and it meant so much for me to hear this. David doesn't like getting his hair cut, so I said thank you to him back into the mirror and kept up my speed. I clipped and Robin cried; I felt her sorrow but kept my feelings in check.

Then my last client of the day, an older woman with grown children, arrived, late as usual. By then I was emotionally exhausted. She had been an only child and her parents were independently wealthy; she grew up to be narcissistic and polite at the same time. I took the fact that she was late for most appointments as control, and lack of respect for other people's time. On the other hand, I enjoyed our conversations and hearing about her travels to third world countries. Somehow she and I worked well together—partly because I would schedule her appointment fifteen minutes later than I wrote on her appointment card. She told me she had read about Jeff's death in the obituary column and we began to talk about what had happened as I began my chemical services (hair color). She was asking questions that were personal and painful, but sincere. I sidestepped answering as much as I could. Then she said, "Well, it is all for the best; he has always been a thorn in your side."

The verbal shock plunged a knife through my heart, and the hairdresser next to me snapped her head towards us and looked at my client with such hatred that I thought she might do something physical. I stayed calm and got through the service, finishing her color and cut and styling her hair. We calmly walked to the desk, and as she wrote her check, I was writing down the names and phone numbers of three local hairdressers she could try. She handed the check to me, and I handed her the piece of paper. As she read it, she became agitated and stuffed it into her purse before she left. We connected a few years later and she came back to me, but I could not have her as a client at that time. My blood pressure was best kept under control.

Those first few weeks, my life was split into two sections: For three long days I worked and took care of my salon; then on the fourth day I'd get the kids up and head towards the bus, then drive the two hours to Lakeport to spend the day tending to my father in the critical care unit, then drive back home.

I would cut, style, blow dry, do foil highlights, smile, chat, joke around, then more cutting, sweeping, and making return appointments. Each day I'd gather the dirty towels into a duffle bag, walk to my car, sit down, and let a flood of tears run down my face. I'd cry all the way home, stumble into the house, flop down on my bed, and feel so sorry for you and for myself. Your brother and sister would start dinner, and then one or the other would come in and gently ask if I was okay. They became the parents and I the child. This went on for months. Sometimes I managed to put meals on the table. Sometimes I'd drive through a hamburger place or stop for pizza. Thank goodness I had taught you kids how to cook.

On my way to my car after work one day, I saw a familiar face walking towards me, a girl who had gone to school with you, Jeff. She said she had heard about you and wanted me to know that she had seen you downtown once "and man, was he ludded out on ludes." I had no idea what that meant except that you had taken something and were high on something. All I could say was "Oh." Maybe she thought describing that scene would help me understand. I already knew that many kids dabble in drugs, and that you played around with drugs as you and I had many long talks about this. I said thanks for talking to me and continued to my car feeling sick.

Jeff, one Friday night when you were about eighteen years old, I couldn't sleep because I could hear the television on, low but constant, and I wanted you to lower the sound even more. It was late, but I got out of bed, went down the hallway and looked through the cutout into our living room. There you sat, staring at a *Saturday Night Live* skit, and then I noticed your leg. You had balanced a stack of about ten pieces of buttered toast on it. I knew that smoking marijuana will typically result in the *munchies*. I stood in the hall watching for a while before I walked around the end of the wall and over to you in the living room and quietly asked, "What's that on your leg?" You looked up to me and replied, "Toast, have one." I told you, "No thanks. Can you turn down the sound a little bit?" Then I went back to bed. The endless lectures of drugs vs. brain matter would be a mute subject that night. But the next day I would take great pleasure is asking you to replace that whole loaf of bread.

For some reason, despite all of the warm thoughts and sincere wishes about you, the one sentence said by the girl who stopped me on the street stays with me. It is as though she tossed something really dirty and sticky on your memory, a vivid picture of you being downtown and loaded. Memories are much easier when you disguise them with a pretense of goodness, although that stack of toast on your leg was too obvious to disguise.

In fairness, there were many kind gestures, and cards that I have read and reread through the years even though I still have no idea who some of the people who sent them are. Most clients and friends said little. Phone calls from my hometown were always heartwarming and sad because they brought you back to life. Townspeople who know me as a business owner avoided conversations and when they did say something referred to you as *your son*. One long-time friend I'd lost contact with walked into the salon and handed me a book titled *Good Grief*. I still read this thin booklet from time to time. Still, I longed to hear your name spoken aloud, I needed to hear it and put into the universe.

In the spring I sat on my porch steps and remembered back to three little happy faces peering over my arm and into the saucepan while I stirred homemade play dough. You kids love to work with the warm, fresh play dough, making designs and sculpting figures and objects with your little hands. Jeff, you looked at the recipe in my cookbook, made a funny sound, and looked up at me with a big smile on your face. I can still see the freckles across your nose as you smiled, because on the top of the page I had written in bold letters: **DON'T EAT.**

Seems like yesterday you sat next to me on the couch, with Dana on my other side, watching me do a latch hook *Spiderman* wall hanging. Dana tried to pull the hook with short wool strands through the mesh squares. I helped her do a few, but her fingers were too little and she was content to watch. But you, Jeff, took over and finished it. You didn't miss one square and were mesmerized with the results unfolding as you worked. Today our *Spiderman* latch hook shag carpet still hangs in my office. I am either torturing myself with this piece of '70s art, or I keep it as affirmation that you existed, that this happened one summer.

I had too much on my plate as a hairdresser with a full clientele, owning the business, raising two young teens, and dealing with my dad in grave condition in another town, and let's not forget that I still cared for my mother who by then lived in a rest home. I was delighted when a close friend and client of mine, a stockbroker who had once been a math teacher in Arizona, volunteered to drive out to my house in Durham after school, and tutor the kids so they wouldn't fall back in their studies. He told me he stopped by a couple of times and worked with Dana and Spencer, explained what to do and checked out their homework, but today neither of them remember him stopping by at all. I had too much on my mind to keep track of this detail. My front porch, with a view of trees and old kiwi bushes in the center of my circle driveway, became my refuge.

I have no idea how Spencer managed to stay on the Jr. Varsity football team, getting himself to practices and games. Your death made motherhood a jumbled mess, and I can only assume we went about school and appointments on auto-pilot. I remember waiting for Dana in the car outside the three-story Masonic building downtown. We were waiting for her *Rainbow Girls* meeting to conclude. She had become the youngest *Worthy Advisor* at age fourteen. After you died, I didn't even know that she was still attending meetings nor how she got there from our place out of town. Her step-mother, Carolyn, was instrumental in getting her involved, and Dana had made new friends and found and expanded many hidden strengths while in *Rainbow Girls*. Jeff, you and Spencer teased her without mercy when she put on her formal for a meeting, or when she kept her book of hidden secrets in an unknown place. You brothers tried all tactics to get the secret information about the *Gerber Girls*, as you called them. Nevertheless, you attended Dana's installation ceremony at the Masonic Temple.

Dana also joined a peer counseling group in high school and began to help fellow classmates by listening and giving suggestions. Helping others promoted her own healing process. Spencer did show signs of anger towards his local friends who didn't know what to say. That was understandable for freshman boys who had never met you, but after he wore your black leather jacket to school one day and the kids teased him, Spencer told me he didn't want to hang out with a bunch of farm boys anymore and decided to move back into town at the end of the semester.

One warm fall afternoon he and a friend played ball in the front yard. When his friend left for home, your black leather baseball mitt was missing. Spencer confronted his friend, who at first denied taking it, but after he realized the mitt had belonged to you and the circumstances, he brought it back and apologized. All seemed well, but Spencer was even more determined to switch back to his original school district. He made arrangements to live with his dad and step-mom and attend school the coming January with his childhood friends who were able to address the issue of your death. These friends knew you from coming to our home and swim parties as little kids, so your death had an impact on them as well.

I began to see more depth in Dana and Spencer, who struggled with your absence. Both were by nature well-adjusted happy kids, and I never had problems with them. In fact, you three kids never got into fights or yelled as I hear about in some families. The only arguing in our home during your early years had been between your step-dad Don and me. We supplied enough drama for the whole family—not daily, but frequently. We'd butted heads about parenting. Specifically, I felt the way he disciplined you was too harsh—maybe this is why the younger kids did not argue with each other.

Our household had been mostly smooth sailing and loving sibling relationships. Daily laughter, jokes, noises, and mimicry filled our walls. You three were always busy, not so much with toys as being outdoors building ramps or forts, swimming, playing in the mud, or being indoors building forts out of quilts and blankets and watching TV. I remember when Dana used her *Barbie Perfume Maker* to make perfume out of flower petals. You and Spencer helped by picking the flowers and stinking up the house with this play station. I was secretly relieved when you kids outgrew the *Barbie Perfume Maker*.

After you died, I watched your sister and brother, these once happy kids, become more guarded, restless, and serious. A quiet home is the worst. Spencer watched TV, stayed in his room at his desk, or he'd play music on the stereo and have friends over, friends from town. I felt like an outsider as your sister and brother didn't respond to long serious talks about you. To survive, they tucked your memory away for awhile. I backed away, and each of us did what we had to do to heal. We lived together, but were apart.

It had been only two months since your death in September and just weeks since my dad's death in October, and fall was in the air. Dana was asked to go to the *Fall Ball*. The day of the Ball, she asked me to cut her hair short. I didn't question her; we simply headed into town and I did as she asked. Every junior girl in her class wore their hair in long permed layers, their bangs sprayed up high. The day of the *Fall Ball,* I cut her hair very short, above her ears, buzzed up the back, and gave her long razored bangs, then I tinted her hair a dark copper auburn mix. When we heard a soft knock at the door that evening, I welcomed her date inside. Then Dana walked down the hall in her short cobalt blue strapless formal, and when she stepped into the living room, he fell backwards onto the wall by the front door and put his hand on his heart. Her new appearance was a great shock to her date, and this made Dana giggle and feel full of confidence. She looked stunning.

The following year a friend and classmate who made Dana laugh asked her to the prom. Her best friend, Denise, also a senior, asked Spencer, a sophomore, to go with her. Jeff, can you believe your sister and brother double-dated? It was a real treat to see your sister all dressed up again, and your brother in a tux for the first time. We took many pictures before the foursome went into town for a nice dinner then on to the dance. When they arrived at the high school gym, they discovered to their surprise and horror that John and I were the chaperones. The kids danced on the opposite side of the gym, as far across the gym floor as possible to avoid our watchful eyes. All evening long, we could only see the tops of their heads bouncing to the rhythm of the music:

Can't Touch This by MC Hammer and *I Like Big Butts* by Sir Mix-A-Lot. Our family was moving forward, and we were having fun again. This was a magical evening. Your brother and sister were finally kids again, Dana a mighty senior, earned new status and respect. She seemed to be treading water much better than I.

Dana graduated the next month and started a job the morning after her all-night grad party. Sleepily she drove into town to learn how to make milkshakes and work the deep fryer at Big Al's. She eventually moved into town and roomed with a couple other girls. Spencer moved back home at the end of summer. My front door seemed to be a revolving door. For his junior and senior year, Spencer continued to attend school in Chico and graduated from there rather than the country school Dana had attended and graduated from. Spencer and I commuted into town each morning, driving past almond orchards and taking a shortcut through the country club before I would pull out onto the highway, and we would yell, "Turbo tardy!" and off we'd go. Spencer would yell again, "Turbo tardy, Ham!" I could almost hear you yelling along with us.

As you know, Spencer is a character, a funny boy. He is always busy and has many friends so our phone rang a lot, and he drove into town frequently, or had friends over. He also stayed at his dad's house some nights as it was easier than coming back out to our place. Spencer and I became very close and he was developing into a wonderful young man. I bought him a blue pickup and he and his friends all had mountain bikes.

He had a blast his junior and senior years. Dana had begun to date Bill so she was happy too. The tide was turning.

Shortly after my break up with John I met Paula, a client at my salon. We began to go out on weekends and get together on Sundays to shop or redecorate our homes. She was divorced with two sons and we had much in common. We took our sons on a train trip to Santa Cruz for a Mother's Day getaway. The train went from Chico through Sacramento, stopped in Davis then went on to San Jose, where Paula rented a car and drove us to the beach town. We stayed for two nights and the boys spent the day at the Boardwalk. On the train, I walked back to the end of the car to see how the three boys were getting along. They had already met some girls and were playing poker using candy (Skittles) in place of money. They were laughing, then Spencer said, "Hey mom" so I balanced myself and returned to my seat to report back to Paula. We also took the boys snow skiing to North Star by Lake Tahoe. I had a friend to hang out with, talk to, have drinks with, and life was not so bad after all. She and I were both suffering from being *dumped*.

In the beginning, Paula and I did a lot of whining and crying to each other on the phone at night. This insanity lessened as we began to focus on our own lives. Sometimes people are put into our paths to help and bring comfort. This was the basis of our friendship. Her father originally named her Selma, so we called ourselves *Selma and Louise*. She and I even had *Selma and Louise* t-shirts made while in Santa Cruz. We have since both married and now live in different towns, but remain friends even though years go by between visits. When we do see each other, we are comfortable with each other, with no pretense.

Of course, I unloaded to her all about you, Jeff, and she listened to my stories repeated many times, then one day she said I needed to move on and not talk about you so much. This hurt my feelings, and I stewed about it for a long while, but I knew she was right because I was on the verge of obsession and was not moving forward as Dana and Spencer had. I displayed framed photos of you everywhere, and even hung up your baseball bat. I was afraid that your memory would fade away and that I'd leave you behind if I moved too far forward. Grief has its own power, and some people heal faster than others, some feel peace by tucking their memories deep inside their wounded souls. Dealing with grief is a personal journey, your own journey; how you heal from the death of a loved one is intense and private.

I knew my kids and I would survive and move forward. I did listen to Paula and tried to reel in my lingering grief and tried, in vain, to heal. Psychologically (this is my own summation), I didn't want to outgrow you, Jeff, or move on without you, or excel financially and be in a place where I could have paid to have you professionally treated, and I didn't want your sister and brother to mature past you. My situation was tri-fold: first I was grief dominated by your suicide, coupled with the death of my father; second was the empty nest, when your sister and brother moved out; and third was the loss of my long-time companion John. This girl had no safety net, but I found something much better: *will power.*

One by one my children returned home, and we joined back together as a comfortable family; they took classes, new jobs, and moved in then moved out, and together and as individuals, we began to face life and the harsh reality of your death.

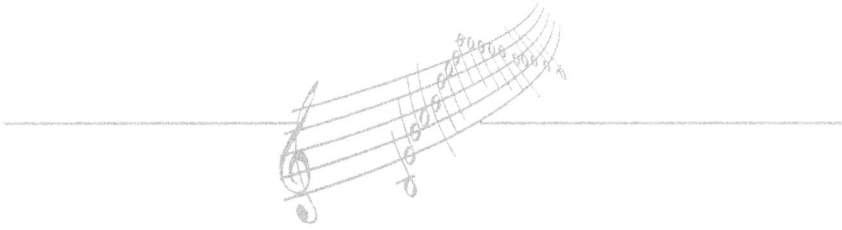

Mommy, if I toss a penny up in the sky,
will Uncle Jeff be able to catch it?
Audrey Howes, age 5

KALEIDOSCOPE

JEFF, YOU HAVE NO IDEA how many times I attended group sessions for parents whose children have died. This is the deal: all parents were grieving for their children, from infancy to older adulthood, but all of their children had wanted to live. The misfortune for those children was to be in the wrong place at the wrong time—perhaps a car accident, drunk driver, random murder. Or they were ill-prepared for a situation—perhaps in water or while climbing. Or they got cancer or another devastating disease. Or they were killed while defending our country. Most were well-adjusted kids who wanted to live, looked forward to a future. At these group sessions, each parent took his or her turn telling about the child who had died. Naturally I felt like a bad mother because my child had ended his own life. My turn was getting closer as the circle of grieving parents relayed their personal heartfelt stories. I knew I was in the wrong circle for healing, but I hadn't been able to find a group for parents who had experienced your particular cause of death. My turn was up, and I made it through telling your story, but decided to continue searching for a different group.

The next public session for grief support was in Yuba City, a 45-minute drive from home. I remember wearing a long wool coat because it was a cold night, so this must have been only a few months after you died. We sat in a circle and again took turns introducing ourselves, saying the name of our deceased child, then telling our story. When my turn came around, I heard my voice coming from outside my body: "My son's name is Jeff …" And those, dear boy, were the last words I uttered. I cried, sobbed, sniffled, blew my nose, and choked for an hour. A few people came over afterwards and patted my back, and I could see their mouths moving but no sounds reached my ears. I found my way to the parking lot, located my car, and somehow managed to drive back home. It was late, raining, and very dark.

The next grief session I attended, a month later, was through a Hospice program held in a two-story Craftsman-style home two blocks from the local hospital. We sat in a circle once again, in what had been the living room. The room had all wood floors and retro curtains, and the atmosphere was very comfortable. I didn't cry as much, but once again felt a huge twang of guilt, as I was the only parent who had lost a child to suicide. I recall listening to one mother's story that really got to me. Her son was her only child, a stand-out athlete, handsome, and popular. He had just graduated from high school and had gone with his class to Mexico for a graduation trip. He was on the rooftop of the hotel next door and didn't notice the skylight that didn't have a white glass top. He stepped onto the opening and fell directly down to the lobby, about ten floors, and was killed instantly. She cried and retold this story. I could tell that she desperately needed to heal, and I knew she never would.

Somehow I got through this meeting, but searched for a better avenue to help with my own grief, to learn how to cope with being a survivor of a suicide victim. Then, a month later I read in the newspaper about a group meeting specifically for parents of suicide victims. The address was, of all places, the lunchroom where you'd attended junior high. This was harder than the others because all we did was cry, one person after another. No one knew what had happened to motivate their child to end his or her life; not one parent saw it coming; not one recognized the warning signs. Each parent was shell-shocked, and for some it had been years since the child's death. It surprised me that grief had such longevity. Obviously, I was new to this type of grief and had imagined I would be miraculously cured any day now. We, too, took turns telling our stories and crying. I didn't feel out of place in this group, but I was too weak emotionally to listen to so many suicide horror stories. I left after the meeting was over and decided to visit a medium and delve into the spiritual world of telepathic information, not to say I didn't also try other routes to relieve the intense pain in my heart and burning red eyes.

Only two people delivered food to us during our time of grief. Maria, a tall attractive Mexican woman, called from my salon, drove to our house one evening, and cooked a wonderful Mexican dinner. She and I had worked next to each other for many years. She simply walked into the kitchen and took over, making her famous tacos, and were they ever crunchy and flavorful.

The other meal was delivered by the lady who lived behind us, whom we'd only met once. Jeff, do you remember the time you were on our back deck petting the neighbor's Husky and your hand slipped under the dog's fur? You came into the house in a panic to show me your bloodied hand. You washed up, then carried the dog to the family and told them you'd discovered the huge wound where the fur on the dog's entire back had peeled back. The next day they came to our door to thank you, and sadly told you they had to have their dog put down because it had been kicked by a horse. Two years later, this family heard the news about you, or read it in the newspaper, and brought dinner to us. No one else, not one other friend or client or fellow hairdresser or neighbor came to our aid. I truly expected more help, but little came from any direction, just those two wonderful meals.

After the kids were gone to various places, I'd often sit on my porch, with a view of the orchards. It was so peaceful and quiet, my dream home that John had built for us in the country. I had enrolled my kids in that particular school because of the academics and high test scores. I'd wanted them to experience a different way of life, what seemed a better way of life. Suddenly it seemed so desolate, my acre needing more work once I was alone, more work than I was able to keep up with. I just sat on the front porch and thought, where'd everybody go?

Now what will I do with this house? It takes a lot of work to mow and water, and it's too far away from my work. You were right, Jeff, it is too far out. These years my kids were displaced were the hardest times for a mother. I walked back inside, to my bedroom, to take a nap. As I lay on my bed, I began to think about you and this came to mind:

I remember so clearly walking to my car after work, when you ran up quietly behind me like a ninja and grabbed the heavy bags of towels from me. We walked together to the car, and you hitched a ride home, and we had a great dinner together with your brother and sister. A simple sort of memory, but it's the small things in life we recall. After your death, walking to my car became a trigger that made the tears begin. I'd walk and wait for you to run up behind me and grab my bags of towels, but you never did and never will again. Still, on my quiet walks to the parking lot, sometimes I turn around and look.

You were always popping up behind me like that, or looking at me as I worked upstairs by the window, when you were at the coffee shop across the street. Or I'd see you at *Hey Juan's*, that little Mexican hole-in-the-wall on ground level below my salon, *One Cut Above*. We used to say, I'm going to run down to *Hey Juan's* for lunch; if I'm not back in fifteen minutes, call a ambulance. Jeff, do you remember their great cheap breakfast? Scrambled eggs with cheese, beans, sautéed red potatoes, and a tortilla—all for one dollar.

Like an ever changing kaleidoscope, memories like these come and go, and are a soothing gift, but I wonder now what you see in the spirit world. Have you met with your Grandpa yet? How about Sheba and Marvin, our dog and cat? Have you met up with them yet? What does your spirit do these long days and nights? Have you been to the Inca Mountains and played the flute? I hope you've been to Easter Island and have looked at the statues from all angles, and to Stonehenge where your sister once went. Did you go to the darkest and worst parts of cities and join thugs to witness the dark side? Have you been able to watch, from a vantage point, the gardens in a palace? Did you go to the Himalayas with your brother? Did you do the world's longest bungee jump in New Zealand with your sister? Did you go with her to London when she worked there for two years? Did you travel with her to Greece, Turkey, Amsterdam, Portugal?

I sometimes wonder if you have ridden a giraffe on the plains of Africa. Or have you been riding dolphins across the waves? Have you ever seen a mermaid, or do they even exist? I bet you are more interested in taking a taxi ride on a whale; or knowing you, you've looked at a shark square in the eye. How about Gandhi—is he on a plane with you, or maybe on a second plane higher than most of us? How about Jesus? And have you met God?

Jeff, your actions turned us into survivors. No one wants this label tagged on them. To outlive a child is the worst possible fate a parent can imagine. It was hard enough when I lost my first son to adoption as a teen mother, but your death created a wound that will never heal. At least I know that my first son David is alive on this planet earth and faring well, and knows the same news concerning the world as I do. He is the person who phoned me early one morning to tell me about the Twin Towers being hit by an airplane. He lived in a Southern state, two hours ahead of us, and we listened to the news together, long distance. Jeff, you never knew about the 9/11 tragedy and the war that sprung out of it. That terrorist attack changed everything.

It is comforting to imagine you seeking adventure and experiencing the wonders of the world as we survivors live out our lives and move along in it. Hopefully each of us will meet our end at a decent age, say goodbye to friends and family in numerical order, oldest first, and that no more young ones will go ahead, out of turn.

Your beautiful sister met a boy when she was age fifteen, a few months before your death. Do you remember her mentioning Billy? Bill was twenty and wouldn't date her until she turned eighteen. Anyway, one day after high school graduation while at work she spotted Bill across the parking lot, walking towards the screened window. She told everyone, "Stand back! This one's mine." He placed his order then asked her how old she was. She smiled and said, "Eighteen." Finally they began to date; and they eventually married after a six-year courtship. Their two beautiful daughters are full of life and full of questions. They know all about their Uncle Jeff.

Dana's first daughter, Audrey, was born on the thirteenth anniversary of your death. Dana was in labor that day, and she and I watched the clock with extreme intensity as it inched towards midnight. The doctor noticed this and finally said, "Yes, this is a good date to be born." We could only nod in agreement. Now, instead of counting how many years you have been gone, we celebrate Audrey's birthday. She looks like Dana, with thick wavy reddish-brown hair. Her birthday being on such a sad but powerful day is actually a blessing, a wonderful diversion, and we thank Audrey for this gift.

Dana and Bill's second daughter, Gemma, was born on New Year's Eve. She is quiet and favors Bill. She is going to be tall like her sister, but has light hair and big blue eyes. You would have loved your nieces, as they are both very funny and creative. They attend a Spanish Immersion school, kindergarten through sixth grade, so they speak Spanish and will retain this second language all their lives. Both are taking Judo lessons, and Gemma takes horseback riding lessons while Audrey plays the cello. You would have had two little ninjas to deal with: a ninja cowgirl and another ninja playing classical music.

Your little brother has grown to be a looming man of great height with a deep voice. He still wakes up every day as if it were a party, just like when he was a kid. He is happy and sees joy in everything nature has to offer. He has a quick wit and is an amusing storyteller. While he was working as a mountain guide, he met a girl who worked at a coffee shop. With the influence of Cassie, he settled down and continued college, but has never given up playing drums and longing to be in a band. This is one of his favorite vices. I can hear the jam sessions now, you on lead guitar and Spencer doing a drum solo. After college, Spencer landed a job as a science and math teacher close to his home, and his students love him because he is upbeat and straightforward, and they are learning a great deal from him. Oh, the fun you would have had hiking in snow, and camping with your brother all the way to the summit of Mount Shasta, to 14,790 feet. He could teach you how to dig a proper snow cave, or collect pure water from the headwaters of the Sacramento River. The fun times would be endless.

Spencer and Cassie had a baby boy just this week. Spencer said he looked at his son and fell in love, and he said that at that very moment, everything in his life made sense. Wish you were here to hold your new nephew. You would have been a wonderful uncle, so silly and full of stories and antics. Your brother married the perfect mate for his style of living. She's tiny but strong, and resourceful. They have a green house and she cans, freezes, and cooks meals for Spencer each day, and works alongside of him on their property. For recreation, they hike or ride bicycles. But not right now, because she's a new mommy.

Also your girlfriend Lisa married a boy she and Dana met in Westwood. Yes, we all met your Lisa, and Dana even spent a summer working with Lisa's mother in her video store. The guy they met there was in law enforcement and they referred to him as the *Sheriff of Nottingham*. Lisa is very happy; her husband is a super guy and they now have three sons. A few years ago, Pete and I went to Santa Rosa and met up with Lisa at a coffee shop. During our conversation, she told me that her youngest son had been born on your birthday, which I found quite a coincidence. Later Lisa mentioned that she thought you had died in Lakeport Hospital. When I told her, "No Lisa, he was transported by helicopter to Santa Rosa Memorial hospital." Immediately, her face and neck turned red, and she told me that's where she had given birth to her son born on your birthday. Also, Lisa's husband found work in Santa Rosa, which happened to be the area we moved to with you after the Department of Water Resources project was completed. And yet another coincidence: Gene and I had lived in a small town ten miles north of Santa Rosa called Windsor. Lisa told me that she and her family live in a small town north of Santa Rosa—Windsor. She and I just looked at each other, finding no need to dissect what was apparent to us; there are no coincidences.

My two youngest children, your brother and sister, were both on flights at the same time, crossing different oceans. Spencer was headed to India to climb the Himalayans on his twenty-first birthday, and Dana was flying home from Europe after a two-year absence. This day was too much stress for me so I asked you to be with them, to keep them safe. I've read that when an older sibling dies, the remaining siblings tend to mature slower than they normally would have. This unconscious mind-set is a common occurrence because to mature at a normal rate would mean they would pass you in age, which meant they had out-lived you. That's why it's much often more comfortable for surviving siblings to pretend they are youngsters. Surviving siblings also tend to be fearless, daredevils. They want, unconsciously, to experience all the things in life you never had the chance to experience. It was indeed a difficult milestone for each of them to turn twenty-one, and to move on with their lives. They have now lived twice as long as you and both did mature into successful adults and have become wonderful spouses and parents.

When you died, I didn't expect that most people would not say your name. People very rarely bring your name up in conversation. Either they think it will dredge up bad feelings, cause painful memories, or might be awkward for us survivors. My friend Judy Murray called and we had a good talk, she had distinct ideas about your step-dad and your dad. Rita also called and was very sad, which was very sweet as she still lived with short term memory. Then when you least expect it, someone will say your name. *Jeff.* Joanie called one year to the date of your death and said, "It has been a year today since Jeff died, and I wanted to call you." I'll never forget her act of kindness; when she said your name, it was music to my ears. I am so happy Joanie's son Billy, had once invited you to go with him to a David Lee Roth concert. The warm-up band was *Poison.* We had stopped by to say hello on our way home from a week-long vacation when Billy mentioned that he had an extra ticket. You smiled and looked to me for an okay. Joanie and I worked out the details and we left you there with Billy. That night you and Billy stayed in the dorms at Fresno State and later, you two went swimming. Such a fun night and a great way to end your vacation. He took you to the bus depot the day after the concert and you were once again homeward bound. When an invitation to do something special like that happened for you, Jeff—and believe me, it was not often enough—it brought much joy to this mom. Jeffrey, on our way home, after dropping you off at Joanie's in Tulare, as we drove towards Fresno, a shiny white Bentley with a gold hood ornament passed us. Your brother and sister had our home movie camera and we have footage of this fancy dancy Bentley, we were yelling and waving because we were so sure it was David Lee Roth.

Jeff, one Saturday afternoon Pete and I stopped in at a small Mexican café and when I looked up, facing me in the next booth was your sixth-grade teacher, Mr. Wetmore. He stood up, walked towards us and slid into our booth. We talked about you, and his eyes became red and he began to tear up. You were certainly liked and missed. Mr. Wetmore said he thinks about you from time to time, and wished he had been more helpful. He regrets he didn't save you.

Then Dana told me about your nieces' new art teacher. It's Mr. Wing, your fourth-grade teacher who wanted you in the gifted program. That was the year before Mr. Wetmore had wanted you tested for learning disability. Neither happened, but I think both teachers were on to something—Mr. Wetmore in recognizing a learning disability and Mr. Wing for noticing that you were indeed gifted. I agree with both of them. It is a great gift for me to see your teachers out and about in town, and to talk with them about you.

Another conversation about you occurred when I went with Dana to have one of her girls checked by the same pediatrician I took you kids to. Dr. Wood rolled his stool with wheels towards me and we quietly talked about you. When I told him Audrey had been born on the date you had died, he became very emotional; I could see it in his eyes. Dana said later she felt very uncomfortable, as if she was eavesdropping on a private conversation, so she read to Audrey while she waited.

Eight years later when Spencer graduated from the University of Nevada, your pediatrician came to our house for a graduation party. Dr. Wood and his wife are avid hikers and Spencer and Cassie used to work summers at Devils Postpile on the east side of Yosemite, Doctor Woods' favorite hiking terrain. It was fun for Dana and the girls to see him at our home, instead of in his doctor's office. Your presence was missed as so many people who love Spencer were there, including your childhood friend Keith, who drove all the way up from the Bay Area. Also, your dad Gene was there, along with Patty and their grown daughter Sarah and her husband Andrew. Don, your second dad was there, too, with his wife Carolyn. Even John, my ex-boyfriend was there for Spencer. It was quite an interesting gathering. Wish you'd been there.

Do you remember I used to repeat the same mantra over and over to you? I'd say, "I'm the parent; you're the child." Yet for some reason, you thought you were the boss of me and the kids and the household. The other sentence I said to you many, many times is, "I can't believe you just did that!" Even on the drive home with John after your funeral, I looked at a beautiful fall sunset slipping behind the mountains as we drove east towards Chico and said to John, "I cannot believe he did this." The car radio was playing *Daniel* by Elton John, a song you used to love as a kid. I thought that if only you knew you were taken on a helicopter across those mountains to Santa Rosa, you would have enjoyed that flight so much.

Daniel my brother you are older than me,
do you still feel the pain of the scars that won't heal?
Your eyes have died, you see more than I
Daniel, you're a star in the sky.

Goodnight Jeff.

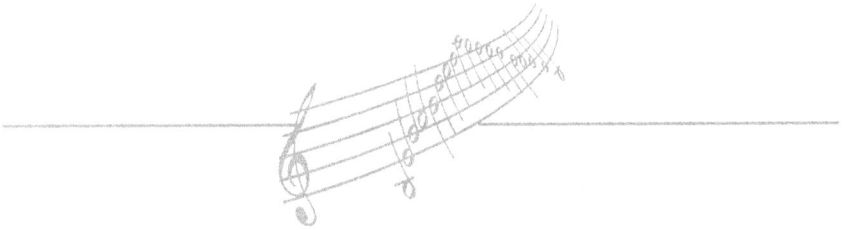

*The heart of a mother is a deep abyss at the bottom of which
you will always find forgiveness.*
Honore de Balzac

ASHES

JEFFREY, WE KEPT YOUR ASHES FOR SIX LONG YEARS. There was a personal struggle to either keep you near or set you free. When I felt it was time to let you go, Spencer wasn't ready. Years later, Spencer said he was ready, but Dana wasn't. Then one day Spencer called to say he felt it was time so I called Dana and she agreed. On a clear sunny spring day your mom, sister, and brother set out to accomplish this painful task.

We decided on Deer Creek Falls rather than the Feather River Falls, which drops into the Oroville Dam. We headed up Highway 32, with your urn on the floorboard, towards the mountains in the direction of Westwood. The pines became thicker and the shadows overlapped onto the winding road as we drove along as if it were any other Sunday. We drove for almost two hours until we saw the sign we were looking for. Finally we were there, yet sooner than I wanted to be. I pulled over to the shoulder, and just as Pete had said, there was a small waterfall and some nice flat granite slabs. He said that this small creek is snowmelt and will eventually flow into the Sacramento River then on to the ocean. We went down the steep ravine towards the gentle creek where we saw a couple sunning in patio chairs by the falls. They needed to know why we were there so I told them. They graciously asked if we wanted them to leave, but I was too nervous to tell them to go away.

Spencer carried your oak urn carved with the two tall redwoods and the eagle above the tree tops, and a quote we found amongst your music lyrics, etched between the trees: *Never ask why, spread your wings and fly.*

We stood on the top of the slabs of rock formations and, with the water shallow and trickling towards the rushing water just before it fell over the falls. This clear cold water was a perfect place to say goodbye to you; our dear brother and son. Surrounded with pines and a bed of pine needles, the sounds of rushing water plunged over a drop of twelve feet and continued to move downstream. We stepped into the creek, and Spencer undid the sealed bottom with a screwdriver, lifted it off, and set it down on the rocks beside us. We took the box and walked into the water, about a foot deep. I knelt down and put my hand inside the box, took some of your ashes, sprinkled them over the water, and watched as they slowly went over the falls. I said goodbye to you. Dana gently took a handful and let the water run over the palm of her sweet hand and dispersed more of your ashes that would follow mine. Spencer let you fall between his fingers very slowly, down into the cold water, watching as it took you away. I will never be able to explain the sadness that overtook me as I witnessed my two youngest children letting you go, their beloved brother. I watched and privately said what I needed to say. We took turns until most of your ashes were gone, then Spencer turned the urn upside down to get the last of the ashes out. That, dear son, was the end of our excursion and the deed of love was completed. We wished you a great ride and journey to the sea.

We then walked around the boulders and sat on the ledge next to the waterfall and watched the water slam into the pond of swirling water. With our feet and legs dangling over the edge, we talked about you and watched the water and the bubbles and glistening rocks below the water. That's when Dana noticed the rainbow. We wondered if it had been there all along, or did it just appear? We talked about your funny witty comebacks, and you mimicking so many of us. We lightly touched on your wants and needs and said how we will miss you. We shared stories about you and agreed how much you'd have liked this sendoff. After a time we sat in silence then trudged back up the ravine to the car; we hadn't noticed that the couple had moved far upstream to give us privacy and to avoid the drama.

In the car we headed back down the mountain. Spencer said he was thirsty and needed water. Dana remembered a water fountain made of stacked rocks in a circle on the bottom and a natural bubbling fountain of fresh ice cold water; she thought it was coming up around the next curve or two. We rounded the curve and saw a parked truck; a guy was bent over and drinking out of the faucet. I parked under a pine tree and we walked towards him as he filled his jug with ice cold water and wiped his face. This stranger, in the middle of the mountains, in the middle of nowhere, looked up at us and said, "Dana, is that you? Hi, do you remember me?" Spencer and I looked towards her and saw a puzzled look on her face, then slowly a look of recognition, then a huge smile crossed her face as she replied, "Yes I do remember you; you're Lisa's brother!"

Yes, Jeffrey, it was amazing to run into your girlfriend's brother, with whom you were friends when you lived in Westwood. A random encounter, or was it? When he asked what we were doing in his neck of the woods, Dana told him about you; and yes, he reluctantly admitted he had heard about your death from his sister. Dana told him we had just let your ashes go into Deer Creek Falls. He talked about you, Jeff, and he told us he was real sorry and that was a good place to let you be. Then we felt awkward because of the topic, and what else was there to say? He nodded and tipped his baseball hat, shook Spencer's hand, and told us to take care. He was a down-to-earth man, dirty from head to toe from working on something we didn't ask about. We told him to say hello to his mom and to Lisa.

We got back into the car and agreed, *wow, that was weird,* but decided there are no accidents. Back in the car we continued down the shaded winding road towards the late afternoon sun. By this time we were hungry. Further down the mountain, off to the left, and up another winding road is a small town consisting of cabins of all sizes, two bars, and a café called the *Bambi Inn.* We drove there, sat on the patio and had hamburgers, fries, and sodas. It was a quiet meal for us; emotional exhaustion is harder to overcome than physical. We ate, looked up at the tall pines and fir trees, took in the cool fresh pine scented air, and listened to a dog barking in the distance. We watched a few kids playing and people milling around their camp sites. I was hoping for no more surprise encounters, and none came our way. It was late in the afternoon so we finished, with very little talk, and headed home.

I dropped Dana off at the big corner house she shared with several friends; she walked up to her porch, waved back to us, and slowly went inside. I drove towards town and dropped Spencer off where he was renting a room downtown on Broadway above *Starbucks.* He pushed the security numbers, waved, and went inside. I watched his legs through the glass door as he disappeared upstairs. I drove home and crawled into bed though it was only 5:00 P.M., still light. The next day I called each of the kids to see how they were doing, and both had also crawled into bed about 5:00 P.M. We had been drained of every shred of strength we had, and all three of us had slept soundly.

Jeff, I swear sonny boy, you have given me gray hair. When you died I had a full head of golden reddish brown hair; now my hair is short and pure white in the front and top, and the white is creeping into the sides. Some of my spunk had been squelched too. Your death changed not only me, but you broke many hearts. Spencer closed down after we tossed your ashes and said he didn't want to talk about you and your death for awhile. Dana remained quiet, too, keeping her feelings to herself. She likes to process in private. To this day, she can barely talk about you or hear stories about you.

As for me, no matter what you have done, I carry half the blame. My job now is to keep your memory alive and fill your little nieces' and nephews' heads with stories of their talented Uncle Jeff.

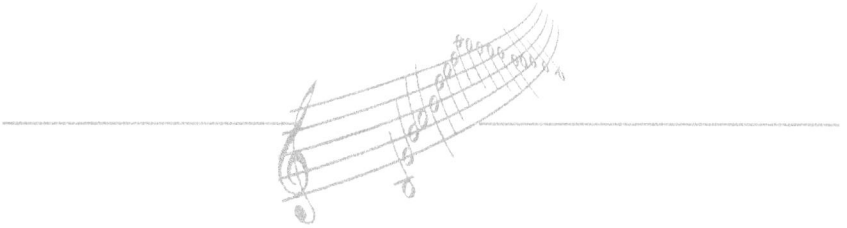

There is nothing wrong with holding beliefs, just do so lightly.
But the deep work is to release your grip on belief and
surrender yourself to faith.
Rabbi Shapiro

A COMMON THREAD

I HAD TO FIND AN ANSWER TO THE QUESTION that kept swirling in my head: Where does your soul go when you die? Jeff, what's become of you? I didn't visit every religion, nor did I delve into God vs. evolution, and I don't have a degree in theology by a long shot. Realize I was simply a mother on a spiritual quest, seeking peace of mind. My simple question was answered in many different ways.

It has always seemed absurd to me that loving Christians bicker and claw at each other, or worse, make snide remarks towards others' beliefs. Some *Christians* remind me of cliques in high school, clinging close together and talking about other religions in jest, acting as if they and only they have a free pass to heaven.

2013. A close friend was asking me about my search, interviews, and faith. She attends church every Sunday and sometimes in the evenings, and has attended *Bible* study for years. She listened as I told her about my questions and my search, then in a very polite voice she told me that I am agnostic and an atheist and will never find my answer. This made me smile. I asked her, "Well, which one is it? Am I agnostic or atheist?" She said she wasn't sure, then when I asked if she knows what these words mean, she answered, "No, not really." I had to stifle my laugh as I told her she shouldn't toss words around if she wasn't sure what they mean. I also pointed out the obvious omission: If you are going to study the *Bible* every week for years upon years, study all of it; study with an open mind; study with different groups of people; mix it up and study with new faces, new thoughts; and don't be afraid you might soil your beliefs by opening your mind. I was flabbergasted that a lifelong believer did not know the difference between or even the meanings of agnostic and atheist, which in my mind is as important as learning about *The Last Supper* and the meaning of *Easter.* She assumed I wouldn't notice because I don't attend church on a regular basis and have a negative view on churches that squeeze the breath out of me.

It appears to me that every religion selects snippets from the scriptures, hence each has a different idea about the correct way to live, believe, and die. Some of their rules to live by are strict; others are casual. Hang on, because this is where the arguing begins, and also explains what I was up against. Swallow hard, because I am not agnostic nor am I am an atheist, but I must give off this air because I enjoy learning about different faiths. And one thing I've learned is that most religions are leery of others' beliefs, and allow no bending to even imagine the possibility of a different route. This baffles me, as we will all end up in the same place anyway, wherever that may be.

I once read that if we all wore white caps, we'd look like a flock of geese.

... And now, back to my quest.

Spring of 1991. Panic set in about six months after your death. "Where did Jeff go?" seemed like a straightforward question to ask clergymen, counselors, and healers. I mean really, the cliché described in the churches I had attended as a child didn't seem the logical answer, or an answer that was believable. Your son is living in a beautiful mansion with gold trim surrounded by gold-lined streets and beauty that you can't imagine; your son is dancing in the streets of gold and rejoicing in the Lord with family and friends who passed before him. How do streets of gold sit on clouds? What happens when the clouds disperse? Why is he dancing with my grandma? This pat answer, always tied up with a tidy bow, is the same one I've heard all my life: Never question the *Bible*; don't let the devil turn you into a *doubting Thomas*. But here I was, questioning anyway.

First I made an appointment with the priest at the Episcopal Church, which we'd attended as a family for years when you three children were young. I felt comfortable there. Thoughts filled my head as I waited for the Priest. I recalled when you were an acolyte at age thirteen—dressed in a white robe with a gold sash as you boys led the procession down the aisle on Sunday mornings. I remembered when Don and I decided to be baptized as a family, and I told the priest in conference that you, my oldest son Jeff, had been baptized when you were three months old. We had been living in Bakersfield at the time, and the Seventh Day Adventist Church was directly across the street from our house. I figured God is God, no matter what roof you're under, so off we went on the Saturday of your baptism. I held you in my arms and the minister touched your head with water and baptized you. It was clean, simple, and quick.

Oh boy, this revelation thirteen years later put a wet blanket on our plans as a family. Absolutely not, I was told. Once you are baptized, you can't be re-baptized. Jeff, you already felt odd man out of our family since you were older and your father was living in another town. You also left for holidays to be with your dad Gene and Patty, sometimes with and sometimes without your brother and sister. I wanted a family baptism, all of us together, that would anoint us as one tight family. *No way. Nope, he cannot be baptized again.* I argued that he'd been just a baby, only twelve weeks old. The priest and I talked at length, but my pleas went unheard. So instead of baptizing you, Father Sterne gave you the honor of standing in front of the congregation and reading a scripture from the *Bible.* It was sweet to see you do this for us, but also sad. We celebrated afterwards with a great meal; and even though it was a joyous celebration, you knew you had been left out of the baptism loop. I mean, after all Jeff, you had water dribbled on your forehead as an infant. How could you possibly consider doing this twice. What was I thinking?

Back to my interview with the Episcopal priest. The secretary opened the door and held it as I walked into his office. The priest was clean shaven, graying hair on the sides, had a pleasant face and I suspected he was about fifty. In his office he gestured for me to please sit down, so I did. My eyes scanned the massive wall of dark mahogany bookshelves, a dark maroon desk (color is called *oxblood*), and an ornate rug with an old English design. So this is where our offering goes, I thought. Nerves led me quickly to the facts: I explained you were not only an acolyte in the Episcopal Church, but you were in the youth program and were one of the boys who were instrumental in the carving of the huge looming cross that still hangs today above the church gables. I began my speech concerning you and our family's relationship to the church. He sat behind his large and tidy desk. The office windows framed three willow trees blowing in the spring breeze.

I began to speak to him straightforwardly and to the point: My son died six months ago, and I want to know if you can explain to me where his soul is now. Where exactly is the Spirit that lived within him? The Priest didn't skip a beat either. He walked around his desk towards me, stood at the window for a minute to compose his words, turned and said he was very sorry for my loss, then stated, "No one can be sure where the soul goes. Perhaps you should read the *Bible,* pray, and receive an answer from God." I tried to remain polite and appreciative, but his answer fell flat. After all, knowing about love and death was his profession; his job was to save souls, but he just told me he has no idea where the soul goes after death. Naturally he mentioned heaven (though not the streets of gold) and hell, and maybe he suggested a scripture to read; but I went deaf and watched the willows out the window.

He went on to tell me that he had a teenage daughter who had been causing him and his wife a lot of grief with her lifestyle as well. He droned on for about twenty minutes, saying that they had been praying for her return, as she had just run away from home. He described going to the city with a friend but having no idea how to find her. He ended by telling me how worried they were and saying how very difficult a task it is to raise teens these days. I squirmed as I listened to his story about a girl I didn't know, nor did I care about. My own child's death was still raw; I was still reeling. We shook hands and I managed a smile as I thanked him for his time. I left thinking, if he doesn't know, then who does? He had brushed off my question, like lint on his lapel. But he was clear on one count: no one knows for sure. It was clear to me that I needed to gather more information and come to my own conclusion.

Final answer: **Read the scriptures.**

The following week on my day off I went to visit the Jehovah's Witnesses at the Kingdom Hall. I spoke with a man in his sixties, an Elder I believe, who seemed fairly high up in the "hall." He was clean-cut and tidy, very polite, and seemed eager to help. Okay, here goes: I repeated the story about your death and my quest to find out where your soul is today—Jeff's spirit, if you will. This handsome older man gave me a serious look, and said this: "We know that when we are put on this earth we have only this life; we must get it right, live well, and do right by our fellow brothers and sisters. You must be a good person, a helpful person, a loving servant, and one who attends meetings at the Kingdom Hall. You must spread the Word to those who don't know or understand (via *The Watchtower*). If you live a good life, after you die, Armageddon will come one day, and the souls of the good will return to earth, which will be a paradise where you will live for eternity. I was unsure what question to ask: Who will be here in Paradise? Who is up there? Just the good people from the Kingdom Hall or others like Mother Teresa? He went on to say, when your life is concluded you become dust and that's it. Dust to dust. No coming back, unless you led a good decent life as a Jehovah's Witness and are ready for the end. I tried not to reveal my thoughts or let him see my throat, which was too dry to gulp air. I was speechless, unable to put into words what I so badly wanted to ask. *Why not a second chance? What about life everlasting? And the spirit is where exactly? Gone like the physical body?* He said if you live a good life as a Jehovah's Witness you will return one day to earth.

Dust to dust was pretty clear, cut and dried. There is nothing out there. Jehovah's Witnesses, I thought, have many rules to learn and live by. I knew I'd need to study this religion much more to understand it, but I actually didn't want to.

He and I shook hands, though I was shaken to the core. I drove toward the airport, where there are no sidewalks and only dried weeds as far as you can see, and pulled over at the first shade tree I saw alongside the road. My hands clutched the steering wheel, and I bit my lip. The elder had been very gracious and gave me what I asked for: an honest answer, the answer he believed to be true. Black and white. My mind could not comprehend and accept or feel good about my son's premature death. I tried to digest what the Elder had told me and get my bearings. I sat staring and taking deep breaths, when a delivery truck whizzed past, engulfing me in dust.

Final Answer: **Dust to dust**

I had to continue on, taking in all the different beliefs and cultures, something like eating at a Hometown Buffet. I figured, what will come of this is more knowledge, which gives you a better understanding of and tolerance for others. I love that I'm not afraid to seek, and to learn. I already knew that Jesus died for our sins and God is a patient and loving God. So my search led me next to a Fundamentalist Church, where the pastor reads scriptures and gives a sermon while the congregation listens. There is much excitement in the air and no one ever questions either the scriptures or the sermon. I enjoyed the pastor's air of confidence and friendly manner. I knew, right then and there, that he was going to talk about heaven and hell and Jesus and the Holy Ghost. I'd been brought up with this belief so I listened and was grateful for the familiarity. In fact, when I was in fourth grade I won a plaque at the Assembly of God church that read:

Christ is the head of this house, the unseen guest at every meal, the silent listener to every conversation. Matthew 18:20

So at age nine, I'd studied the words, tried to understand the message, stared at the face of Jesus, and became afraid to talk at the dinner table. Now I knew I was being watched day and night, and although this brought security, I craved privacy and felt I couldn't even whisper to one of my cousins.

Winter of 2013. Recently I discovered a friend from high school on *Facebook*. We privately messaged one another and I learned that she is also a grieving mother who lost her teenage daughter to an illness. Because she is also a Jehovah's Witness, I told her about the man I'd interviewed at Kingdom Hall twenty-four years prior, and how his answer to my question really threw me for a loop. She wrote back that God gives you a soul (on loan) and when you die, it still belongs to God. One day, after Armageddon, you will be resurrected and you will return to earth where there is no pain or suffering or evil. If you are one of the good ones, God will return your soul, and you can reside on earth for eternity. She suggested I read these scriptures: *Genesis 2:7, Psalms 104:5, John 5:28,* and *Jeremiah 10:23.* Because of my insatiable curiosity, I read them all.

Final answer: **Borrowed soul and possible resurrection**

Early spring of 1991. On my way home from my interview at the Kingdom Hall, I stopped at the grocery store. Going through the checkout stand, the checker happily asked me how I was today and I told him my son had died. He stopped, looked up at me and said he was sorry; everyone in line behind me stared down at their feet. I have no idea why I blurted this out to the guy who was being polite, probably asking the same question all day and expecting the same "I'm fine" response. I guess I just needed to tell him how I really felt, to yell this news from the roof top.

The following week I called my Mormon friends Susan and Kay, both clients, and Susan had been my neighbor at one time. I loved Susan, and enjoyed having her kids at my house—especially when I needed care during my pregnancy with my youngest son Spencer, and Dana was just a toddler, and you, Jeff, were almost seven and a handful as always. Susan was a not like anyone I'd ever met; she had a great twisted sense of humor, and she had strong faith and conviction. My friend Kay knew you as a kid, too. She had once tried to teach you piano, but you learned only by ear; she tried to teach me, and that was impossible; but she did succeed in teaching Dana how to play. Anyway, when they drove to my house in Durham the spring after you died, I was still suffering terribly, so it was a sad moment between old friends. They both hugged me and felt my suffering as another mother would. I felt safe asking my Mormon friends about my concerns on your whereabouts. Both knew you well and cared enough about me to visit and help.

I laid out the same question about the spirit world, braced myself, and waited for their honest response. I knew Kay could be especially blunt. These two ladies smiled after I asked them about your soul. Susan looked towards Kay then looked back at me and spoke about their faith and healing. I can still see Susan's sweet smiling face and big round eyes as she said, "We believe our heavenly father welcomes you after death. Heaven is not a million miles away, Judi; it's right here. Not high up into the sky or across the world, but right here. Imagine a veil right next to you. Jeff is right here, on the other side of a very thin veil. He can see you, watch you, and he loves you. Jeff can almost reach out and touch you."

I began to tear up.

"Your Heavenly father loves you too," she added. This was the salve I so desperately needed on my open wound. They didn't get too complicated nor did they get preachy; they didn't go into the heavens and the levels you can achieve. They simply answered my question. I didn't say much except thank you so much for caring and driving all the way out here. Kay spoke up and told me in her stern but motherly way that their church believes in baptism of the dead. "Mormon churches have the ability to perform this, and our Ward uses the facility at the Oakland Temple. We take turns doing this for people who have passed on, including babies and the dearly departed who were unable to be saved while on earth. Some names are submitted and others are acquired." I told them about having you baptized when you were a baby, in a Seventh Day Adventist Church. They suggested I have your name submitted so that as an adult you could choose whether to make Jesus Christ your Savior. I thought about this and figured it wouldn't hurt to cover all your bases. Again my theory was: God is God no matter where you are. So here you go, Jeff. Seize the moment!

Final answer: **A veil away, very close**

One week later, after some soulful pondering, I phoned Susan to inquire about the baptism for the dead. She suggested I ask your childhood friend John, who is the same age as you Jeff, and I asked him to do this. His family is Mormon, his father a bishop, and John was an especially nice, polite, and a well-adjusted kid. I remember you two playing together in grade school, before our family started going to the Mormon Church, then you two friends joined the Boy Scouts at the same time. Also, you boys went to the county fair together one year, and Jeff, you did the dime toss and won a crystal carved cake dish. You ran all the way home, glass cake plate under your arm, to give it to me. Having your friend John submit your name for baptism seemed like the correct choice.

Do you remember when we attended the Mormon Church–Second Ward? It was in 1976, when you were seven years old, Dana was a toddler, and I was pregnant with Spencer. I was having so much trouble staying on task that I felt I was in jeopardy of losing control as a mom. I decided that if I joined the church, you had a fighting chance of becoming an *Eagle Scout*. So I attended the Mormon Church for about two years, until the pressure came from the missionaries to convert me and they set a date for my baptism. I'll never forget those two young men in long-sleeved white dress shirts, ties, and slacks standing in the doorway between our living room and family room as I began to explain my stance. Don watched me squirm, waiting to see how I would backpedal and get out of this one. I decided the truth was the best way so I was honest and told them I just don't believe the part about the tablets falling from the sky. They asked me if I had read the *Book of Mormon* as requested, and I replied, "You told me it was considered the second book after the *Bible* and the *Book of Mormon* was a continuation of the *Bible*." This was the opening I was looking for. "I can't read the *Book of Mormon* because I have not yet read the *Bible*, and I can't read Part II before I finish Part I." They looked at each other, grabbed their bags, and very politely left. I felt terrible but also relieved from making a huge commitment I knew I could never fulfill. It had nothing to do with the wonderful people I'd met; I simply couldn't commit to their lifestyle, even though I was halfway there since I didn't drink coffee or smoke. But just because I couldn't make the commitment doesn't mean you couldn't, Jeff.

A week passed since my friends were at my house to help me, and I thought about your passing and the baptism of the dead and called Susan, who contacted John, who agreed to do this for you, his friend. He mailed in the paperwork, and then he called to tell me the exact date this was going to happen. This was an awesome deed for you, Jeff, and it helped heal my heart so much. John, twenty-two years old at that time, went to the Mormon Temple in Oakland, waited until your name was called, then was submerged under water in the name of his friend Jeff Harris. This is a good thing, Jeff; all you have to do, for eternal life, is accept Jesus Christ as your Savior. I'm supplying you with every chance you might need. Later I got a letter from John, who wrote from his heart thanking me for asking him to do this for you, Jeff, and saying it was an honor.

Final answer: Read the *Book of Mormon* and be baptized at the Temple

After your posthumous baptism in the Mormon Temple, I pulled back and didn't continue my quest for twenty years. My quest resumed when I reconnected with a grade school friend through mutual friends. I had not heard his voice or seen him since we were kids playing and running through fields. I knew he'd served our country in Viet Nam, lived through many trials and errors, and is now a Sikh. Anyway, I phoned my old pal from fifth grade, Gurujiwan, and asked him to help me find the answer. His positive attitude was energetic and infectious as he told me this:

"Chant or sing God's praises, and the soul travels back to God when it leaves the physical body."

"A true Sikh has already died while alive, and lives in service. True, I am a yogi and learned from the master of Kundalini Yoga, Yogi Bhajan. His teachings can be paraphrased this way:
When the soul leaves the body, it can choose one of four decisions:
1. Return to this physical body, 2. Return in another form, 3. Come back as a ghost, or 4. Go with God, which is the most difficult because we are pulled by the tie to our family and friends. The journey in earth time is seventeen days, during which the course of the soul can be benefited by the prayer from the mother of the loved one. A yogi understands that this life is part of a much larger journey, that death is not an all or nothing experience."

The Sikhs practice a gentle religion, and their journey is simple and straightforward. Thanks, Gurujiwan, for taking the time to share this. Now we all can learn from a Sikh.

Then I delved a bit into the world of the Hindu. George Harrison must have ignited my curiosity. I read his autobiography, *Here Comes the Sun,* and was intrigued with his Hindu faith and his calmness as he crept closer to his imminent death from cancer. I didn't really know how to go about studying eastern religion. I read what I could understand, but it was so foreign to me, I kept getting lost in the layers of Heaven.

In my backyard is a wind chime of the third eye (intuition, insightfulness, and imagination). I also have Marion's 1950s gold Buddha in my shade garden. I felt I was on my way.

Also, my next-door neighbor Aram and I, both recently retired, were becoming friends. We both have young dogs that run around and tackle each other on our lawns while he and I stand for hours watching and laughing. Aram has led group meditation for thirty-five years so one crisp Saturday morning I asked if he could show me how to meditate. Aram took me to his meditation room, which at my house is the guest room (our floor plans are identical). He told me how to place my hands, palms up, my feet flat and relaxed. Soon my mind did go into another place and I did achieve total peace. We sat in total silence, breathing in the aroma of incense for fifteen seconds, then exhaled. I felt completely relaxed and my mind had a nice rest from its hyperactive owner. Total time: 25 minutes.

I believe people are put in our path for a reason. Aram, my new neighbor, isn't pushy or preachy or judgmental. He is not trying to indoctrinate me. I ask Aram questions, and he tells me what he has learned.

Aram has opened up and shown me a way to rest my mind, and a way to slow down and enjoy the beauty around me. While our puppies continue to romp and play from winter into spring, he has continued to answer my questions. He is not a Hindu, but he loves the people of India and their loving peaceful way of life. He said the Hindu religion believes there are many layers after death; after the physical plane (Earth), there is the astral plane (the spirit world). We are separated from the astral plane by a thin veil of delusion. In other words, souls living in the astral plane are, in truth, very near to us. Our separation from them is basically a matter of consciousness and perception. This reminds me of the Mormon veil. Many of us get tastes of this world from time to time, and every major religion throughout the ages recognizes it as *heaven*. On occasion, when the situation and your consciousness warrant it, astral beings can *visit* us on the earth plane.

The higher plane above the astral plane, the highest plane of existence is called the causal plane. This is where you live permanently with God. This is the final resting place where one merges into God's brilliant white light. I suspect Mother Teresa, Gandhi, Paramahansa Yogananda, Billy Graham and perhaps George Harrison, are up there, along with a few chosen others.

My head swirls with explanations received, and each provider of information speaks from the heart. Question ten people, and you will get ten different answers. It is clear to me that I need to come to my own conclusion. Still, this was an amazing experience, and I am grateful that there are so many wonderful people in this world of ours who are willing to share their heartfelt beliefs and who anticipate their last days as a glorious journey.

Final answer: **God waits for us**

Perhaps Madam Ruby, our local spiritual advisor, said it best: "All paths lead to the same ending."

or

Robert Arnett in *India Reveiled:*
"All religions lead to God, and it does not matter which path you follow, the multicolored lamp of each faith burns with the same white flame."

"Everyone who is dying is not dying for the first time." This quote heads a chapter in the first book of Neale Donald Walsch's New York Times bestseller *Conversations with God.* I'm now reading his third book, on loan from Aram, titled *Home with God.* The questions and answers are very clear and easy to understand. Aram also loaned me his coffee-table book *India Unveiled* by Robert Arnett. Inside are large amazing photos of the colorful culture, fabrics, and scenery. In it I found this quote by Albert Einstein: "Science without religion is lame, and religion without science is blind." He could have been describing contemporary America and India. India has become overbalanced spiritually and cannot adequately provide for the material needs of its own people. America leads the world in consumer comforts but has veered sharply off course morally.

My quest was renewed when I realized I'd missed the Catholics, so I put my question out to two long-term friends who are my age and raised Catholic: Joanie, a high school friend from my hometown of Porterville, and Deb, a client from my current town of Chico. Each attended private Catholic girls' schools and both married in the Catholic Church. I asked them what the Catholic Church beliefs are concerning dying and the soul. They gave essentially the same answer: Deb said, "If you are not baptized in the Catholic Church, you will go to purgatory no matter what." Joanie said, "It's been so long I don't remember exactly, but I do know this: Stay out of purgatory!" Then she laughed. Is purgatory funny? I looked at her and asked, "What IS purgatory exactly?" She replied with one word, "Hell." Now I am assuming my two different friends meant there is a heaven and there is a hell. Deb said,"You can never, and I mean never, get out of purgatory once you go there. Never!" Good lord, Jeff, I hope you didn't take a wrong turn and end up in Purgatory! Then I phoned Joanie who said sweetly, "You can get out of purgatory if you pray and try really hard." The Catholic religion seems to work on fear. I know the fear worked on me because I was too afraid to ask a Catholic priest my questions about dying and the soul, and purgatory.

Final answer: **Heaven or Purgatory.**

I asked a friend who is Jewish my question: "Where does your soul go when you die?" He quickly, without hesitation, replied, "Our faith is vague about life after death." He did, however, stress that Judaism teaches you to be mindful and respectful of others. For one who has been a good loving person while on earth, the rest will follow, which I assume is Heaven. The here and now, how you live while you reside on earth, is what matters. The rest will unfold when the time is right.

Final answer: **In death, the truth will reveal itself.**

Jeff, I phoned your dad Gene, to forewarn him about this book concerning you and your life. I mostly wanted to prepare him and your step-mom Patty for this particular chapter. Patty asked me if I had read the true book, The *Holy Bible*. Many of you who are reading this book may wonder also. Yes, many of the answers came from churches that read out of the same book, The *Holy Bible*. But I have to add, this is simply my personal search, which led to a potpourri of beliefs and customs. You can't acquire multiple answers and ideas by asking one person.

I also talked to Lutherans, to the minister at the Presbyterian Church, and to an Amish lady I met by chance when our mothers shared a room at the hospital. She was thrilled to tell me about her faith, which was modest and simple and clear: Love God and you will fit into his plans. I have noticed, however, that a high percentage of Christians are leery of listening to others about their faith, beliefs, and differences. This fear factor is based on the idea that the devil in disguise will lure you away from the truth. Oh dear, I disagree. You are not being led astray; you are opening your mind!

There are thousands and thousands of beliefs—far too many for me to research. Also, my Christian upbringing has me fighting some of these ideas, and my lack of faith yearns for concrete answers, and my youngest son's science degree keeps me tuned in to still other possibilities.

I have put my quest and search for spiritual knowledge on hold. I have received many answers to digest, a mish-mash of intertwined beliefs from many cultures. I wish I could have met an Indian Chief since the American Indians seem to embrace the land with compassion, clarity, and respect, and send their people to the spirit world with a loving farewell.

In conclusion, I feel more at peace now than I have for a very long time. I'm not convinced that organized religion is the answer for me, the ultimate free thinker. I guess I believe a messy jar full of multi-colored beliefs set out on my counter is better than a clean jar locked in a cabinet. And I have no idea what that means.

On a Sunday afternoon this last May, I entered a church to attend a graduation recital for my granddaughter Audrey, who plays the cello. Some of the violin pieces were very moving, and the cello has a deep rich sound. It was very touching to watch the little ones play such heartfelt music. As I sat inside the walls of the church where the recital was held, I felt comfortable, not at all squeamish, and found myself thinking that maybe one Sunday morning I'd stop in to check out this church. This is the first twinge of softness I've felt towards organized religion in a long time.

Perhaps it is time I digest the answers my search yielded and accept my longstanding rebellion against organized religion. I have crumbled some of my childhood walls, built by misguided do-gooders and Christians who live for one day of the week. My aversion to gathering with like-minded worshippers is easing up; maybe it is time for me to lay down my armor.

I haven't yet talked to the Quakers, nor have I attended a gospel church or a tent revival. (Do these still happen?) Even with a degree in theology, one couldn't grasp all the different opinions and origins and concepts. I did not delve any deeper into Eastern religions. I touched on fundamentalist churches where I had been brought up and attended. All I can remember about Sunday school was the smell of glue, and I still remember a few songs which I used to sing to my children when they were young. *Deep and Wide* and *Jesus Loves the Little Children* come to mind.

My twenty-year quest ended abruptly. Much like Forest Gump when he began to run, *one knows when it's time to stop.* I feel that after all my snooping around; my chatting with friends, family members, and strangers; and my devouring of books, I can clearly see a common thread which binds all faiths together. This is comforting.

Most people I talked to, whether inside a church, or in open air, or on the phone, all share this common thread: All people believe, with every fiber of their body, that their faith is the correct one, the Truth. The Truth is, I believe what works for you is your Truth, but not necessarily someone else's.

I recently went to San Jose to my uncle's funeral. The unity of family, cousins I grew up with and aunts and uncles I visited with, filled the void in my search and I found my roots. Visiting my grandmother's grave with four adult female cousins was an amazing moment of comfort. The minister summed it up at the end of the service when she said: "Death ends a body, but the spirit can go everywhere."

I have been asking, "Where did your spirit go?" I realize now that you didn't go anywhere, Jeff. You are everywhere.

And Jeff, you are at peace now; or I should say, I am at peace. I haven't had any weird coincidences with birthdays, deaths, towns revisited, or random messages from someone who once knew you. While writing, I have had to stop and compose myself from the depths of sadness and memories. This chapter was more difficult than I imagined because to bring you back to life meant I had to let you go again. The other day I had to push away from my computer and rest my mind. I sat down in my clean, organized living room, took a deep breath, and laid my head back on the cushion to compose myself. I took some deep breaths, wiped my eyes, and looked out the window. Then I noticed a tiny white paper square on the side table, a very little white triangle sticking out from under a coaster. I pulled the corner of this paper point, turned it over, and realized that it was your kindergarten picture. I looked at it closely, wondering why it was there. I studied your face, remembering with such clarity the day we shopped for your new *Garanimals* brand t-shirt with matching slacks, and I knew why this photo revealed itself. I smiled and put it down before I left for the market, and your favorite song was on the radio: *Free Bird* by Lynyrd Skynyrd.

Jeff, thanks for stopping by again. Yes, I will add your kindergarten photo to this book. I thought it was so cute that you flipped your collar up, but a bit disappointed that you didn't take off your jacket and show the world your new outfit. Well dear, so much for new clothes on picture day.

I feel your presence and my quest is over. This peaceful aura that surrounds me is long overdue, my boy, and I know you are at peace too.

In Peace, Jeffrey Jetstream ...

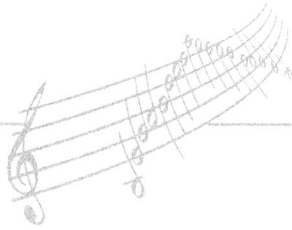

In every walk with nature one receives
far more than he seeks.
John Muir

WALKING IN CIRCLES

ONE YEAR AFTER YOU DIED, I put the salon up for sale. Finally, a couple purchased it, and part of the agreement was that I stay and work for another year. After the year was up, I left and worked in a small salon and had no worries or responsibilities except to keep my own clients happy. I was trained as a color technician and taught the ins and outs of chemical services to licensed hairdressers. I kept myself very busy. I was afraid to have too much down-time. Dana took her driver's test as planned when she was sixteen and got an A. She could drive herself and her brother wherever they wanted to go. Life quietly moved on without you.

My life was better, but being single again was like flying on a trapeze without a safety net. One morning, sitting on my front porch with my morning coffee, the silence seemed the loudest noise sound I had ever heard. I stood up, walked into my bedroom and sat on the edge of my bed. Soon I slipped to the floor with my arms on the bed and began to cry. Then I prayed. First I reintroduced myself, "Hi God, it's me, Judi. Yes, Judi from Porterville." I began to ask Him for forgiveness and patience and to show me the way to a happier life. I boo-hooed and begged for inner peace. Then I got right to the point: *Can you send me a husband? All I want is a nice guy, one I can trust and one who is normal and, well, I want a man who can cook. I really want someone who likes to stay home and relax too. This unconditional love I hear about would be a must. I'm lonely and need a companion.*

Three weeks later while working at the new location, Pete walked in with his two kids, a twelve-year-old daughter and a five-year-old son. I walked into the back room to rest and put my feet up while my timer was on, and he came back to get a drink of water while his kids took turns getting haircuts. We discussed fly fishing. I checked him out and could tell he was checking me out.

He called me three weeks later, June 29th of 1993, and we met for a glass of wine, talked and laughed. As I looked into his blue eyes, I knew I'd met my match. Two days later he invited me over, put a really cheesy CD on his stereo, and said that one day we should get married. I pretended to be shocked and told him this was really fast. I then thought about my prayer and recanted to, "Okay, but let's not tell anyone. They'll think we are crazy."

Dana stopped by the salon one late morning, soon after I'd met Pete. I told her I'd just met the man I am going to marry! Dana, who you know is usually very quiet, said very loudly, "Mom!" Then I noticed Pete was walking up the steps to the salon carrying a bouquet of pink roses. When I introduced Dana to Pete, she turned pink, Pete turned pink, and I turned pink just like the flowers. It was an uncomfortable moment, as time seemed to stand still in a totally pink room.

After a fun summer and into fall, Pete and I had a plan: put my house out in the country up for sale; then in the coming year, after it sold, get married and build a new home. My house sold in five hours. God works really fast. Spencer and his friend Finney moved us to Pete's duplex and I moved in with my two cats, Marvin and Kiki. This was the new beginning I'd asked for, and my life was moving incredibly fast. *The power of prayer.*

Jeff, you have never met the man who would have been your stepfather. You two have much in common. Pete prefers a quiet setting and is shy in a crowd, but he is very funny with a biting sense of humor, like you, and he is also talented with landscaping and is a great cook. I remember when you wanted to be a landscaper, and I remember when you used to make dinner for us. Pete could have shown you so many things.

Life went on, and I continued to have meltdowns in front of Pete. I recall standing at the stove stirring dinner when I had a breakdown. Pete simply walked over, took the wooden spoon from my hand, and began to stir so I could have a good cry. I was so relieved that I never lost it in front of his kids who lived with us every other week. Although it happens less often now, I still sometimes feel overwhelming sorrow that takes over my presence, and I never know what will trigger this.

Soon Dana had left the nest, first moving to Montana; then she came back home just long enough to regroup before she was off to Nebraska to work with a friend from high school, and to explore this new state and life. She was finding herself and growing up. She drove my Honda to Nebraska and asked permission to take Marvin the cat with her for moral support. I agreed to this but had to get sleeping pills from the vet to keep poor Marvin sedated. One bright Sunday morning we watched as she drove down our driveway with a groggy cat looking at us out the back window, turned the corner, and was gone.

She told me about her trip across the states and described being somewhere in Western Utah very late at night, when she stopped to gas up the car and get some hot coffee. It was pitch black outside and Marvin was passed out around her neck like a furry scarf. She went inside to pay and casually walked back to her car, never mentioning the cat asleep on her neck. She was alone in the middle of nowhere and very scared. She laid Marvin down in the back seat of the car and drove into the darkness. As she headed towards the unknown, driving on a dark winding road, she suddenly felt weird. Then when something touched her shoulder, she screamed and spilled hot coffee in her lap. It was Marvin touching her to say hello. She put him back around her neck and continued to drive through the mountains.

I recall being so afraid for both of them, but knew Dana had to grow up someday, and no one could stop her from moving across the states.

Dana returned one year later by plane and Marvin, again sedated, sat on her lap in coach. He was as fat as a pig because she kept him locked in her bedroom all that time so he wouldn't run away and get lost.

As Pete and I began to plan our wedding, Dana, back from Nebraska, moved in with us. Pete and I stood at the landmark Covered Bridge with only our kids in attendance. We had a big reception at a local restaurant on the patio. My friend Paula was the hostess. Then Pete's kids, Kari and Alex went with their mom that week, and we took off for the Oregon coast, which was a bad choice because of my memories of you kids playing on the beach. I began to get melancholy so Pete and I made an exit and headed through the redwoods south down the California coast instead. I still imagined complete healing was around the next corner. I had no idea that healing is accepting, and I simply couldn't accept your fate and let you go.

Your sister continued experiencing life to the fullest. Dana landed a job and continued her education. Then after Bill broke up with her, she sold her *Karmann Ghia*, and with this money moved to Paris, and then to Spain where she ran with the bulls. She called to let me know she was in Pamplona so I could watch the running of the bulls on CNN, just in case she went flying through the air. Then she was a waitress at an outdoor bar in Portugal called *Bad Moon Risen.* Eventually she went to England, lived in London and delivered sandwiches and sodas all over the city, riding a bicycle and toting her food in a trolley. She visited Turkey for three months, then Amsterdam, Greece, and so many other places as she continued to bloom and discover herself.

Jeff, you would have loved this. For Christmas I gave Spencer a plane ticket to visit Dana. She in turn surprised Spencer with a bus ticket to Scotland. They went with a group of friends and partied at Edinburg castle to bring in the New Year. I was on the Internet trying to be with them; but when I read that 80,000 people were partying at Edinburg Castle, I clicked off the computer and went to bed. It was too much to take in, and I knew I'd never get a glimpse of them in that crowd. Neither your brother nor your sister have said much about this trip to me. I guess it's their private adventure and not mine. Spencer did relate that when he was in the midst of the crowd outside the castle, he saw something moving high up in the dark sky. He watched it sway back and forth, move closer and closer, and finally drop on his head. A wool plaid scarf. Did you drop this for your brother?

Dana's last adventure was hitchhiking in New Zealand. She was all the way around the world, at a crossroads waiting for a ride, any ride, because the sand fleas had begun to jump onto her legs. No matter how many times I'd told my kids not to hitchhike, reminding them that Ted Bundy was a handsome man who inspired trust, the bottom line is they should never get into a van with a stranger.

As Dana told the story, the sun was beginning to settle down behind the mountains. A van pulled up and the driver offered her a ride, and she got in. I had warned her about getting into cars with a man she didn't know; I warned her car doors would lock. She told me she carefully felt for the handle, and it was not there. She told him she wanted to be dropped off at a youth hostel. He began to drive. Dana looked at his hands on the steering wheel and noticed he had a tattoo on each knuckle. Not *Hate Love*, oh no such luck; his inscribed tattoos read *Hate Hate*. He drove her into town to a youth hostel, pulled the van over then he leaned across her lap and reached into his glove compartment. Dana braced herself for something bad. She said he reached in and grabbed a book, handed it and a pen to her, and asked her if she would write something in his journal—you know, like if she liked his driving and the experience.

Whew, you kids! And a very lucky girl you are, my dear daughter. Jeff, I hope you were with her on that journey! Dana finally came home. She was quiet, seemed tired and introspective, but she wore a new confidence I hadn't seen in her before. She had found herself and knew who she was. A few years later she gave Billy boy a second chance. He said he'd let her go so she would experience life. Boy, did she ever! Spencer had moved to Mendocino after he graduated from high school, where he said he'd tasted the best bowl of soup in the world and wanted to eat clam chowder every day for the rest of his life. Move he did, and so did his best friend Geoff. You'd remember him, Jeff. He and Spencer have been best buds since kindergarten. They parked their VW buses next to each other in a state park, one facing in and the other backed in beside it. Then they opened the sliders to make a double-wide. No, son, I'm not making this up. They went to the humane society and each got a dog. Spencer named his tri-colored dog with pointed ears Raven. Spencer got lost in his new world with his dog Raven and loved it. He and Geoff kayaked in the ocean that led to outlets deep into the forest and the boys deep-sea-fished and dove for abalone. Geoff landed a job building houses, and one day he became a contractor. Spencer needed better shelter and more money and bounced around looking for the best place to live. You would have loved this part of his life, Jeff. Spencer finally did land a good job at *Wind and Weather,* where he boxed and shipped upscale expensive yard art all over the world. He lived the good life and named his VW bus *Shiny.*

After awhile, Spencer was doing dishes in a high-end restaurant and grew tired of this nasty job. Besides, everyone he met called him Stewart. His lifestyle was growing old and was not as much fun anymore. He was also growing tired of clam chowder. He came home, worked at a UPS postal center, and then he got a job delivering soaps to restaurants, prisons, and larger companies. Finally, he decided to take classes and become an emergency medical technician (EMT) and was thinking of becoming a paramedic. He moved back in with Pete and me and landed a great job delivering medicine to in-house patients, sometimes through a feeding tube. Coincidentally, he delivered morphine to my friend Annie. She had wanted to be in Hawaii to find peace from the chemotherapy, but her doctor wouldn't allow her to fly. Your sweet brother sewed fresh flowers together to make a Hawaiian lei, which he took over to her on his delivery. When she died fourteen months later, she had left the lei for him. Oh Jeff, so many things changed. Sometimes I forget how much you have missed.

Dana took classes to be a Certified Nurse's Assistant; she got the highest score but never set foot in a rest home again. This was not her calling. She also worked at Woodstock's Pizza where she was the girl in the front window spinning pizza dough on her fingertips, tossing it into the air, and transferring it to the other hand. She wore her short hair in little pigtails. Jeffrey, just think, you could have had all the free pizza you wanted. Plus free entertainment from your sister.

Dana also started taking business classes and graduated with an AA. Then, out of the blue she called me at home one day and said she was going to enroll in Beauty College. I am a talker by nature, so she wasn't prepared for the phone to go dead. I couldn't speak. I had never thought this was a possibility. Jeff, I thought of how many times I cut your hair, and realized that you could have had a mother and a sister to serve your needs.

One weekend, before Spencer moved home, Dana and I took a much-needed road trip to the ocean; actually it was more like a rescue mission. We parked after we spotted Spencer's blue Toyota pickup (Shiny was sold then wrecked, RIP). Soon your brother crawled out of his camper shell to greet us. I rented a room for the three of us, with a view of grass then a sandy beach. Spencer took a long hot shower and a our rescue mission was a success. After dinner I dropped your brother and sister off at the movies so they could have some alone time. It was great fun to be a family again; this visit was long overdue, and I can tell you that your name came up many times, Jeffrey.

So much more changed, Jeff. After your death the kids scrambled for security and normalcy. They each graduated then made drastic decisions, as though they didn't know which way to turn. They needed time to heal, but this would be a long road for two kids who were ill-prepared for the jolt they had lived through. I had a major breakdown after John broke off our relationship. I had one too many losses to cope with and although Paula and I had some crazy fun times, I was suffering inside; your loss was always right there in my face and heart.

Your brother has also had some very dark times, too. Once, when he was well into his thirties, he told me he was driving along and began to think about you and he had to pull off the road. Just the thought of you popped into his mind and he sat in his truck and sobbed. He is so sad deep inside and no one would ever expect this as he is a very upbeat funny guy.

Your grandma has been in a care facility for so long I can't believe she is still with us. Today she doesn't remember people very often, including me. Except you, Jeff. She remembers the baby I had when I was young, and when I ask her, "Mom, do you remember Jeff?" she always nods and says, "Oh yes, I remember Jeff." She is clear on this. I wonder, when you visited your elementary school and maybe your other schools before you left for Lakeport, did you visit your Nana too? Were you saying goodbye to your childhood, Jeffrey?

I purchased a memory bench and dedicated it to you with a brass plaque placed in the concrete. It has your name, dates of birth and death, and this description: *Brother, Son, Musician.* It's in Bidwell Park, one of your old favorite spots as a kid. It sits next to the lawn overlooking One Mile swim area, right by the jogging and bicycle path, under a canopy of shade trees. The homeless people like this location too.

Sometimes I stop by with spray disinfectant and a cloth and a whisk broom and clean the bench and sweep the concrete. Occasionally I'll sit and visit with gnarly dirty men, and sometimes I just sit there and think of how much you would have loved the location and the view of the natural setting and dammed-up swim area. Jeff, my friend Annie died nine years after you. Annie also has a bench dedicated to her, with a plaque that reads: *Annie loved this park, so rest your weary tush* (short version). On some of my trips to the park I bench-hop, cleaning both memorial benches.

Dana put together a wonderful scrapbook of postcards and photos of you that she has been collecting since you two were very young. You sent her a postcard when she attended church camp at Camp Noel Porter in Lake Tahoe, another from Alaska, and letters and postcards from your days in Westwood. You have to be careful what you send to your sister; she keeps everything.

Spencer was a mountain guide in Mt. Shasta for a few years. He and his hiking partner have taken many clients up this snow-covered summit. He has completed over eighty climbs. One of his climbs was for you, Jeff. He hiked and ice-climbed to place a prayer flag on the summit. This selfless act was an endearing tribute to you, his much-loved brother.

Now this is a weird happening: *The City Lights Opera House* began to fundraise for new spectator seats by advertising that patrons can purchase brass memory plaques for the arms of the chairs. I had a suspicion you would hate this, but I bought one anyway. Oddly, the volunteers could not get your plaque to stay on the arm of the chair. I was told that it popped off each time or curled on one end. When they walked away, it would shoot off the arm and land a few feet away. They tried everything from glue to nail guns. I told them that obviously you didn't want to attend the opera and that was that, so they tossed the twisted brass plaque with your name on it into the trash, and I got a refund.

Dear Jeff, sometimes I have this crazy notion that my door bell will ring one day. I will open my front door and there, standing in front of me is a young woman holding hands with a young boy, your son. I know this is crazy talk, imagining that you have a child out of wedlock and here he is, but whatever it takes for me to sleep or dream future thoughts of you, I do.

I suspect you had no idea how much you were loved. It was you who kept pulling away, drawing a line in the sand. It was hard to watch you becoming more and more isolated and anti-social until we were unable to grab your hand and pull you back. I will feel responsible for you and your death for the rest of my life, no matter how many people, trained professionals or family members, tell me it wasn't my fault. No matter how much I spend on counseling, which is not that much since Dale made his exit, I know I could have done more for you.

I do feel your presence and sometimes have an idea or a notion to do something, or call someone for no apparent reason; and I have to wonder if you are with me. On a Friday night, the night before you killed yourself, I was asleep, and for an unknown reason I sprang out of bed. It was pitch black and I shoved the bedroom curtains open, but in the wrong direction, and exposed a bright ray of light. I stood for a moment in the spotlight, and then dove back into bed. I crouched as low as I could get, feeling like I needed to make myself smaller, and I said to myself, "We have to stay low or we might be shot." The next morning I woke up, and seeing the mess I had made out of the curtains, verified that this did indeed happen. I woke up Dana's friend Sonja to take her home, up north towards the ridge. When I told Dana and Sonja about my nightmare and fixing the curtains, they both said, "Wow, that's weird!" I woke Spencer up early too, because John was coming over to drive us to the Bay Area. Then on the drive to Sonja's house, I was telling her about Dana's older brother Jeff, and then we both saw a guy walking down the side of the freeway who looked just like you—same clothes, size, stride, and hair color. I looked back to see his face, but his head was down. I told Sonja about you and your problems, and she told me about her brother and her mom and all of their struggles. Sonja shares a birthday with Dana, same day and year, and they have the same set of drama in their home. I later realized that I'd passed that guy who looked like you at 10:00 A.M., the time noted that you killed yourself.

Ten years passed before I had this memory, and I thought, why was it so bright in my bedroom window that night? I went on the Internet to research this, to see if there was anything special about the night before you died, the night I woke up and messed up the window dressings. I learned there was a huge blinding Super Moon on September 5, just two days before I jumped out of bed and was blinded by that light on September 7.

George, my step-brother, said he'd sat with you that evening, Jeff, outside by your grandpa's pool patio area. He told me you two visited and you seemed the same, nice and calm, and talked about life and ideas. He said you had applied for a job that day, which I find odd. Why did you apply for a job in Lakeport? You also told George that you wanted to sleep outside by the pool under the stars, which you did. This meant you saw that Super Moon, too, Jeff. We both looked at the moon. I believe your intense thoughts of shooting yourself transmitted to me that bright night so long ago. Our connection, so strong and ever-present, was in full force that night.

Your cousin Kristi said her friend told her that you had visited a pawn shop in Lakeport on Friday and that you had looked at a gun. So Kristi went to talk to the pawn shop owner, who told her you'd been so scared that your hands were wet; he had to wipe off the gun after you held it. These events tell me you were applying for a job, were on your way to find Lisa, and were frightened to hold a gun. This doesn't add up, but I think you were a bit confused too; you weren't sure what you were going to do.

I also had an intuition a few weeks after your death when I went back to Lakeport to visit my dad. While I was at their home, Marion told me that you had stolen your grandpa's watch. I stood up to her and said, "No, he did not take my dad's watch. He wouldn't do that." She argued back, "Then why it is missing, and where could it be?" I stood up, walked into their bedroom, opened the double doors in the armoire, went directly to the third drawer, reached in and pulled out my dad's watch. I have no idea why I did this or who led me to its safe resting place. I handed dad's watch to Marion and she said, "Oh," then apologized, and I accepted. But you could have cut the air with a knife, it was so tense.

She and I had our differences, but I played along as I didn't want to ever disrespect my father's new wife. She was very generous and nice to me until she tipped a few in the evenings, then her son, my cool step-brother George, would come to my rescue and tell his mother to be nice. But, after your death and my dad's death, I always wore full armor, ready to defend myself and you and also my dad. I found and began to use my voice. Although I made a few enemies doing so, I realized I should have had this confidence years and years before.

After you died, your cousin Roger cleaned up the garage, hosing down the blood and putting everything back in order. I was a bit upset as I desperately needed closure. I wanted to see the garage as it was. I needed to study the scene to confirm your death in my mind and to say goodbye. I talked to George about this problem I had about feeling like maybe it was another guy, maybe it was an intruder, maybe there was a mistake, and Jeff is still alive. George took me by the hand and together we went into the garage. We stood and looked around, at my dad's work bench where the tools hung above, each placed over the shape of that tool, which he'd painted in blue, and I looked at all the storage boxes of Christmas and party things. George pointed to a puddle of dried blood and a splatter on another box. I stood and gazed at the dark maroon puddle as he stood close to me. We said nothing. I stared and imagined the scene, then nodded okay and let out a sigh. George showed me the hole in the garage door frame from the bullet that had pierced my dad's lung, and said that Roger took out the bullet and has it. Even as numb as I felt, I found myself thinking that was a strange souvenir to take. I looked at the room, imagined your last minutes, then I looked across the street at your last visual before we walked out. Our oasis away from home was gone; everything had changed forever.

It felt as if a scene from a movie was fading. I remembered all the weekend trips to Dad and Marion's, all the swim parties, dinners at the long table. Dad's sign *Ban the Bra* still hung by the fence surrounding the pool, his silly garden art was still randomly placed, Marion's gold Buddha in its strategic location, and I even remembered that someone had plopped my wedding veil onto its head. The ceramic boy was still peeing into the pond that rotated the pond water to a wooden wheel my dad had made, then to a waterfall and back to the little pond. Aunt Harriett's colored resin balls still hung on ropes with knots in a long row and decorated the backdrop under the pergola over the pond. Dad's vintage bar still stands, turquoise and silver sparkles and designs, as though waiting for a drink to be made; but now it is empty and dusty and a catchall for things no one wants to put away.

I remember Marion in one of her bright floral muumuus bringing out another dish of food, and my dad mixing drinks. Jeff, I even remembered that you never liked to be on the air mattress when it floated across the mosaic mermaid on the bottom of the pool. It scared you. I should have taken a picture of her.

Now the pool sits with leaves floating towards the edges. No laughter, no music, no screams from kids splashing about in the turquoise water after taking a ride down the water slide on their back and landing on an air mattress. No one is there. The parties and the fun weekends in Lakeport came to abrupt halt when you and your grandfather left us. When people take their own lives, they may want to be liberated from pain, they may want to end their ongoing thoughts of failure or peer pressure, or they may just want to be free. What is not considered is that now, the ones left behind have the pain to sweep up, and the memories to deal with.

As much as I love you, I also want to shake you and tell you that killing yourself was a very selfish act. It is devastating for the ones left behind; the trauma and shock is a lasting emotion. Oh, how I wish you had waited! Or here's a novel idea: you could have poured out your heart to me, told me about your darkest moments, and shared the idea of ending your life. Lord knows this would have made me wide awake and got me to stand at full attention. But no, that isn't your style; you were aloof, silent, and quiet. And if you were waiting for me to notice, you picked the wrong person. I need to have ice water thrown in my face before I notice something is amiss.

What you seek is seeking you.
Rumi

MADAM RUBY

1993. JEFF, MY QUEST TO FIND YOUR SOUL made me more confused but determined to proceed. Your mom is a steamroller when on a mission. Yes, I did find comfort with my Mormon friends, but I found much more on a fluke visit to Madam Ruby, our local *spiritual reader*. Madam Ruby has been in our town for as long as I can remember, in the same house on a busy commercial street, with the same neon hand in the window. She had called the salon and wanted a hair appointment and asked if I would consider a trade. I am all about the barter system, and a reading was more than a fair trade, just so I could say, "I did Madam Ruby's hair."

Jeff, when it was my turn to collect my half of the barter, I waited about three weeks then called for an appointment. I cautiously walked towards her front door, looked at the bright neon hand in the window, and entered with no expectations. To my surprise and amazement, she was not only accurate; she actually went beyond the reading and asked politely whether she should proceed further into my life.

Madam Ruby held my palm and did an analysis, telling me things about my life and my journey. I thought I would remember everything she told me, but the second part of her reading was so mind-blowing that the palm reading part went out the window. She sat back, looked at me, and began straight up with information: "A dark-haired man has broken your heart" (oh my gosh—John!) "but you will meet him again on your path. He will come back to you and want another chance, but don't go towards him. If he broke your heart once, he'll do it again. Don't go towards him on the path," she repeated. "You have recently met a fair-haired man." (Pete, oh my gosh!) "He is the one you should be with; he is honest and will take good care of you." I sat stone-faced and played the *void of expression* game as I didn't want to give her any clues into my past. Surely most first-time clients play dumb just to see what the palm reader really knows. I wanted to see how far she would go on target, and she went all the way.

She proceeded with "The fair-haired man has two children." (Yes he does. How did she know that?) "They like you and enjoy you and always will be close to you until you cross them or tell them no. That was a shocking thing for her to say. "They are used to getting their own way—you must always keep this in mind—and they do not want you to ever tell them no." I sat in amazement with a twinge of worry. I had met Pete's kids about thirteen months prior to this visit, and we were beginning to bond as a family during the weeks they lived with us. Our household was happy, but with unique turmoil I'd never dealt with. We were establishing a healthy and warm relationship, but I noticed a few quirks in the family dynamics.

For example, Pete made Kari clean her plate at dinner, or no dessert; but he didn't have this rule for Alex. When I pointed out the inconsistent rule for dessert, he was surprised. I also noticed Kari had a lot of baggage for a twelve-year-old girl; she still had many concerns about her parents' divorce, and she talked often of the sadness in her young life. She also had a stubborn streak. I had raised three kids and knew the signs and caught her in many little white lies, which she certainly didn't appreciate. She definitely didn't like it when I came on too strong.

Five-year-old Alex was somewhat in a daze, following all the rules, doing his homework, and staying close by. I remember telling Pete, "I am worried that one day Alex is going to blow a gasket. He is too well-behaved, wound too tight." Alex was also closed off and afraid to show his feelings, keeping his true self neatly tucked away. Only when he played football or soccer in the middle of our street, or rolled around and wrestled on the floor with his dad did he show some determination and aggressiveness. I decided to let Pete raise his own kids, but sometimes I had to step up and be the voice of reason because Pete wanted to be their friend, not their parent. Madam Ruby was right, but I didn't tell the kids that I had been guided and pre-warned by Madam Ruby until they were older.

Madam Ruby snapped me back to attention, and I began to listen and admire her predictions and suggestions. After our talk about the dark-haired and the fair-haired men and Pete's two children, she paused, ad-justed herself in her comfortable overstuffed chair and began to speak about something I could tell would be an uncomfortable topic. She shifted the cushions to support her back and tilted backwards, until she was re-laxed and composed. She put her hand on her dress, on top of her belly button, and began to rub her fingers around and around on the floral cotton dress. Her fingers were mesmerizing as they slowly circled, and I began to relax and wait with wonder.

"Do you mind if I tell you something that is very important and per-sonal?" she began. "Someone very close to you has passed on. This person is not there yet."

I decided not to play this game of silence any longer and chimed in, "Yes, my son died two years ago." Madam Ruby continued with her hand on her dress going around very slowly with her finger, circling her stomach, and she spoke with caution. "He was not ready to go," she repeated. "He wasn't supposed to leave this earth and he is now in limbo, which means he is not on earth and he is not in the heav-ens. Maybe by this fall, perhaps in September he will find his way."

I thanked her for telling me this but didn't even ask her what limbo meant, I was so distraught. Actually, I had a vague idea what limbo was, so asked, "Is he lost? Scared? Is he trying to get out?"

She went on to repeat that he was not supposed to go; it was not his time. "Once he finds his way out of limbo, he will be able to contact you," she said.

This reading and revelation that were my part of the barter made your passing somewhat disturbing, and knowing you were in limbo made me frantic. I felt this soft, gentle, but explosive information as a punch in my stomach area. At least you weren't in hell, yet I wanted you to get out, to come back to us, or be on your passage to the next realm, heaven, whether it is far away or a veil away. I could sense Madam Ruby didn't want to dwell on this information, but felt compelled to let me know.

How did this stranger know about dark-haired John breaking up with me, and about my new relationship with fair-haired Pete? And how did she know Pete had two children? And about your passing? I thought back to her hair appointment and knew I'd said nothing, seriously not a word. She asked me no questions about my life, and I offered her no information. She sat quietly while I applied and timed the color and completed the service. I have no photos on my station that might have supplied clues. She rested.

I have never been back to see her (or she to see me).

The information about you, Jeff, was truly disturbing but insightful. The other significant spot-on revelation she tossed at me wasn't her warning and caution concerning the two men I have loved, not John's apology and his regrets, but her reading of Pete's kids. I had sensed from the beginning they were not being their true selves when they were in our home, their home every other week. These kids were too polite; they didn't laugh like my kids. They seemed like poster children for good behavior, which to me is a ticking time bomb. They watched instead of lived. Pete roughed-housed with them on the living room floor and every time, this wrestling ended with one of them crying, usually his daughter. When I told Pete not be so rough when he played, he said he wasn't; but they were children, and no match for Pete's strength. I do know that the wrestling was great father attention time, and I suspect the crying was a good way to get away and go to their rooms to escape the tackle.

I was on shaky ground with Kari and Alex from the beginning. While with us, they didn't know what to do with themselves without organized schedules and activities. One Saturday afternoon when Alex was about seven years old, he told me that he was bored, and I told him he needed to use his imagination. He looked up at me and I could see he was dead serious when he replied, "I don't have one." I laughed out loud, put my hand over my mouth and choked back more laughter because this statement was so bizarre that I didn't expect it. I gathered some composure and told him that was the saddest thing I'd ever heard in my life. Then, I dug into my orange vinyl box of *stuff*, pulled out a huge button, and put it on the bulletin board in his room. It was a picture of Albert Einstein with his crazy hair, and under the photo were the words: *Imagination is more important than knowledge.* Alex looked at me, reread the button, thought about it, then turned to me and said, "I like that a lot. Thanks, Judi!" He kept that button pinned to his bulletin board for the next ten years, and Alex began to bloom. He began to use his mind, to think and plan. I'd see him digging in the dirt to make a bridge and create a war zone with ditches and huts and people it with all of his army men. He got really dirty building ramps and forts, and he had friends over, and all those boys and Alex seemed happy.

Eventually Pete's kids began to ease into our family dynamics; they realized they could joke, poke fun at me, and be silly. We shared many laughs while at the dinner table, especially the evening I told them that my three kids helped me hand water all our small trees on the Durham property on a weekly basis. I said that I had two big jugs and explained in great detail about the watering process. Pete, Kari, and Alex were laughing and red-faced so I again said, "Well, I did! Honestly, I did all of this with only my two big jugs." Finally I realized what I was saying, and we joked about that for years. Slowly our relationships intertwined like vines around a big old tree. It was fine to ask questions, complain, tell personal stories, be themselves. I knew they felt I'd disrupted their relationship with their dad—not his marriage (Pete was already divorced when we met). Soon they realized that all was going to stay the same—except for me, the elephant in the room. Once Kari and Alex felt safe in our home, and realized that they wouldn't lose their dad, we began to be a family.

Dana and Spencer now had a younger brother and sister, and we all began to move forward.

Naturally when Madam Ruby mentioned the children in my reading, warning me to be aware and to tread lightly with my two new step-children, I became a believer. I tried not to command them (not too much anyway). Once the kids became more comfortable and independent as teenagers, I became more assertive. That went over like a lead balloon.

One Saturday while I was in the kitchen, the front door slammed. I peeked around the corner and there, standing in our entry, were three young neighborhood boys about six or seven years old. Alex was showing them the wall with all the kids' framed photos clustered together, and pointed at your 8 x 10 picture. Alex asked me if was it was okay to show them Jeff's picture, and asked again for reassurance with his story. "He shot himself, right?" I said, "Yes Alex, he did," "And he's dead, right?" "Yes he is." The other two boys looked closely at the photo, looked towards me, then back to Alex, and then their gaze went back to you, Jeff. I felt that from their perspective you were on display as an oddity. If only they knew what a funny guy you were, they'd have enjoyed you so much. This hurt my heart, but I didn't want to make this into something more than a photo and a story so I kept quiet. I could see the innocence in Alex's eyes. He was proud to show his new friends something none of them had in their homes or lives; he had the best story of all. This moment has stayed with me every since, and makes me love Alex even more.

Even castles made of sand fall into the sea, eventually.
Jimi Hendrix

SWEET MEMORIES

ONE OF THE CUTEST *mom calls* from you, Jeff, happened on the Oregon coast, you were about nine years old. We were at Nesika Beach playing in the damp sand. It was an overcast day, the kind of day you can still get sunburned and then be surprised. You began to build a sand castle, and I joined you to teach you about the different types of castles. We made a moat and tall buildings with a walkway to help ward off the enemy. I left you to go watch Spencer and Dana, who were writing ABCs in the sand with a stick of driftwood, when you desperately yelled for help. "Mom, come quick!" I raced over to where you were on your knees, looking up with worry and begging, "Mom, can you stop the tide?"

You got your first lesson about the moon and tides. The tide was creeping closer and closer to your masterpiece, and you learned that we were both powerless to stop it. So you decided to let the tide enter; the collapse of the castle was going to be your idea, not the tide's. While you dug an opening at the end of the moat closest to the ocean, I took Dana and Spencer by the hands and we all stood still and watched the water slowly fill the moat, circle the castle, and eventually crumble it—but not before you kicked the top off the lookout point. It was a lesson in nature to watch the tide overtake the castle and slowly pull it back to the ocean.

Life was never dull with you; it seemed you were in some kind of danger every day. I remember when you were in fourth grade and being chased by the neighborhood bully who tried to beat you up as you walked past his house on your way home from school. You described him to me: "He has really big blue eyes and he looks like a grouper." Did you perhaps mention this fish comparison to him? I bet that's why he jumped you!

When you were ten we enrolled you in a gymnastics class at the YMCA. With your athletic body and sure-footedness, you were a natural and loved it. The third week the coach told everyone to find something to hook your toes under and do thirty sit-ups. He pointed for you to go the locker across the room, which you did; but because the locker was on wheels it began to roll as you pulled with your toes for leverage. Someone had left a barbell on top, which rolled forward and landed on your foot, breaking it and leaving you in excruciating pain. After another trip to the emergency room, you had a cast on your foot, crutches, and pain pills. You hopped around the house and became the focal point at home and school because of someone else's senseless mistake. The YMCA paid all medical expenses, but good grief, it was always something.

You made your next trip to the emergency room when you were twelve. Your friend was snapping you with a wet beach towel at the swimming pool. After several tries, you managed to grab the towel in mid-snap. He jerked the towel back and your knuckle was torn apart. You ran into the house clutching your hand and off we went. You came back home with your finger taped to a splint and were told to be quiet and still. I recall thinking that this was like expecting leaves not to blow on a breezy spring day.

I only know what you and Spencer shared with me, but I do know that in your clubhouse you used the magnifying glass to look at spiders and flies. Fortunately, our next-door neighbor Roger was my saving grace. He kept you kids busy, either in the swimming pool or on his ranch.

I love to tell about the time you moved to Lakeport and worked at Roundtable Pizza. You asked the manager if you could have the discarded tap beer vintage nozzle. He said no, absolutely not; the company will want it back. You were told you couldn't buy it or have it. Then you made a deal with your boss, that if you ate a fist full of anchovies in front of the other employees, then he'd give you the nozzle. You called that night so happy with your prize. Apparently after the pizza parlor closed, everyone gathered around and began to clap as the manager made a ball of anchovies, rolling it nice and round and tight. He handed it to you and you began chewing the salty fish that was so disgusting, the smell so overwhelming, that you said you almost vomited. You told me how you chewed and swallowed it as fast as you could. Now sonny boy, that's crazy. You kept that vintage nozzle for many years; and after your death, I gave it to your brother. I hope Spencer still has it.

Many more tales surfaced with you typically in the middle of the action. As the oldest child I raised, you were supposed to set a good example and protect your brother and sister. They loved you, adored you, and looked up to you. What kid wouldn't, Jeff? You had a very active mind and keen sense of humor. By the way, Dana never told on you—at least she didn't until she was in high school and told me about you stuffing her into the toy box. Spencer never told on you either, until much later when he spilled the beans about your rooftop jumps into the concrete jacuzzi when I thought he was play watching *Scooby Do*. I also know now that when you were in about sixth grade you would quietly take off the screen and climb out the window (Spencer thought it was at about 5:00 A.M.) to meet your friend Jason and hike up to Horseshoe Lake and fish. I learned about your adventure and sneaky exit when you phoned from the golf course collect. I accepted the call, expecting an emergency, but you came on the line, said you were too tired to walk home, and then had the audacity to ask me to pick you up! I ran into your room and yes, your bed was made and the screen was off. I swear, Jeff, this was such a shock to me as I thought you were sleeping in on a Saturday morning. I didn't want to stir the kids, and I also wanted you to learn a lesson, so I told you to walk home. You arrived in about an hour, moseying back across our lawn with your head down—hot, hungry, and tired, and you hadn't caught any fish. Why didn't you just ask me if you and Jason could go fishing? You were a pill in many ways, but also so endearing.

Few days went by that you were not in trouble for one thing or another, mostly for arguing. You just had concrete ideas and arguing became the most annoying habit you developed. If I said this rock is black, you would show me little gray specks and call it tweed. If I said no, you can't go to Keith's house, you would tell me why it was important while on your way out the door. Then—drum roll—you would tell me when you could be back or how long you would stay; sometimes you'd compromise and say you'd be home early just to have some sort of control. One thing I repeated over and over is "I'm the parent; you're the child!" How many times did I say this? Did you ever actually hear me say that?

Most of the time, I now admit, you lost me. You would argue a point and I would get hung up in profound statements and details and actually forget why we were having a disagreement. There were times when you were actually right, but I was such a staunch reflection of my father that I'd continue trying to prove my point, even when it was incorrect, and try to out-argue you. One such time is so clear in my mind. We were standing in the doorway between the kitchen and the hallway. We butted heads about something—I no longer remember what—and you said your piece and I explained to you why not and you added, "but what about the time you said okay?" to which I retaliated with an answer that made no sense. Suddenly we both started laughing. Simultaneously, each of us lost sight of whatever point we were trying to make and forgot the fight. It was such a silly time, you and I laughing together. You were so comical. You did a little dance, and I sat down on a kitchen chair laughing so hard I couldn't breathe. To this day I don't know if I said okay, go ahead and do it, or what. You really wore me down, buster.

When you were three years old, I bought you a little blue Bible with a picture on the front of Jesus playing with little children. I began to read to you and the word Yahweh appeared. I tried to pronounce this with Yaw-we, ya-ya, Ywaa, and you looked up at me with a typical three-year-old grin and mimicked my long drawn-out word: "yah WA." We laughed and laughed, and I was embarrassed that as an adult and mother I couldn't pronounce this word. You and I shared this Yah-wa word for your entire life. When you were a teenager, I recall that if I hesitated even a second while thinking of a word to complete a sentence, you would yell from the next room "yah-wa?"

Jeff, do you remember the round rubber soap holder that I stuck onto the tile on the inside of the bathtub/shower? Well, after you tossed it in the air, it became perpetually stuck on our bathroom ceiling. It stayed there for so many years that I lost count. I also found a dozen pin holes in the wallpaper next to the toilet. Your doing? And in the kitchen, I remember finding what looked like a piece of salami after your little fingers squished bread so tight. And do you remember tossing our cat Helen into a bag of ashes from the fireplace, not knowing that ashes take days to cool down? This caused Helen tremendous pain and agony, and cost me a hefty vet bill when we had to have her paws cleaned and wrapped and medicated daily. You were surprised, and sorry. Yes, buster, you definitely kept our daily lives on high alert!

I so miss the times you helped me cook a Christmas dinner. Events such as these seem insignificant to the average family. But to us, they are priceless as we will never again make more memories with you. I used to worry because you liked to be home with me so much, and I was sure you would be the one to care for me when I grew old and frail. This was more of a worry, however, than a happy thought. I am sure we would argue about the shade being up or down, whether the blanket on my lap is too heavy or too light. But still, I knew you would have been there for me.

Once we took a trip down south to visit family, with my mother, her suitcase, and her walker. The ride home turned out to be a trip like no other. I should have gotten a ticket for unsafe conditions and child endangerment. We stopped off to visit my old friends Robert and Dennis on their ranch. They handed you kids some paper bags and said you could pick all the grapefruit and oranges you wanted. To have bags full of fresh citrus fruit to take home was like discovering a gold mine. We got Mother settled into the front seat, her walker in the back. You kids jumped into the back seat and worked yourselves around her walker (which you loved to play on) and off we went, waving goodbye to my good friends from high school. I remember Robert looking at the sky and saying, "It looks like rain."

We were only ten miles into our five-hour drive when it began to sprinkle. This was more a nuisance than a worry because it never rained in the summer. I just wanted to get home, plus there was dust on my windshield from driving down their dusty road, I didn't mind a *little* rain. But soon the sprinkles turned into a downpour with raindrops the size of quarters. Thunder tumbled in the distance and the wheels of cars in front of us blew water all over us. I turned on my wipers and watched the left one, driver's side, which moved like something dead trying to get up. I had to open the windows to see where I was going, which meant more rain blew inside the car. My mom only said, "Oh dear," and Jeff, you said you'd look out the passenger window for me. We continued down Highway 99 north when one of the kids asked for a grapefruit. I said okay and my mom said that sounded good too. Jeff, you reached into the bag between my mother's feet, got out a nice big grapefruit, peeled it and tore it into slices to share. The grapefruit juice shot me in the eye so I couldn't see out of my right eye. I thought about stopping, but it was still pouring and we had no jackets, plus the side of the highway was a muddy mess. Dana rolled off her dirty sock and offered it to me. I began to wipe my eye and held it to my face. Jeff, you took off her other dirty sock, slipped your hand inside and wiped the dashboard, helped my mother dry her hands, and suggested you could wipe the steering wheel if I needed you to. The car was a sticky mess when finally we landed back on our turf, dropped mother off, and returned home for baths. Just how long it poured and how long it took me to regain my eyesight is unclear, but I do remember thinking of the trip as a nightmare that kept getting worse. Looking back now, though, I see what a funny scene it was.

I will end this sweet memory story with the best one ever: you and Keith in the Talent Contest. I let you wear my pink turtleneck sweater and I bought some bright pink material and sewed a long tube, put a stretched-out wire hanger inside, curled it up on one end and pinned in to your blue jeans butt. While Keith played *The Pink Panther* on the piano, you came out on your tip-toes and snuck around on the stage. Then you reached behind a plant, picked up the pink strawberry yogurt pie I'd made. You were supposed to smash Keith over the head, but he saw you coming and ducked so that when you tossed the pie, it landed on the American flag. We helped clean the pink whipping cream and gick off the floor, but I heard they never got all the pink stains out of the white stripes on the flag. The school stopped all talent shows for years because of you boys. But what a funny skit that was!

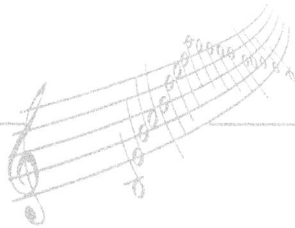

The highlight of my childhood was making my
brother laugh so hard that food came out his nose.
Garrison Keillor

OH YOU KIDS

THE ROOF OVER OUR HOME WAS OUR CIRCUS TENT. I suppose I was to blame as I laughed so much of the time, and fueled the imaginations of my children. I also joined in with the games and set the mood for fun and adventure. But Jeff, you were the *Ringmaster* and also a key performer. You lived in our home with a built in audience; your younger brother and giggly little sister also performed and had many acts of their own. *Let the show begin.*

Jeff, when you were five you gained a baby sister and you were very un-happy about this as you had specifically ordered a brother. Soon, I placed her in your arms and you sat on the couch, your legs stuck out off the cushions and your little leather cowboy boots moved up and down as you settled into a position to hold her for the first time. I sat next to you watched as you looked back up at me, then smiled and stared at her little face. In a few months you were down on all fours playing with her, you put stuffed toys into her crib, and showed her your hot wheels. You became the watchful big brother.

Twenty four months later your order was fulfilled and your brother arrived on the scene. Joy was smothered by dismay when you had to wait for your baby brother to crawl, then walk before you could actually play. This was a very long wait for an impatient big brother. I love the photo of you and your brother, standing at the chalk board I'd hung low so he could write on it. Spencer was a toddler and you would draw a picture, then watch with glee as he wiped it off with his sweaty hands and do a dance with his fat feet moving at record speed, standing there in his diapers. You, on your knees, kept drawing and laughing all the while. Your sister kept smiling and watched from my lap.

Jeff, you had serious worries and needs. You were seven when you came up to me in the kitchen and asked me if I could make your sister stop smiling. You said you just didn't like it. I suggested you relax and enjoy her sweetness. You then made faces at her and she laughed, you jumped off the couch with monster arms ready to pounce and she giggled, you got under quilts and moved towards her in a threatening way, growling and she laughed. Finally you gave up and the three of you played together for the rest of your lives, she smiling all the way.

Taxi. It was 1979, and, as every morning we drove to school, and in a hurry. There were no seatbelts required and you kids were all over the car. I confess one morning to be running really late, we took off, taking a right turn, then another right; I was too close to the curb which moved the car and jolted us from side to side. Jeff, you yelled, "mom's the *Dukes of Hazard*" and I heard little hands clapping in the backseat, I kept going.

Jeff, you began to grow tall and continued to play games with your brother and sister and sometimes your youngest sister in Potter Valley, Sarah. You'd color Easter eggs then point with your pointer finger but you kept yourself out of view of the camera Patty held. What you will see on this video are three happy little kids, smiling and proud of their egg designs, and one finger pointing down at the eggs. Jeff, you always created your own game, and I have to give you credit, you always made the most of hanging out with the little kids.

We were at the baseball field—Chico's Westside Little League, you are about nine years old. You're playing short stop and this is the team to beat. Bleachers are packed with parents—little kids line the wire fence behind home plate to get a closer look though the holes. The game has started and I notice you're talking to the center fielder, you two are talking and looking and comparing your mitts. I stand up, cup my hands around my mouth and yell, "Jeff Harris, pay attention!" Later in the game I'm talking to a mother sitting next to me and I hear this loud kid's voice coming from the field, "Judi, pay attention!" Everyone looked up at me as I had been the mother to yell earlier in the game and most parents snickered and some outright laughed. I looked at you and did thumbs up, as a sign of *touché'*. Boy, you really got me that time Jeff.

Your creativity as a young teen was again apparent one Halloween when you dressed me up as *Joan of Arc*. I put on a burlap sack for a dress; you tied a rope around my waist and put some kindling on my backside as if I was burning at the stake. I wore orange nylons. Jeff, you hung a wooden cross around my neck and slicked my hair back. I won second place and shared my prize with you, we went to Oy Vey, you ordered steak Diane and loved it, I had an onion bagel with crème cheese. *Two happy people.*

The first Christmas in our newly built home in Durham, I bought you kids what I afford that year, about three gifts each. To make this a better and different take, I bought empty tin cans, put a note with clues in each one, then sealed the cans. Each of you had to get a can opener to find your gift. Jeff, I still remember this part of your note:

> *Don't catch a cold,*
> *You might sneeze,*
> *Life is a breeze,*
> *If it doesn't freeze.*

You finally ran towards the kitchen, opened the freezer and found two frozen solid faded 501s, just your size. Each of your cans contained clues, a new key chain with a key to our front door, and money. While your brother and sister were scurrying around the house, looking in closets and under beds, you stood by the wood-burning stove thawing out your blue jeans.

Life continued like any other family and the conversations grew to new heights. Dana, the quiet listener continued to smile and enjoy her brothers. Every now and then she found her voice and said something profound, and we all chimed in with, "That was funny Dana, good one." Spencer was easy to laugh and the one with an extended vocabulary and endless stories kept us on our toes, while you Jeff, the eternal mimic and king of one liners that never failed to entertain us.

A special treat was when we went on a road trip, Jeff you were the one who always called *shotgun* and road in the front seat, before we reached the end or our driveway you lightly touched the newly sagging skin under my arm, then began to sing a song you made up on the spot about *Jell-0.*

Soon after we moved into our new home out in the country, so did the Flickers. These pests are a cousin to Woodpeckers. The unwanted guests pulled off the vents from under the eaves and moved into my attic. My friend John, who built our home, replaced the vent wires with industrial strength and that was that. The next day these strong vents were also pulled off. I called the Nature Center and they suggested I use mothballs. I bought ten bags and Jeff, you climbed up on a ladder and Spencer handed you bag after bag, while you tossed the mothballs into the attic, as far as you could. Now, that's the end of that.

Next morning our circle drive way looked like it had snowed during the night. Those Flickers dropped mothballs on the driveway, no place else. I called the Agriculture office and he laughed, then suggested *Tangle Foot.* This super sticky substance will capture a bird and that'll be it.

Jeff, you climbed back up the ladder and squeezed the sticky gooey stuff onto the opening where the wires had been pulled back. We sat down for dinner and in no time; we ate to the sounds of thumping inside our attic. Not a pleasant sound. Well, that was that, we never saw another Flicker again. All the Flickers told all the other Flickers not to go near that brown house with green trim.

Next day I had a *freeze frame, a* scene I will never forget. I stood at my kitchen window, looked out to the walnut orchard to see my two sons, sitting back to back with a tree between them, same tree. Not moving a muscle, they sat and waited, each with a BB gun. They waited and waited. Two snipers, waiting for just one Flicker to dare fly into a no Flicker zone. Forever etched into my mind, the brothers, sitting and waiting.

Jeff, thanks for saving our attic, for entertaining us and for all the frown lines.

No matter how hard the past,
you can always begin again.
Buddha

KARMA PSYCHIC

TWELVE YEARS AFTER YOU DIED I visited a medium, and one by one my children followed my lead. Her name is Mary Kay, which I first thought was a bad omen because I am allergic to *Mary Kay* products. But on the day of my scheduled appointment, I took an extra long hot shower to relax and prepare. I passed up breakfast and lunch and instead drank two bottles of water. I was so incredibly nervous I was shaking inside and couldn't control my emotions. I sat in my car and waited in the parking lot. While there, I spoke to you, Jeff: "Okay, I am going in there, and if you want to tell me something, I'm open."

I went upstairs and knocked on the plain white door. No answer. Fifteen minutes passed so I called her cell phone. She forgot. As far as signs go, this was a huge negative. How could someone with special skills as a medium forget? I reluctantly made a second appointment for the following day. I ate a hearty breakfast, threw on my blue jeans and a top, and headed to her office. Hopefully, she'll remember, I thought. Mary Kay came in, introduced herself, lit some candles, and sat down. She was in her mid-thirties and was a natural beauty. She apologized for the previous day, and began to stretch her neck and relax her body. Then she looked towards me, actually over towards my left shoulder, and the first words out of her were, "There is a young man standing next to you. He has light sandy golden hair, and he is about twenty. He is very excited, over the top with joy, and he is very animated. He wants me to tell you that he has waited a long time for you to reach him. I see the letters J, no ff, Jff."

I replied, "Jeff."

Mary Kay expressed that she had never seen a spirit so excited. "He is telling me to tell you it was an accident." I was dumbfounded, and a little scared of the process. I began feeling anxious as I jotted notes very quickly and received long-awaited information through Mary Kay's relayed messages. "He wants me to tell you 'I'm okay, I'm in charge. I can do as I please and go where I want to go. I have the power I've always wanted.'" I was quiet, and stunned. Mary Kay went on, "He wants you to know you don't have to be here; you already know what is going on. There's no need for you to come back to see me because you could do this yourself. He wants you to know he is in a powerful place and is watching his family. He asked me to tell you not to be so sad. Jeff also wants me to tell you to say 'Hi' to Gene from him."

This is crazy, I thought. No one here knows Gene; he lives in another town. I finally spoke up and said aloud so Jeff could listen (if that is how this works), "I can't do that. Jeff has been gone from us for twelve years, his dad will think I'm crazy if I tell him, *Jeff says Hi.*"

Next she told me, "Jeff says he is has been watching David and likes what he doing."

I was even more dumbfounded. It had been ten years or more since I'd spoken to David, the son I gave birth to and gave up for adoption when I was a teenager, and who now lived in Arkansas. I'd called him when Jeff died, and he'd called me back after he regained his composure to tell me that he'd gone out to his parents' porch, sat on the top steps, and cried like a baby for the brother he had just met and was just getting to know. Because Mary Kay had said Jeff liked what David was doing, I later phoned and asked David what he had been doing and explained about the medium. David told me he had been building condos in Branson, Missouri.

The medium spent over an hour with me, and the messages were from Jeff only. She said many older women and a man, a tall man with gray hair, was standing next to me, but Jeff wouldn't let anyone else in. How had this message arrived from my deceased son to me, I wondered. There are so few people who know his real dad, and no one knows his older brother's name. Mary Kay was quick to continue. She said she was relaying messages to me quickly as this spirit is very active and has much more communication to share. She said, "He wants you to know he has Sheba with him too. He is very clear on his demands." Mary Kay continued by saying, "He wants you to be happy for him, not sad." As she talked, I jotted notes as quickly as I could. I am now looking at my messy handwriting and the disjointed phrases I'd scrawled on a yellow legal pad as I type this for my book. My dad was never mentioned in this session although I suspect he was the tall graying man next to me.

Mary Kay miraculously picked up on one more detail. When I had a birthday, our family all met in Nevada City where we walked around town. Dana took her daughters into a fairy store and bought some fairy dust which she sprinkled on Audrey's head. Mary Kay chuckled as she said, "Jeff wants me to tell you something very unusual. It makes me laugh, sorry. He wants me to tell you that he liked the fairy dust. Does this make any sense?" Oh yes, it makes perfect sense, I thought. When my session was over, Mary Kay asked me if I was interested in working with her. She told me that I have potential to read and be clairvoyant. This didn't surprise me as I can recall having visions of scenes that couldn't have happened yet they did indeed happen; but at that time I was too invested in my own quest. Plus I was shocked with this reading. I think I answered with a "maybe."

She continued with "He wants you to refer to him as Uncle Jeff when talking to his nieces. He said he sees a male child in the future." I thought at the time that meant Dana was going to have another child. Then just recently, Spencer and Cassie welcomed a baby boy into their lives.

Note to readers: I had never met Mary Kay before. She didn't even know my last name, or that I had children, and certainly knew nothing about my son who had passed on. Not even my closest friends know Jeff's father's name is Gene. David was the baby taken from me when I was fifteen. His name was unknown to most of my friends at the time, and this reading with Mary Kay was before I wrote a book about David's birth. I am going through this with you so you can grasp the power of my medium visit.

Jeff, you then said, via Mary Kay, to prove it was really you, "Remember the tractor and the baseball hat?" Jeff, one of my favorite photos is of you and Grandpa Harris coming down the drive from the orchard on a tractor, and you are wearing a baseball hat. You were about five years old.

After hearing about my experience, Dana went in to see Mary Kay a few weeks later. Her appointment was such an astounding and accurate exchange of information that we decided Spencer had to go visit Mary Kay too. Indeed he did, but it took us two years to get him on board. He kept saying he was too busy. He was in college at the University of Nevada in Reno, a three-plus-hour drive away, and because of his studies and weekend job, we had to wait. Dana and I didn't nag him too much.

Well Jeff, when Dana sat down across from Mary Kay, the medium looked at her (not knowing she was my daughter and not knowing about your passing). She told Dana that she saw many ladies with gray hair around her, including one very short woman with curly hair and a little dog (this had to be Grandma Harris), and one with pure white hair (this had to be Marion). Mary Kay said the woman with white hair was surrounded with gold and shiny crystals. (Remember Marion's gold flocked wallpaper in the living room and dining room? And her chandeliers?) Mary Kay said, "They are happy and want to visit, but there is a young man who won't settle down. His spirit is taking over the session. He is a young man, fair-haired, and he says you are gullible. He tells me that when you were a young girl, he said for you to look into the hose to see why the water won't come out, and then he turned the water on." Dana remembered that incident very well. Mary Kay also asked Dana, "Do you remember a gray cat? He wants you to know he has your cat, Helen (named after Mt. St. Helens). He also wants you to remember gathering crawdads." Then Mary Kay said something extremely startling to Dana: "This young man with light-brown curly hair thinks you are doing a good job as a mother to his nieces. He loves his nieces and wants you to refer to him as Uncle when you talk about him." Much more was said, which is private, but Mary Kay really hit it. Dana said she was amazed and naturally moved by your requests, she stayed strong and listened carefully.

How could she know this stuff?

Spencer finally went in for his appointment. Two years we waited. Jeffrey, your sister and mother are very tricky. Neither of us told her about our relationship with this new tall man who came in for a reading. Then in walked Spencer. He said she lit some candles and he could smell incense. His reading is for the most part private, but the gist of it was as follows: Mary Kay told Spencer there was a young man next to him. "He wants you to know that he has been with you all the way. He was with you when you traveled to India. He, your brother, was with you each time you climbed a mountain and he sat next to you on the summit." Mary Kay also told Spencer, "Your brother walked across the stage with you when you graduated from college, and he wants to thank you for living the life he would have wanted." She said that you also really like Spencer's girlfriend (Cassie, now his wife). Spencer was shocked and very open to her about your death, Jeff. She kept repeating that you really liked his girlfriend and his dog and that you are with him on all his travels.

The three readings of the medium—for me, for Dana, and for Spencer—each had a different feel. Mine was full of profound statements and requests, indicating you still order me around. Dana's reading was heartfelt, including many childhood memories as well as her life today with a focus on her two daughters, the nieces who will never meet you, their Uncle Jeff. Spencer's reading stressed brotherly love and a kinship in your activities, and was also very heartwarming.

All in all, Mary Kay's readings were so complex and full of personal information that I do believe she has a true gift and the ability to share these moments with your spirit with our family. I have tried to use my *untrained ESP gifts*, sometimes attempting to summon you when I'm feeling lonely. Nothing happens. But when I least expect it, your picture will be on the floor next to my bed, or I'll get a message on the desk at work from a girl who "knows Jeff" and wants you to call her. This message appeared twenty-three years after your death! Or I will stumble on to a poem you wrote, or I'll think I see you. I watch and wonder, and at the same instant, one of your favorite songs comes on the radio, *You're Still the One*. Maybe I'm looking for tiny droplets of hope through these *sightings*. It's okay. I'm not hurting anyone. It's my journey and my choice.

When I think of you, my son, as a spirit, the animated spirit Mary Kay encountered, I want to be happy, but still I have doubts. I just do. I have no idea how Mary Kay knew all this information. I guess there is much we don't understand in the universe and the spirit world.

I was so wrong to think that a medium can't forget things, such as my first appointment. I was also wrong to think a medium can't know details of my life. Thank you, Mary Kay. We are so lucky that you chose our town to open up your business and share your gift with us.

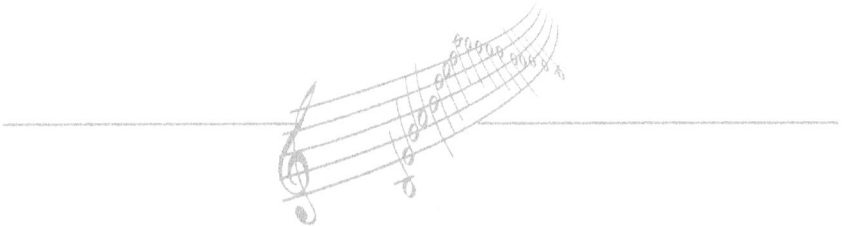

Learn how to see.
Realize that everything connects to everything else.
Leonardo da Vinci

A Hero's Luncheon

DONORS ARE REAL HEROES IN THIS WORLD OF OURS. If the deceased is brought to the hospital in time, or kept on a ventilator at a hospital, a team of doctors can quickly remove the organs and soft tissue, which is called harvesting, and they will have recipients waiting for these organs and tissues that will give them life or health or sight. The parent or spouse often has to make the decision to allow harvesting within minutes. There is no time to have a hot cup of tea and ponder this idea. Jeff, I had mere minutes to give permission after I'd been given the news, over the phone, that you had died. I don't regret my decision—I know this is what you wanted—but it was still a very difficult choice to make, at least it was for me.

My friend Joanie's grandson Beau was hit by a car one Saturday night as he crossed a busy street in Fresno. He stopped, looked, waited, and after the last car whizzed past, he stepped into the path of a car hidden from his view on the far side. His mom, Kristi, whom I've known since she was born, had to make this same decision. But, unlike the decision I made in 1990, she received information. She knew her son's gift would help a high school boy in Alaska, who was fighting for each breath he took, and who desperately needed a new, strong heart. After he received Beau's donated heart, and after the recipient healed, Kristi, her daughter, and her parents and her brother met the recipient. He and his parents flew in from Alaska to meet them for lunch. Joanie said he seemed healthy and very grateful for Beau's heart. Joanie said he looked so sweet and happy, he is forever grateful, and now has a bright future. He let them feel his chest and Beau's beating heart. Kristi gave him photos of her handsome son Beau, knowing that a part of him still lives on and that he saved this boy who was on the brink of death. After lunch the recipient and his parents repeated thank you many times, and they all hugged. I haven't followed this too closely, but Joanie did say that the boy in Alaska is still in contact with Beau's mom Kristi, who continues to share intriguing stories about Beau, whose heart still beats.

Eighteen years after your death, I began to investigate the transplant banks and to seek answers. Where did everything go? Where are the recipients living who received your gifts of life or sight? Unfortunately, I was unable to locate your recipients as too much time had lapsed. But I believe they must have files somewhere so will try again.

The Donor Transplant Association invited us to a Donor Appreciation luncheon in Sacramento. When we walked in, 300 donor family members were seated at round tables, six to a table. We sat next to a couple about my age, but perhaps because we were smack dab in front by the stage, no one else sat with us. We learned about the couple's son Jason, a Marine who returned from deployment, his second tour of Iraq. Four months after he returned from his tour of duty, he was riding his motorcycle when he was hit and killed. Then I shared my story about you. Both you boys were so young when you died.

We each received a booklet with photos of all the 100 donors accompanied by a short synopsis of their life and how they died. I opened the booklet and found your photo, and reread the synopsis to be sure it was printed as I'd wished. Then I noticed the young man's picture on the page next to yours. I showed the couple next to me that our sons shared a page in the booklet. Jason's mother thought that was a weird coincidence, but she didn't know me very well, and weird is my middle name.

For page after page, I looked at faces and read about lives cut short—a guy tubing down a river with a friendly smile, his red hair in a ponytail; an older man dressed in a suit, killed while on vacation; a little girl with a birthday party hat, who was killed in an auto accident a few months later; the portrait of a once-functioning person in her work place. These pictures, taken when these people were very much alive, really put the tragedy of their death into perspective.

We each had to stand up and say the name of our loved one who was a donor. For some reason, when I said your name, as usual my eyes began to burn. The lady next to me could only whisper her son's name.

Then a line of people came on stage—kids, men and women of all ages and races. All were recipients who thanked us, and gave us a round of applause, and thanked us again for the gift of life. Then a man came out on the stage and placed a very large photo of a young boy with freckles, short dark hair, and a wide grin on an easel. He told the story of his nine-year-old son who was attending a birthday party, running and playing chase with the other kids. Suddenly, the father heard a loud crack and watched as a large tree branch snapped and hit his son as he ran around the tree, killing him instantly. It was tragic and random, and within hours the boy's heart was beating inside someone else. The next speaker was a woman whose shiny shoulder-length brown hair swung from side to side as she stepped up to the microphone wearing a red dress and matching heels. She appeared healthy and was glowing, then introduced herself as a recipient of that boy's heart. She told the crowd about her heart condition and impending death as she'd waited for a donor. Since she received one, and got her life back, she now tours donor luncheons telling her story to bring attention to the gift of life. She told us she was grateful she had received the heart from the little boy killed at the birthday party.

We got in line at the buffet table and shared stories as we waited for our food. A young man in front of us turned and asked me to show him which one in the booklet we were related to. I flipped the pages and pointed to your photo, Jeff. He looked at me and said, "He looks like you." Then he flipped back a few pages and pointed to a photo of his three-year-old daughter, Megan, who had a big grin and messy golden wispy hair. After telling me she drowned in their backyard swimming pool, he pointed towards their table, specifically to a boy about twelve years old who was waiting for lunch. I assumed it was his son, but he said that the young boy over there has Megan's heart.

The day was overwhelming, informative, and exhausting. Massive information was being shared in all directions; everyone wanted to show their relative's photo and tell their story. I overheard people thanking families, saw others shaking hands and hugging another who now had their mother's liver or had gained eyesight through a corneal transplant. I noticed that most people knew each other from attending annual luncheons, but once was enough for me. It was nice, and did bring some peace, but I only need one heart-wrenching booklet. I realized that day was the first time I truly felt thankful and proud. I usually squawked, moaned, and whined over your loss and desperately wanted you back. But your gift to others meant some recipient got something very valuable from you.

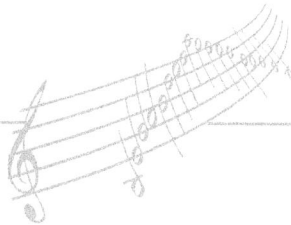

For more information, you can go online to www.dcids.org
There is also a Donate Life California organ and tissue donor registry:
www.donateLIFEcalifornia.org and www.doneVIDAcalifornia.org

A mother's love for her child is
like nothing else.
Agatha Christie

SUICIDE PREVENTION WALK

THIS PAST FALL, I ATTENDED A SUICIDE PREVENTION WALK with family members and a host of other survivors. The Suicide Prevention Memory Walk in downtown is an annual event of respect to the departed. Many people love you, Jeff, but on this day, just the few of us who had the time walked together to honor your memory. My neighbor had helped me make tags to hang around our necks, with your name printed with a background of a Scottish plaid, so everyone who saw us could plainly see who we were walking for. I'd stayed in emotional neutral gear, or so I thought, as Pete and I slipped into the car and headed to the City Plaza on that crisp Saturday morning. I held the placards on my lap and carefully kept the twine from becoming tangled, ready to hand these to our family before the walk. I secretly hoped so much that Dana would be there too.

As we parked a few blocks away and made our way towards the plaza, I was not expecting such a large number of survivors and walkers to be milling about. We stood around and waited for the group of walkers to get together as more people began to slowly walk towards the center area and meander around. While we waited, I saw Pete's daughter Kari, who would have been your step-sister if you'd stayed around, walking towards us. She seems uncomfortable but pleased to be with us, and I was so impressed that she made it. Pete and his daughter Kari are two people who never met you, but feel a strong family connection.

Your sister Dana had said she would try to come. Still, I was feeling okay, mostly solid though a bit apprehensive because this was new territory. This composure and sure-footedness all changed when I spotted Dana walking towards us with her arms folded. I know her body language. She wore sunglasses and she didn't want to talk. Instantly my eyes began to burn. Waves of sadness flew in and out of my head, and we avoided each other's eyes.

There was a group of college kids with large clumps of tin foil twisted like a chocolate kisses and the little paper at the tip of the Kiss wrapper had the name Kelly on it. This big sparkling shiny chocolate kiss was glued to the backs of their sweatshirts. Most family and friends had some sort of unity with a photo on a t-shirt or hats, or pickets with a photo of their loved one which they held up with pride as they looked for more family members. The group gathering was unnaturally quiet, and the fall morning with gusts of frigid air kept us close together.

There were speakers on stage, including a woman who read excerpts from her book about her son's death. Kari got teary-eyed as she now has three young sons of her own, and could relate to our loss. Next speaker was the anchor guy from the morning station; he is of medium height, with thick black hair and a round face, and he seems like a cheerful guy. He addressed everyone standing in the middle the city plaza, saying that he suffers from depression and has thought of taking his life many times. He was very emotional, and he choked up and became red-faced, but he continued to talk about his internal battle with these reoccurring thoughts. He is Mr. *Happy* on the morning show, and I never imagined he suffers so. He is a local celebrity and his speech, given prior to the walk, was very moving and heartfelt. He announced to the crowd who began to gather close to the stage that this was the first time he has admitted his dark thoughts and depression, being a public figure and all. His confession was impressive, because he had the courage to admit in public that he had such a dark side.

The announcement echoed over the plaza that we were to head out, and the walk began. Pete and Kari walked in front, Dana and I directly behind. All four of us wore your name around our necks, fastened with white twine. The mass of people took command of the sidewalk as we walked silently north to the end of Main Street then turned left onto First Street. Our mass of survivors continued to walk towards the University campus, then past Laxson Auditorium and the tall red brick buildings on campus. We walked next to bright green sprawling lawns and manicured hedges. The huge trees that line the California State University campus provided a canopy of shade and the fall colors of orange and yellow leaves blew across our path and circled around us. This part of our walk was very soothing. Then our massive group took another left turn, onto Ivy Street, and headed towards Fifth Street where we made yet another left and walked on until we could see the Plaza once again. Guides at each corner pointed the way. Bystanders gathered on corners or watched from the sidelines in respect.

There was little talking amongst the walkers. It was essentially a massive silent walk for the memory of our loved ones. The eerie and haunting part of this walk was the mass of people and the silence; no one was talking out loud, only whispering. If someone not involved with the walk was coming towards us, they silently stepped off the curb and let us pass.

I saw groups of college kids and what were obviously families walking together. I saw some loners wandering around looking lost and deep in thought. Many people shed tears; some openly cried and wiped their faces. Many were holding hands or hugging. I noticed one photo on a t-shirt worn by all the members of one group, that of a middle-aged Hispanic woman, and I wondered why she had left her children. Dana and I talked quietly and wiped our eyes, recapping your life as we walked along the familiar streets of happier times.

As we stepped in the direction noted, we filtered like a funnel of pebbles onto a path. Thoughts exploded inside my head, and to my surprise, my thoughts of you were a mix of regrets and pure sadness. I found myself thinking that, by taking your life, you left behind the message that your family and relationships meant nothing to you. You preferred being dead to watching your little brother grow up and your sister bloom into a beautiful woman. In taking your own life, you took away their innocence. Spencer, only thirteen-going-on-fourteen, admired you so. He looked up to you as a mentor and friend. Dana, heading towards sixteen and looking forward to getting her driver's license, had no sadness or stress in her life until you died.

You must have been in a state of mind to end it all. I wonder if the last thing on your mind was your family, regrets, and goodbyes. I can only imagine your terror and the trance you must have put yourself in to proceed with your plan. I hope you were somewhere else, far away in thought, because if you were thinking about us when you ended your life, it would be even more painful for me to comprehend. I suppose this violent act unfolded as the right thing for you to do; it was either your way to end your pain or the curious place your mind had gone. If only you knew, if only you had waited, I swear, Jeff, your life would have unfolded and worked itself out.

Jeffrey, dear boy, by ending your natural life and changing the path you were to walk, neither you nor anyone else will never know your potential as a human being. The children you might have had will never be born, the love of your life is with someone else, your potential as a fabulously talented musician remains untapped forever. Sigh ... I recall being angry with you as I walked, thinking of all the times I made you brush your teeth when you didn't want to. Heck, if I'd known you weren't going to live a long life, I'd have let you eat ice cream and trot off to bed. Why did I bother? Because this is what my mother taught me. You learned how to behave on a date, to let the ladies go before you, to open car doors; and you knew how to be respectful and to speak the King's English with proper grammar. You would have an edge on kids who didn't know etiquette and didn't smile with sparkly white teeth, which would help you in job interviews and your future. But this was not to be.

Lisa told me that when she was your girlfriend in high school, you sent her red roses with a beautiful note. She was so pleased to show me the photo her mom took of her sitting at her dining-room table covered by a lace tablecloth beside the roses. I looked closely at this picture and gasped. Granted, the roses were beautiful, but I zeroed in the red t-shirt she was wearing. It was the one I thought I'd lost. So you took my favorite top and gave it to Lisa! It's okay now, it's all okay. Now the missing shirt mystery has been solved. When she showed me the photo of her with the roses, she went on to say that you were very polite. I melted a little inside, proud that you did listen after all. Thoughts such as these rattled around in my head as I walked with so many strangers, all wearing special t-shirts, or signs around their necks that bore the names of their loved one.

Jeff, you knew you were loved but were very angry the last year of your life. People reached out to help you, but your stubborn streak got in the way. Will this memory of you and of your death ever float away so I can be truly happy? Let's be honest here; I know the answer: a survivor of suicide will never be without a swinging pendulum of sadness and regret.

Suicide changes everything; birth order of siblings, trust, confidence, and spiritual beliefs. Some survivors go deep towards a church and God, while others drift away and are angry with this so-called loving God. It dims the light in the hearts of the innocent who are left behind to cope. Did you think about all that before you took your life, Jeff?

We hope, weather permitting, to do the Suicide Walk every year. It's a wonderful way to remember you, to keep your memory alive, and to help to bring suicide prevention to the attention of the general public. Spencer said he'd join us next year if possible, and we are hoping Cassie will too, with their new baby. Dana said your nieces want to walk for you too. Lord, the little ones walking for you next time, Uncle Jeff, will be a bittersweet sight. Tammy, your cousin, said she will walk with us next year too.

Before we left the Plaza, I bought three t-shirts with *Out of the Darkness* printed in light gray on dark gray. There were also tables with brochures about suicide prevention and many counselors on hand, and books for sale. And lots of breakfast foods, including really unhealthy things like donuts, bear claws, and jelly rolls, plus free bottled water, coffee, and hot tea.

Walking silently in the steps you had walked so many times really brought this home to me and your sister. Jeff, for eight years I owned a business on Second Street, where you worked for me on weekends, and, well, it was just that everywhere I looked on this particular day I saw you around every corner and felt your presence with every step. I know you were indeed with us.

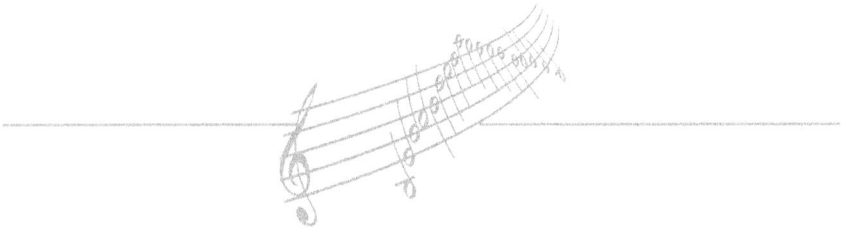

I love me boy
–Mom

THE BIRTHDAY PARTY

Unedited messages to Jeff on his 40th Birthday:

Today is Jeffs 40th birthday, so hard to believe, he was a darling little boy. I remember him lying on a blanket in the backyard and he was happy and smiling. He melted my heart. When he was bigger, Kristi and Jeff like to play together.

When Jeff was older and lived in Lakeport he had a cute little apartment. He would come to Papa and Marions and play the piano, so good looking. I wish I had tried to be closer to him then, Love, Aunt Shari

Dear Jeff,
When Aunt Judi told me she was going to have a baby I was so excited! Visiting in Bakersfield, the anticipation was overwhelming. I wasn't allowed to go into your nursery, for fear of germs, only peer inside from the door! This only added to the mystery. When you finally arrived, I finally had a baby to play with. You were the most beautiful baby. When you moved to Windsor I came for a visit and pushed you in the swing which seemed like hours! You just smiled and laughed. Who knew what a hysterical, funny young man you would become.

    You were so quick and funny and you always got the last laugh. I wish I had been closer to you, but miles kept us apart.
I cherish the times we were together and memories of you always make me laugh! You were just so darn funny.
Love and miss you,
Your cousin,
Tammy

There are certain people that come into your life and you just want to claim them. Jeff was one of these people. Every time I think of him it is as vivid as if it were yesterday. I remember hanging out at your house and Jeff sitting there making wise cracks and busting us up. He had such a wonderful irreverent take on everything. I always loved running into him. He was so much like you. I always had secret plans that one day he'd get together with my sister.
Katie Longoria

Dana, Spencer and Keith

To whom it may concern,

Hello, I'm Keith. Friend of Jeffs! On this day, which would have been Jeffs 40th birthday, being 40 myself, met up with Judi, Dana, and Spencer after about 17 years of not seeing each other. What a blast! Feeling old now—but still young at heart.

Memories of Jeff are all good, and with today more good ones come back—some I had forgotten all about. Anyway—rambling trying to say something to go down into history—

First game with Jeff—trek ball.

Best movie to watch with Jeff—Poltergeist

Best song to listen to with Jeff—Stars on 45

Song Jeff liked to tease—New Years Day U2

Jeff best played classical song—Invention # 4 by Bach

Jeffs crazy faces: the demon, the bug, the iguana, Madame Livingston, blip,

Back to Poltergeist, Jeff memorized the entire speech of that midget lady who was the exorcist, did it word for word with the perfect accent.

Jeff quickest wit funniest guy I've ever met, often in thought—

Keith

Dear Jeff,
My memories of you are very sweet and special. You were my
boyfriend in the 10th grade. Every time I hear the song
Hotel California I think of you, and when you did the lip sync in
front of our school and sang it for me. You threw me a necklace that
I still have. I loved seeing you play the guitar and ham it up on stage.

Everyone wanted you in their song.
You cut your hair because of my dad. (That was so big). But I liked it
long. I was happy when it grew back... Whenever I think of you, I
always smile. Thank you for showing me how a boyfriend should be.
You set the standards high for me.

Now I have my little boy who was born on your birthday, he has
red hair and brown eyes. And yes he's a non stop, on the go kind of
kid :)
Thank you for this time
Lisa.

Jeff and Lisa at the Prom

My brother Jeff was easily the funniest person I ever knew. He was very clever and witty, and was very good at impersonating people (like Dana and me). He was wild! We were always playing practical jokes on each other, and doing things that we should not have done if we had known better.

Jeff was also an incredible musician. It seemed like he could play any instrument that he got his hands on, and that really inspired me to play music. To this day, I continue to play music, and try new things. I think that is a direct result of Jeffs influence on me.

As my big brother, I always looked up to Jeff, and wanted to be like him. Later in life we saw each other less because of competing forces of life (friends, work, family), and we both had changed. Jeff was always exploring and pushing the boundaries, and in a lot of ways he felt that the rules for everybody else didn't apply to him.

As I sit here writing this on what would have been Jeffs 40th birthday, I feel thankful to have had him as a big brother, but also sad that he isn't here to celebrate this day with us.

Some people live an entire lifetime within a few short years. Jeff was one of those people. People like that always leave a mark on the people who are around them. Jeff made quit a mark on everybody.

Spencer wearing Jeff's leather jacket

I will always love, and miss my big bro, but I will also do my best to help his memory live on.

♡

Love ya Dude!

Spencer

Spencer, Dana and Jeff
Castle Construction

Judi, Spencer, Jeff and Dana

"Hi mom" I heard
haveing a birth
Happy birthd
happy birthday
happy birthday
happy birthday
I love me mom
I love me

Protective Jeff, Dana
and Spencer

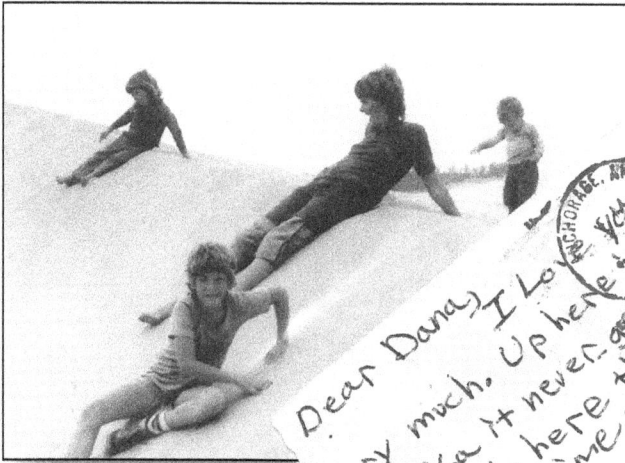

Dana, Judi, Spencer and Jeff

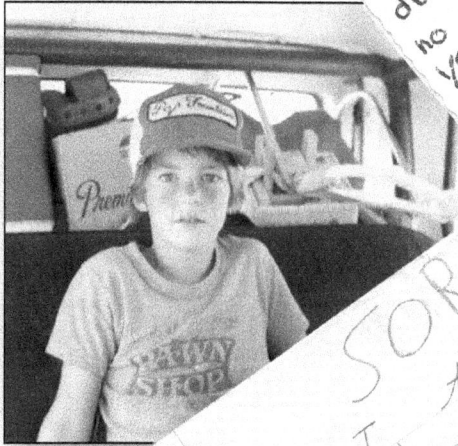

Jeff

Dear Dana, I Love you
very much. Up here in
Alaska it never gets
dark. Up here there is
no nighttime. I miss
you.
                    Love Jeff

Dana
#2

Dana, Spencer
and Jeff

SORRY

Mom
I threw a rock at
I she was bothering me
            mean to hit her
                to scare her
                            not

                                    sorry
                                    her lip
                                            see
                                    and
                            ships
                        nered
                    to thro
                        but
                    axede
dirt
    to
                and the lips
                                SORRY

Kids at the lake.

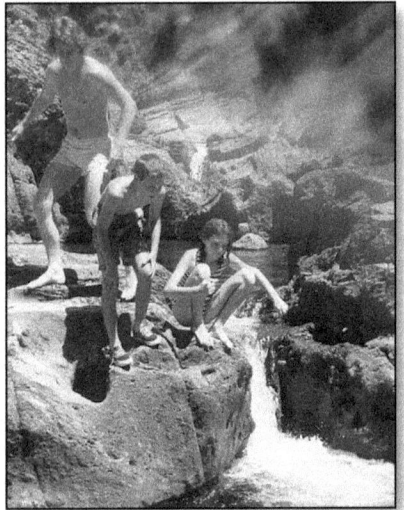

Jeff, Spencer and Dana
at Lake Oroville

Jeff playing piano
for Sarah

Judi and Jeff at the beach

Day at the lake

Spencer, Jeff, John and Dana

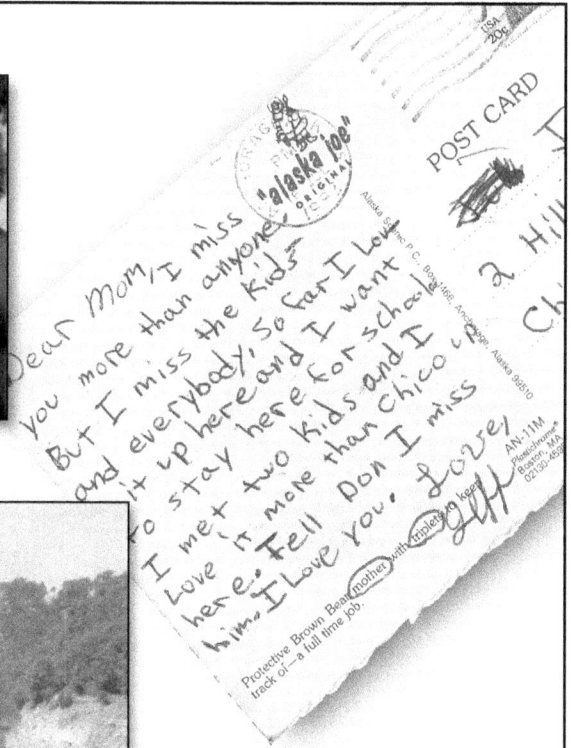

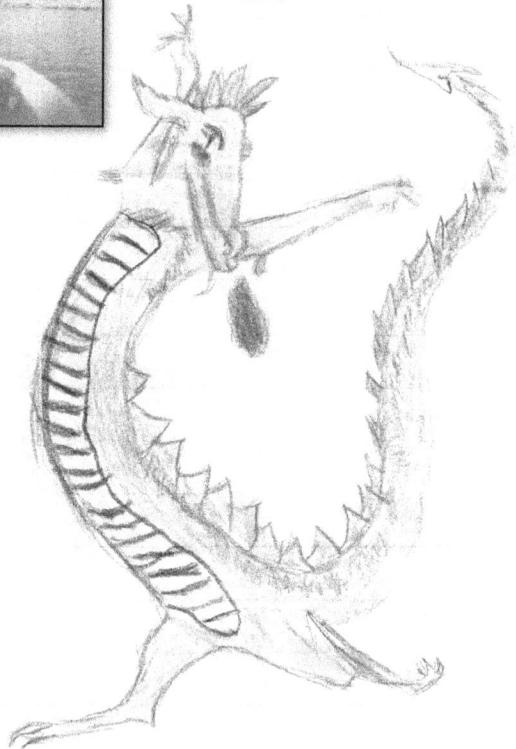

Dear Mom, I miss you more than anyone. But I miss the kids and everybody. So far I love it up here and I want to stay here for school. I met two kids and I Love it more than Chico up here. Tell Don I miss him. I Love you. Love, Jeff

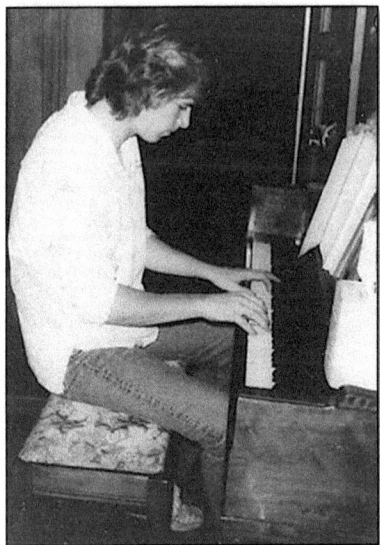

Jeff playing the piano

Drama Class performance

Pool Antics

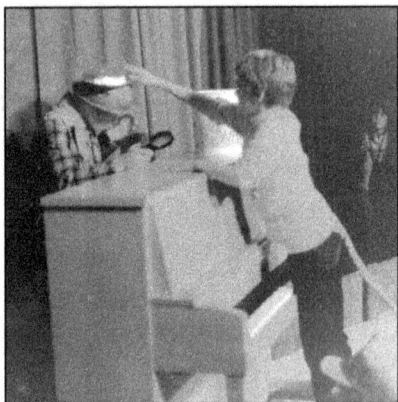

Infamous Pink Panther

The Totem Pole

Dana, Jeff, and
Spencer

Jeff and little sister, Sarah

Dad's Patio Bar

At Dana's piano recital

Dana, Spencer, and Jeff helping Nana

Jeff and Gene

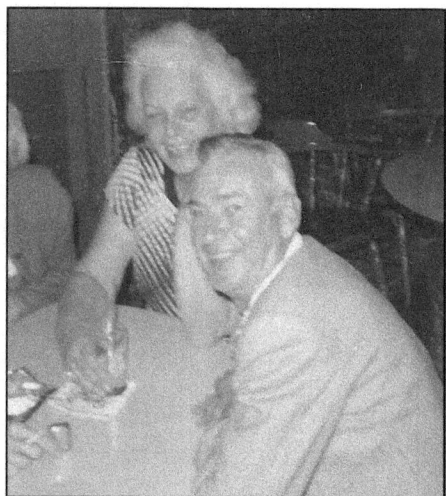

Marion and Dad

"I hope the recipients who received his eyes will see what wonders in the world he didn't see, the one who has his femur bones will *run like the wind* or walk for the first time, and the beautiful skin will give new and beautiful confidence."

Judi Loren
Mother of donor, Jeff Harris

Spencer, Cozumel

Dana and Lisa, Cozumel

Worn out kids, Cozumel

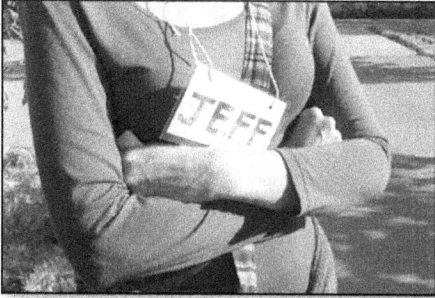

Dana at Suicide Prevention Walk

Dana, Sarah, and Spencer

Dana

Dana, Judi, and Spencer

Spencer and Shiny

Dana

Dana traveling in Turkey

Spencer mountain climbing

Spencer's Graduation

Dana and Spencer

I mean the heart and the spirit are connected to this God force and source, and you have to be quiet and listen to that.
Al Jarreau, jazz singer

THE NOTEBOOK

I TURNED ON OUR TELEVISION ONE DAY when you had just turned thirteen years old. Jazz singer Al Jarreau was singing *Mornin'*, his delivery as smooth as silk. You jumped off the couch, sat right in front of the screen, and asked, "Who is this? What kind of music is he singing?" We listened until the song was finished, and I explained to you about jazz. Later in the week I bought you the 8-track of Al Jarreau that you listened to over and over again. Jeff, you were fixated on this new sound. I could almost see the wheels turning in your head, and could see the joy in your eyes. I told you what information I could to satisfy your curiosity. I played *Dave Brubeck*, *Sérgio Mendes*, and *Aja* by *Steely Dan*, and some other long-playing albums, and I watched you lap it up.

Today, while *Dreamscape in A minor* was with the editor, I decided to return your box to storage, but first I sorted through papers you'd saved so long ago. All that was yours now tumbled out of a manila envelope onto my kitchen table. There was a certificate showing that you had taken and passed a gun safety course. Also there was a key chain you'd received from Narcotics Anonymous for being clean, with a white tab for perfect attendance. At the time of your death, you were forging ahead even as you slipped into darkness.

I still have your wallet, dear boy, the one you carried all the time, which left a faded square line in the back pocket of your blue jeans. Inside were your driver's license, $75 cash, a picture of me, and a photo of you and Brandi in a photo booth at the local fair. There was also an application from the DMV for a donor card.

Then, along with greeting and birthday cards, saved papers, and other evidence of a long ago active life came your maroon flip-page notebook. The last few months of your life, I watched from afar as you jotted down notes in this booklet, sometimes writing fast and furiously, occasionally stopping to look up and think before continuing to feverishly write your private thoughts. Within days after your death, then again a few years later with your brother when he was in his early twenties, I'd sat down to read your entries. It was gibberish—sometimes quotes and lyrics, sometimes crazy words on a page that made no sense at all to me. It had bothered me to some degree, but mostly brought sadness, as I was still too overcome with grief to fully grasp its contents. This changed today, twenty-four years later, when I began to read your notes with new fresh eyes.

I calmly sat down and read every page in an effort to decipher the scribbling, to grasp your thoughts, and to understand you. But this time, instead of starting at the front, I began reading from the back of your notebook and flipped forward. I suddenly realized that was the way you had entered your thoughts. Then as I grew closer to the end, the front of the notebook, I had a moment of clarity. You, dear son, were losing your grip on reality, hanging on by a thread. You'd scribbled down lyrics and words about friends and girls and death. Only a few words referred to *mother,* but one such entry was very sharp and hostile. Some of your scribbles are notes, such as a reminder for a job interview you had in Lakeport. This appointment was to be on Saturday, the day you died. It seems you were confused, slipping between reality and fantasy, and were still trying to cover all your bases by applying for a job.

You questioned many things in life, and most of your entries are hostile and disturbing. I read all the names or words along the sides, phrases squeezed in next to each other. I followed the arrows you drew towards other entries when a sickness like I had never felt before invaded my body. A dark shadow seemed to hover over me. You were done; you wanted to die; you were angry and didn't make any sense, at least most of it made no sense to me. But maybe to you, these notes made sense.

Even if I had read this notebook or looked inside your wallet prior to your death, I would never have assumed you were heading towards suicide. Still, I wish I could have somehow stopped the tide. Instead, your silent agony went unheard, and I was in denial. Me, the person at the helm. Because I am a survivor by nature, I made the ultimate mistake of assuming all my children would inherit my inner strength.

I looked through your medical records and came across your autopsy report. I sat down with the paperwork and opened the folded white papers and with a rapidly beating heart I began to read. *Healthy male,* any mother would be proud, but all I can think of is, *why?* Then, the words jumped out at me, the report states that you were *drug free* and *alcohol free. Everything* about you was healthy. You had one tattoo, between your thumb and forefinger; a tiny dot. This killed me, *yes, it is you.* I remember seeing this dot and I was not happy with you for getting a tiny blue dot tattoo. Boy Jeff, you should see the kids today. Tattoos creating sleeves and full body tattoos are the new *dot.* I was fixated on the report; *you did it son, you were off drugs.* You never were one to drink, and you were physically well. Your problem was psychological, this is such a loss. Papers are back in the envelope, back in the box, and back into storage.

Jeffrey, I hear you now. I'm listening. Your life and death had a purpose. Your story, your notes that make no sense yet so vividly communicate your state of mind, will help other families pay attention. I promise.

I thought that I heard you laughing
I thought that I heard you sing
I think I thought I saw you try
        R.E.M.

No one can say how much our lives have been altered since you and your grandfather died. If you were still alive, would we be the same people we are today? How did your actions change our lives and the choices we've made?

Meilani, Dana's friend from *Rainbow Girls*, who was with us that fateful weekend, left our home that evening with a friend and never returned. After the scene in my bedroom, when the phone rang with news of your death and our reaction, the friendship essentially ended. Dana grieved the deaths of her brother and grandfather, and the loss of a friend. Years later, Meilani finally contacted Dana and reflected on her feelings about that ill-fated night. At the time, Meilani was taking a class in psychology at the local University and had been assigned to write an essay on the worst day of her life and to then stand up before the class and read her story. Meilani told Dana that her essay was about the day she went for a weekend trip with our family, and returned to our house to receive the news of her friend's brother's death, and hearing her friend's mother's animal gut-wrenching sobs, while she and Dana hugged each other and cried. This was the worst day of her life. Meilani got an A on her essay.

Jeff, I wrote my story about grief and healing to better understand your life, and to help others in similar situations, perhaps other parents with a child such as you. I'd like to think reading your story might curb the idea of suicide for those thinking about taking their own life, or help their loved ones recognize the signs of impending suicide.

I do feel that I can now move forward. Although I thought I had healed after so many years, and after writing my first book, *The Third Floor*, I now realize I have been suffering for twenty-four years since your death and the death of your grandfather. I hadn't grieved for my father until I wrote this book. I just put him in the background and pretended he was still in Lakeport or somewhere obscure.

The chapters of your childhood to your last days revealed a life that I didn't understand for all those years, but now your life has become crystal clear to me. I can better understand your journey as I remember events in your life and recognize in hindsight the signs that the end was creeping closer. For me, and my personality, tucking this story deep inside obviously didn't work. Facing the reality of your troubled life has allowed me to better understand what happened and why.

Marion never recovered from witnessing the results of a double shooting in her garage. The home she was born and raised in, and lived in until her death, had become a daily reminder of a nightmare. She became angry with me after she lost her husband and her bitterness towards me lasted for years. She never seemed to consider that I had lost my father and my son. Not once did I receive any condolences or compassion from her. Her health began to decline as she continued to lose her appetite and her will to live. She never wavered, however, from the comfort she got from a good smoke from her floral-papered cigarettes and a tall cool Vodka Collins. Both passions began early each day and never waned.

Towards the end of her life, I was visiting her, perhaps because I like to torture myself and because I felt the need to make it right between us. She asked me to please mix her a drink. I went into the dining room, phoned her son George and asked him what I should do. She was obviously frail, and I wasn't sure if a mixed drink with alcohol was a good idea. George laughed, and told me to fill the glass with ice cubes, add the Collins mix only, and then rattle the ice cubes so she could hear them. I did as instructed and walked back into her sitting room. The cubes clanged on the sides of the glass as I held it close to her ear. I placed the cold glass into her frail aged hand, and watched her slowly put the drink up to her lips and sip. She then looked up at me and said, "Oh, that's dandy." Marion lived fourteen more years after the tragedy.

Jeff's dad Gene and Patty kept to themselves. We didn't hear from them for two decades. I popped into Gene's office soon after my father's funeral when I went to a meeting with an attorney whose office was in the courthouse where Gene works. Whenever he sees me, he tears up, probably because my face is a reminder of our son. He and Patty are basically the same people; they still live in their dome-style house on the Russian River that moves slowly towards Jenner by the sea. Gene still works, in Santa Rosa, and Patty goes into town to help your sister Sarah and her husband Andrew with their new baby boy. Patty babysits their grandson Josiah one or two days a week. I give them a call now and then, and we talk about our grandkids and life. We're growing older so we've nixed the Christmas cards.

Your girlfriend Lisa is happily married and has three boys. Her oldest is in college, one in high school, and one coming up to junior high. She is very busy, and talented, and she is the same sweet girl I met so long ago when I watched her with Dana and Denise as they baked in the sun in Cozumel and danced till dawn. She is an artist and she recently painted a beautiful close-up of a red daisy as a gift for me.

Kristi, your cousin, now lives in her Grandmother Marion's home with her husband. She keeps the home mostly the same; your grandfather had remodeled the kitchen and it looks exactly as it did when he lived there, and it is still full of Marion's treasures. Every so often I will get a call from Kristi that she found your granddad's ledger, or his cast-iron frying pan, or a scrapbook Marion put together after his retirement. It is bittersweet to have his things, nothing can ever bring back my dad—your grandfather, or reinvent the flavor of his home, the weekend parties, or the sound of our family get-togethers.

I believe with every fiber of my being that you shot your grandfather accidently. You were sitting on two boxes with the gun on your lap, contemplating suicide when your grandfather completed his six-mile walk, entered the open garage, and raised his arm to wave hello as he usually does when he sees someone. The gun went off from your lap.

The police told me that when suicides are interrupted, this can result with a police officer being shot. The person contemplating suicide is so charged up, and in the zone, that when interrupted, the gun goes off like a knee-jerk reaction. I am sure, from studying the police reports and listening to Marion, that you waited approximately three minutes, and then turned the gun on yourself. You thought you had killed your grandfather. He did die, but not until six weeks later due to surgery for a bleeding ulcer, complicated by a weakened heart from a heart attack years prior.

There are a few who speculate that you were waiting in the garage and targeted your grandfather. This theory is inconceivable to me although no one will ever know for sure.

Anecdote about Your Grandfather: When your grandfather was to be discharged from the hospital after his heart attack in 1983, my sister and I went to his room to bring him home for a Christmas Eve celebration. Everyone he loved was to be there: the barbershop quartet he sang with, and his family. The nurse came in and unhooked his heart monitor, then we continued to wait in his room for the discharge nurse to come back to sign him out. Your grandfather was an impatient man. We watched the monitor flat-lining and we waited. He then said to us, "You girls get my bags; we're leaving." Like two little girls, instead of grown women, we picked up his housecoat and suitcase and quickly trotted along behind him, out the door of his room and down the shiny hallway. When he reached the front desk, he slapped the top of it with his hand and announced to the startled nurses, "Charles Geoble. I've been dead for twenty-five minutes," and off we went out the double doors. He was a firecracker.

Three weeks before the shootings, Dana, Spencer and I drove to Lakeport. Dad was expecting us, but we liked to think we were kidnapping him. I drove all four of us to Fort Bragg. What a great day we had as we drove over the mountains and listened to him share his expertise of the surrounding areas and landscapes, and his knowledge of the American Indians. He pointed out this ridge, and that valley, and

Dana, Grandpa, and Spencer leaving for Fort Bragg

showed us this grouping of natural habitat, that clump of trees; this next curve. "Now," he'd say, "look to the right," then he'd lecture us about the vernal pools. We dropped him off at his brother's house in Fort Bragg, then our plan continued to unfold as we met up with Patty and young Sarah and played on the beach all day. Dana snapped a picture of me and Patty as we stood next to each other pointing our fingers as if to say, "No, no, no, Jeff!" We giggled and decided this picture was for you. Unaware how far you'd slipped into the depths of despair, we were naïve to the darkness that loomed behind the horizon just a few weeks away.

Patty told me at Spencer's graduation party that this photo of us on the beach now haunts her. She confessed that she can hardly look at it, and I told her, me too. I have the same feeling towards that photo. It shows us concerned for you, joking around as usual and not accepting your choices in life, as your two mothers, we were scolding you in jest. This picture of me and Patty, with the ocean waves breaking behind us, is clearly a photo of innocence.

My firstborn, David, came into our lives when he was twenty-two years old and you were fifteen. You two unacquainted brothers roomed together in our garage that Don had remodeled into a large bedroom. You shared this space for four months, and then David was summoned home. It was a rocky start for you two half-brothers, but you did try to connect. You fished and talked, watched shows, but you had been raised differently, so it was an awkward dance for two people who shared no history and had much different interests. I made a huge mistake assuming this was a gift, the two of you rooming together. But you brothers had issues to work out from the beginning. David was jealous of our lifestyle, you were jealous of the attention David was getting. In spite of your rocky acquaintance, David says he is still affected by the news of your death, and like all of us, remembers to this day exactly where he was standing when he heard the horrific news.

Dana and Spencer: These innocents were exposed to the dark side of life, yet each grew up to be functioning, clever, and compassionate adults, seemingly untouched by the tragedy that was put before them. They keep this part of their childhood inside and privately tucked away in a part of their mind where they love, cherish, and remember you. They have never lost touch with their silly inner child. They are each happily married to mates that bring out the best in each of them, they are attentive loving parents, and they are well grounded. Both are into healthy foods and exercise. Dana is a runner and has tried the *Mud Blast* and *Tin Man* triathlon, and she and Billy are raising creative daughters who address you as their Uncle Jeff. Spencer and Cassie enjoy century (100-mile) bike rides, biking fund-raisers, and are also avid snow skiers. Now that they have a new baby boy, I guess they will be running with him in a stroller, and skiing with him as soon as he's big enough to stand on skis. My two surviving kids are very much aware of the environment, they don't lie, and they pay their taxes. As their mom, I couldn't ask for more.

Sarah: Jeff's youngest sister, grew to be a gorgeous woman with long curly golden blonde hair and large green eyes. She exudes confidence, is soft spoken but direct, and has a gentle manner. When I look into her eyes, I can see you Jeff. I can see you in Dana's expressions also, and Spencer shares your quick wit. Sarah and her husband Andrew are the parents of a young son Josiah. She and her family live in Santa Rosa, and she works in the same office as Gene, her dad.

My two step-children are adults now. Kari is married and raising her three little boys. Alex graduated with a degree in Health Science at CSU, then traveled to Europe, came home, and then moved to Australia. He is now engaged to Valeria, a girl from Italy. Though they never met you, they feel they know you well.

To this day, you are a sweet memory, sprinkled with joy and sadness. You left us with the love of music and the sound of your piano playing— *the best gift of all.*

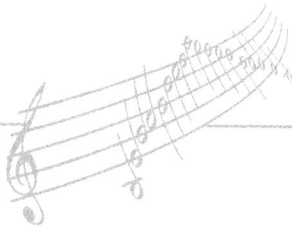

(Dreamscape)

IN THE MIND
LIES THE KEY
TO MAKE YOURSELF
WHAT YOU WANT TO BE

THE CHALICE OF LIFE
WITHIN YOUR SPIRIT
ITS CALLING OUT
~~IF YOU COULD ONLY HEAR IT~~ But you don't hear it

ITS THE DOMINATION
THE MAJESTIC POWER
YOU MUST LEARN TO USE IT
By ~~BEFORE~~ THE FINAL HOUR

I ONCE NEW A GIRL
THIS POWER SHE HAD
FOR A LIFETIME JOURNEY
IT WASN'S THAT BAD

IN THE FUTURE
IS WHERE YOU DREAM
WHEN ONLY AWAKE
THEY CAN HEAR YOU SCREAM

BY: JEFF HARRIS[3]

SUICIDE STATISTICS AND HOTLINE INFORMATION

IN 1977, STEVEN KOENIG WAS JUST EIGHTEEN and suffering, then he shot himself. His mother, Marilyn Koenig, struggled with tears and prayers to keep her household of six other children going. In 1982 she met another mother who had lost her son to suicide. Both reeling and in need of support, the pair founded *Friends of Survival.* They distribute 4,000 newsletters worldwide, provide support to suicide survivors and life-saving suicide prevention education, and sponsor support meetings. Located in the Sacramento area; call 916-392-0664 for information and support.

A Brooklyn-based photographer, Dese'Rae Stage, is compiling a project called *Live Through This,* a collection of photographic portraits and personal accounts of suicide survivors who have a story to tell. The project is looking for volunteers who are survivors—not those who lived on after the death of a friend or loved one, but survivors who attempted suicide and lived. Stage, who attempted suicide herself, says, "We're not that fragile. We have to figure out how to talk about it, rather than avoiding it." Co-chair of this project is psychologist John Draper, director of the National Suicide Prevention Lifeline. According to Draper, about 7 percent of survivors later kill themselves, a higher rate than other groups. But 93 percent go on to live out their lives. The other co-chair is Eduardo Vega, himself a survivor of a suicide attempt. Vega is now the executive director of the Mental Health Association of San Francisco. Note: Kevin Hines, a prolific writer who survived an attempted suicide, is on the circuit as a public speaker to share his experience. Hines survived a jump from the Golden Gate Bridge in 2000. Look up these names on the web and check out their blogs.

Suicide Warning Signs:

Threatening suicide or expressing a strong wish to die

Talking or writing about wanting to die

Looking for a way to kill oneself, such as seeking access to guns, medication, or poisons

Talking about feeling hopeless, having no purpose in life

Talking about feeling trapped and in pain

Increasing use of alcohol or drugs.

Acting anxious, agitated, or reckless

Sleeping too little or sleeping too much

Withdrawing and feeling isolated

Showing rage, and seeking revenge

Displaying extreme mood swings

Prevention:

If you suspect a possible potential suicide with someone you know:

Call the National Suicide Hotline, 800-273-8255

Take the person to an emergency room or call a nearby mental health clinic.

If immediate risk, call 911 and ask that a Crisis Intervention Team (CIT) trained officer be dispatched.

Show you care.

Listen without judgment.

Suicides Statistics

Adolescents: For every completed suicide, there are 100 to 200 attempts.

Young to Middle Age: For every completed suicide, there are 20 attempts

Baby Boomers (born between 1946 and 1964): Suicide is the 8th leading cause of death

BOOKS AND INSPIRATION

Life Instead	Diane Bringgold
The End of Normal	Stephanie Madoff Mack
Proof of Heaven	Eben Alexander
Why Suicide	Jerry Johnston
Good Grief	Granger E. Westberg
Embraced By the Light	Betty J. Eadie
Tuesdays with Morrie	Mitch Albom
Silent Grief	Christopher Lukas and Henry M. Seiden

Schizophrenia is more prevalent with boys between the ages of eighteen and twenty two.